A FINE TEAM MAN

A FINE TEAM MAN

JACKIE ROBINSON AND THE LIVES HE TOUCHED

JOE COX

GUILFORD, CONNECTICUT

An imprint of Globe Pequot, the trade division of
The Rowman & Littlefield Publishing Group, Inc.
4501 Forbes Blvd., Ste. 200
Lanham, MD 20706
www.rowman.com

Distributed by NATIONAL BOOK NETWORK

British Library Cataloguing in Publication Information available

Library of Congress Cataloging-in-Publication Data available

ISBN 978-1-4930-6191-4 (paperback)
ISBN 978-1-4930-3905-0 (e-book)

∞™ The paper used in this publication meets the minimum requirements of American National
Standard for Information Sciences—Permanence of Paper for Printed Library Materials, ANSI/
NISO Z39.48-1992.

CONTENTS

INTRODUCTION

It is my lot in life to be a believer in the great man—or, as it should now accurately be considered, the great person—theory of history. For the unfamiliar, it is the idea that the world's events and occurrences are largely dictated by a remarkable few leaders, blessed with special skills and abilities unique to their time and its own needs.

I learned about Jackie Robinson through Red Barber. My father was an English professor and I was a young sports fan, and we had few things in common, but for the few moments on Friday mornings when Red Barber was on NPR's *Morning Edition*, we found mutual enjoyment. Barber fascinated me again on Ken Burns's *Baseball*, when he told his recollections of Robinson and the changes the great man had made in his life.

Another piece of the puzzle that became this book came when I read Doris Kearns Goodwin's *A Team of Rivals*. As a Kentuckian, Lincoln was another of those great figures whom I admired and studied. I was dismayed over the years to see various historians pick the bones of his historical carcass as so much fodder to support their angle. I've read about Lincoln the writer, Lincoln the man of faith, Lincoln the depressive, even Lincoln the gay man. Some of these books are well founded, and by no means do I intend to detract from the significance of historians continuing to look at the past with a fresh eye, but these books often seemed to drift further away from the reality and essence of the man. Then came Goodwin's book, which showed Lincoln in a new light by showing him interacting with the people closest to him. I read it with great excitement and enjoyment—*this* was the great man who changed the world.

Jackie Robinson has been dead long enough to begin to suffer the same fate as Lincoln. When I read one popular Robinson biography that claimed that the young Robinson had essentially turned the other cheek as a child in Pasadena after a little girl called him a nigger, I was furious. The reality, which I had read many other times, was that Robinson retorted and ended up in a rock fight with the girl's father. As we get further from history, the reality blurs beneath the "need" of an author to present the subject as whatever he or she wishes—the Robinson of reality was supplanted by "the patient black freak," as he himself described the stereotype some held of him.

One day, I was washing dishes in my kitchen and listening to an audiobook that included Red Barber's writings on Jackie Robinson. As I listened to Barber's explanation of the cerebral undoing of a life of prejudice, I found certainty. Robinson, I knew, was a great man. His greatness could be defined by the epitaph on his tombstone: "A life is not important except for the impact it has on other lives." Perhaps, as Ms. Goodwin had done with Lincoln, his greatness could be best contextualized by showing that impact.

The impact goes both ways. Robinson was famous as the loneliest man in sports. To be sure, the burden he carried in blazing the trail of integration was one that only he knew. But while he was alone, he was far from lonely. There were others who traveled the road to glory with Robinson—some by choice, some unwittingly. Some had spent their lives searching for this opportunity to change their society. Some just wanted to play or manage a game of baseball.

If this book does its job in any capacity, I hope it helps people remember a great leader as he was. But my second wish is that it helps people remember those who weren't necessarily great. Because the fear of the great person theory is that it leaves those of us who aren't born brilliant leaders wondering, "How do I fit in?"

We cannot all be Jackie Robinson any more than we can all be Lincoln or Mother Teresa. However, I hope that *A Fine Team Man* offers some consolation to those of us whose destinies are in the dirt rather than in the stars. History is not made by the great people alone—it is made by ordinary people deciding to cast their support, their energy, and their friendship behind the great people. The title of this book is a phrase that befits Robinson, but which he actually wrote to his wife in describing Pee Wee Reese. Changing the world may be driven by a great leader, but over the course of seasons of baseball or seasons of life, it takes a team to follow that leader, to allow some part of themselves to be remade in that image of glory.

CHAPTER ONE

RACHEL ROBINSON: "YOU KNOW DOGGONE WELL YOU'VE GOT A GIRL."

This is a story largely inhabited by ghosts. Over seven decades after the breaking of baseball's color line, virtually none of the principal characters remain. The last of Brooklyn's Boys of Summer are slowly passing away, and the management that formed their team and guided their play have long since returned to the dust. An era in which any facet of American life is lily-white is, if not impossible to imagine, at least fading day by day, year by year.

But in New York City (or the suburbs nearby, on a given day), there is a lady who was very much a witness to those earlier days. Well into her 90s, she retains graceful beauty, a warm smile, and a no-nonsense sensibility that can transmit anyone hearing her speak to another time and place—Pasadena in 1940, or Montreal in 1946, or Brooklyn in the 1950s. Rachel Robinson has this quality because in many ways, she is the last survivor of the firsthand group, those who not only witnessed Jackie Robinson changing baseball and America—or is it America and baseball?—but those who, so to speak, had "skin in the game."

As one-half of the marriage that was forged in the crucible of fighting Jim Crow, there was probably never anyone who either had such a strong impact on the life and career of Jackie Robinson, or whose own life and career were as defined by him. The mutual love and devotion of Jackie and Rachel Robinson shine through whenever she speaks or writes of the relationship and couple at the center of the maelstrom of social change. If we—as a country, as a people, or as individual men and women—seek to gain anything instructive from Jackie Robinson's life and times, then his marriage is a good place to start. It defined his life and Rachel's life, and thus it also tends to define their story.

Rachel Annetta Isum was born on July 19, 1922, almost three-and-a-half years after her future husband, in Los Angeles. Unlike her future husband's hardscrabble youth, Rachel's family background—while hardly typical—was much more rooted, both in attachment to the American West, where the worst vestiges of segregation were at least less prevalent if not absent, and in their solidly middle-class existence.

Rachel's father, Charles Isum, had been a bookbinder employed by the Los Angeles *Times* before a heart condition sustained in World War I left him retired and permanently disabled. Rachel's mother, Zellee Jones Isum, simply picked up the slack. She ran a catering business and worked in the cafeteria of the Los Angeles Public Library. Rachel had an older half brother and a younger brother, and while she would acknowledge that her ill father "seemed to favor me over my brothers," her mother taught Rachel at an early age not only to help keep up their home and to care for her injured father but also to prepare herself for financial self-sufficiency. Rachel would later recall working at the public library alongside her mother at age 10, noting, "I got fifty cents every time I helped. I liked helping, but I also loved the fifty cents. I think that was the whole point."

This self-sufficient streak was hardly a secret. In a June 1951 magazine article she penned, Rachel freely admitted, "I don't know where I got the compulsion to earn my own money." She recalled "pretend[ing] I was a needy student to get jobs around school" and recounted that one year, some local (white) charity workers had been so touched by her work ethic that they determined she must be in dire financial need and they brought her a care basket of food and a small Christmas tree. Rachel and her half brother, Charles Williams, were both aghast, and Rachel feared "those good people would come inside—and see our big new phonograph and the huge Christmas tree with gifts piled under it."

Even writing at the peak of Jackie's baseball career, Rachel's plans for the future still contemplated her own career. "Right now it certainly isn't necessary for me to work," she wrote in 1951. "But I am not satisfied being just a housewife, either." Like her husband, Rachel was ahead of her time in her desire for the self-determinism to define her own worth—an industriousness that her husband apparently found both endearing at first and a little difficult to warm to later in life.

Given her independence and her intelligence, it was hardly surprising that young Rachel Isum was a very good student. She graduated from Manual Arts High School at age 17 and started college at UCLA, where she intended to earn a bachelor's degree in nursing and work in a hospital. But first, her life took a few unexpected detours on that path.

Jack Roosevelt Robinson was the fifth of five children born to Jerry and Mallie McGriff Robinson. He was born on January 31, 1919, in Cairo, Georgia, where his father was a sharecropper on a large farm. Given the system of the time, in which farmers worked for scrip money that could be used only in the farm boss's own store—which naturally tended to feature significant price gouging—Jerry Robinson was a generation removed from slavery, but it was a removal by means of semantics rather than productivity.

Mallie Robinson, frustrated when her husband borrowed a significant amount of money in order to give his family some attempt at a proper Christmas, cornered Jerry. She insisted that he approach the farm boss with a plan to work for part of the sales of the crops he raised. Jerry Robinson reluctantly agreed, and the ensuing agreement placed some money in the family coffers. Just enough money, it turned out, to cause Jerry to develop wandering eyes and roaming feet.

Jerry Robinson left the family before Jackie was a full year old, on a trip to Texas from which he chose never to return. Given the animosity that her superintended arrangement with the farm boss created, Mallie was soon intrigued by the possibility of a fresh start, one away from the southern soil in which her people had toiled without remuneration or advance. It was California that drew her attention, and in 1920, she packed her five children (along with several other family members) onto a train and headed West.

The area of Pasadena in which the Robinson family arrived was a bit less welcoming than the cozy Isum house over on 36th Place. Mallie eventually bought a small house at 121 Pepper Street, despite outcries against her ownership from aggrieved white citizens of the neighborhood. The new life that awaited the Robinsons in California was only marginally better than what they knew in Georgia. Mallie worked as a domestic, stacking multiple jobs and sometimes still feeding her own children only with sweet water and bread, or with whatever extra scraps her white employers would bestow upon her. And while Jackie grew up out of the sanctioned segregation of the South, the de facto segregation of the West was stil sometimes brutal.

As a young boy, Jackie was confronted with a white neighbor girl who taunted him as a "nigger." Robinson turned the tables on the girl, calling her "cracker," which predictably led her to the chant, "Soda cracker's good to eat/Nigger's only good to beat." Confronted with the child's hate, Robinson upped the ante, grabbing rocks and firing them at her. But his advantage was short-lived, as the girl's father materialized and quickly began pelting Robinson with rocks himself. Eventually order was restored, and if the episode was a chilling reminder of the hate harbored against Mallie and her children, at least no one ended up at the end of a noose, as they may well have in Georgia at that time.

Perhaps just as barbarous was the day that Robinson and a few of his friends from the informal but much-recalled Pepper Street gang, denied the advantage of the city's swimming pool except on a specific day of the week set aside for minorities, decided to go for a splash in the town aquifer. The local police quickly rousted the group out, with one officer allegedly complaining of "niggers in my drinking water."

Much more jarring than racial taunts or uneven accommodations was the lack of opportunity that Robinson faced. If he had any doubts as to the issue, he needed look no further than his older brother, Mack. A talented athlete who was restricted to noncontact sports after a heart scare as a youth, Mack became a great track star and in fact won a silver medal at the 1936 Olympics in Berlin, finishing second only to the great Jesse Owens. Mack came home and found the only available employment in his path was as a street sweeper for the city of Pasadena. When he wore his Olympic jacket while performing the embarrassingly menial duties, some residents complained of Mack's attitude in holding such an affront under the noses of his white neighbors. Mack himself purportedly replied that it was simply the warmest clothing he owned.

Young Rachel Isum faced many of the same restrictions, but she had drawn herself a path leading to the sort of solid middle-class existence that was often the ceiling of the African-American experience in the first half of the twentieth century. Jackie drifted more aimlessly. The incident at the aquifer aside, he had a handful of minor misdeeds and run-ins with local law enforcement, more the mark of a boy whose imagination outstripped his opportunities than of a petty criminal. But the uncertainty of his future certainly colored his youth.

Robinson's path might have gone a decidedly different way had a young, energetic pastor named Karl Downs not appeared in his life. Downs, a pioneer ahead of his time, loved his faith but also loved youth and activities—the better to draw the local community into his flock. He gave Robinson not only recreation and moral instruction but also direction and authority within his own community, with the two becoming such close friends that he eventually drafted Jackie to serve as a Sunday-school teacher. Downs saw the leadership ability within Robinson, and the church provided an outlet for the zest for activity and life experience that would become legendary. When that joie de vivre was combined with organized athletics, something magical was formed.

As is the case with most prodigies, it is virtually impossible to pinpoint when Jackie Robinson first emerged as a great athlete. He himself fondly recalled leading a third-grade soccer team that was good enough to beat the sixth-grade squad. Early stories had Robinson telling Mallie that she didn't need to pack him a lunch—that he would barter his baseball skills for the best bargain available on the playground, sandwiches for base hits, as it were.

The myth of the natural athlete is an unfair one, attempting to discredit hard work and competitive fire in favor of God-given talent, and it is often broadly painted onto outstanding African-American athletes. That said, given Robinson's wealth of talents, it may be forgivable to grant the stereotype some latitude. As a freshman at Muir High School, Robinson played shortstop on the baseball team, saw some time at quarterback on the gridiron, was a solid contributor on the basketball team, and was a talented jumper on the track team. A year later, he won the junior boys' singles championship in the Pacific Coast Negro Tennis Tournament. In marked contrast to the difficulties surrounding much of his life, when a ball or a goal was involved, everything Jackie Robinson touched seemed to turn to gold.

After his two years at Muir High, he enrolled at Pasadena Junior College, where he continued his multisport stardom, although he did drop tennis. He managed to compete in track alongside his brother Mack, with the fraternal competition driving the elder Robinson to establish a national junior college record in the broad jump. A year later, Jackie bested that record. He continued to shine in all four sports, but the divide between the glory of athletic victory and the difficulties of his personal life continued to divide Jackie Robinson's identity.

When his junior college days finished, Robinson moved on to UCLA to continue his college career, but the dark clouds that hovered over his personal life continued. His brother Frank died in a motorcycle accident. A minor brush with police after an incident in which he was a mere bystander resulted in Robinson having an officer's gun pressed into his stomach, before cooler heads prevailed. While UCLA admitted African-American students, there were only a handful, and they remained substantially apart from the rest of the university's student social scene. Furthermore, contrary to the big-man-on-campus image one might expect, Robinson maintained part-time jobs to help pay his expenses, even as he starred in football and basketball for the Bruins. He reluctantly lettered in track, and his baseball season was a failure, as Robinson batted just .097. Meanwhile, in his few spare hours, while other UCLA students socialized in Kerckhoff Hall, Robinson swept floors as an assistant janitor. But if a broom wasn't attractive to many young coeds, Robinson's life would be changed by one woman to whom he would not need to apologize for his ambition or station.

In the beginning of his senior season, the first UCLA student to letter in four sports in the same season found himself falling in love. Robinson was watching then-17-year-old UCLA freshman Rachel Isum well before she was watching him. The beautiful Rachel exuded a maturity and charm that intrigued Robinson. Again, despite his all-American athletic pedigree, Robinson was a young man who was relatively uncomfortable with women in general. Whether it was his preoccupation with competition or a social inferiority complex, the dating scene was apparently not one that Jackie Robinson fancied.

Years later, Robinson would recall being wary of white women, as a trumped-up interracial relationship was a frequent basis for running black city workers out of jobs in the Pasadena area. He certainly seemed disinterested in the kind of girls who would chase a star athlete. Youthful friends would recall one dating relationship with a girl named Bessie Renfro, which was somewhat serious, but for the most part Robinson was as ill at ease at a Saturday-night dance as he was comfortable at a Saturday-afternoon football game.

For her part, Rachel Isum was not especially excited to meet Robinson. Her first impression of him, garnered from watching him play quarterback for the Bruins, was that he thought too highly of himself, which she later confessed she based on the hands-on-hips stance he assumed before snaps from center. Her first impression aside, Rachel soon realized that what she had first suspected was aloofness was simply shyness. She found herself drawn in by the "handsome, proud, and serious man with a warm smile and a pigeon-toed walk" whom she found a kindred spirit as "we both were shy and intent on reaching the goals we had set for ourselves."

Rachel's charms were evident to Robinson. As she admitted, she was somewhat reserved, but the effect was that she was sophisticated instead of giggly, which was appealing to Robinson's no-nonsense nature. She was beautiful, with high cheekbones accenting a delicate face and a warm smile. And she was from another world—even the black middle class was a world apart from the friendly chaos of 121 Pepper Street and the single-parent raising that Robinson had experienced.

Their differing identities and perspectives came up very literally on the matter of skin color itself. Rachel was initially put off by the fact that the much darker Jackie favored white shirts that only accented the depth of his ebony color. "I thought to myself, 'Now why would he do that? Why would anybody that dark wear a white shirt? It's terrible!'" she later recalled. Indeed, some biographers have indicated that Rachel's father initially disfavored Jackie as a suitor because of his darker complexion. Not that it ended up mattering.

Robinson won over his lighter love interest. She remembered, "He wore his color with such dignity and pride and confidence that after a little while I didn't even think about it. He wouldn't let me. He was never, ever, ashamed of his color." The depth of this revelation would only grow for Rachel as the years rolled by.

Their first date was the homecoming dance on November 2, 1940, at the ritzy Biltmore Hotel. Robinson wore the only suit he owned, and Rachel chose a beautiful black dress that she augmented with her grandmother's fur coat. Rachel later recalled the evening as "fun but never completely comfortable," and in her own book she admitted that the couple had danced the fox-trot but that she would have preferred something more intricate like the Lindy Hop. Intimidated by the surroundings, at the end of the night Robinson bestowed only a peck on the cheek on his expectant date. Despite the spark of young romance, their paths would take very different routes before they would ultimately pull together.

Only four months after that date at the Biltmore, the week after basketball season ended, senior Jackie Robinson quietly made arrangements to leave UCLA shy of graduating. The decision was unpopular both with his mother and his girlfriend, but Robinson himself later explained, "I could see no future in staying in college, no real future in athletics, and I wanted to . . . become an athletic director." Additionally, the years of being a financial burden on Mallie Robinson irritated Jackie, and he wanted to try to help his aging mother instead of relying on her. Family seemed to have been much on the mind of Jackie Robinson as he grew into adulthood. Only a few days after Robinson withdrew from UCLA, Charles Isum passed away. Rachel and Jackie grew closer as she worked through her grief. Three decades later, Jackie wrote, "In this time of sorrow we found each other and I knew then that our relationship was to be one of the most important things in my life no matter what happened to me."

Rachel observed, "My father's death gave Jack an opening where he could at last be the man, the main man, in a family of his own. . . . Jack could step right into the center of us all and take possession of his own family—at least in his mind. I think it had a profound appeal for him."

While he tried to fill an influential spot in the Isum family, Robinson fell deeper in love with Rachel. "There are few people it is easy for me to confide in," he later wrote, "but when I was with Rae I was delighted to find that I could tell her anything. She was always understanding and, beyond that, very direct and honest with me."

As he grew closer to Rachel, Robinson was hired as an assistant athletic director at a National Youth Administration camp in Atascadero, California. The young Robinson often envisioned a future in coaching, and getting to spend a few months working with young people in such a role was a pleasant experience. It was from this job that he sent Rachel—in a simple envelope that was half-destroyed in the mail—the first keepsake meant to show his devotion to her. It was a charm bracelet decorated with sports equipment, and Rachel later recalled, "I was thrilled to receive it—it was just the sign of commitment and love I wanted at the time."

Their young romance was soon drastically complicated. Robinson moonlighted as a football player with the Honolulu Bears in the winter of 1941. The Bears' season ended in late November, and on December 5th, Robinson set sail back to California.

Of course, two days later, the Japanese bombed Pearl Harbor, and all thoughts of New Deal jobs took a back seat to the immediacy of Uncle Sam. Robinson quickly received his draft notice and was inducted into the US Army in April 1942.

Not that Rachel exactly sat around waiting for his return. First, she was still busy at school, continuing another year at UCLA and then moving to UC San Francisco's School of Nursing for her remaining education. As a student nurse, she worked full eight-hour shifts at the hospital, attended to her studies, and also worked as a riveter at Lockheed Aircraft.

To say that the military was an endurance test for Jackie Robinson is probably an understatement. His court-martial at Fort Hood, Texas, when a bus driver told him to move to the back of the bus and Robinson refused, has become the stuff of legend. But even in the more casual day-to-day experiences of military life, Robinson was tested.

Despite his stellar qualifications, Robinson was not admitted into Officer Candidate School until a few months after Joe Louis, the legendary boxer, happened by his base and may have put in a few well-chosen words to political figures in high places. Robinson eventually became a second lieutenant. During a period in which he was a morale officer at Fort Riley, Kansas, he asked a provost marshal, Major Hafner, about some additional seating for black soldiers at the post exchange. When he was then asked, "How would you like to have your wife sitting next to a nigger?" Robinson predictably exploded. Additional seats were obtained, and Hafner treated him much more respectfully thereafter.

Things did not go as well on the athletic fields. Robinson wanted to play baseball at Fort Riley but was told he should play for the colored team—which did not exist. He was then tapped for a football team, but when he was conveniently placed on leave before an upcoming game against the segregated University of Missouri, Robinson made clear that he wanted no part of such a sham.

For Jackie, the never-ending stream of segregation was intolerable and was not helped by another issue. In a manuscript for a book that was never published, Robinson later wrote, "If you ever want to find out how much you think of your girl, just get yourself drafted into service. I missed Rae desperately. The only relief I could get was through writing her letters almost every night and receiving mail from her."

This desire to be with Rachel motivated him enough to make Jackie take more permanent steps toward establishing their relationship. In March 1943, two months after he was sworn in as an officer, Jackie offered Rachel a tiny diamond engagement ring. But just as Jackie was reaching a point in his life when his desire to commit was driving him forward, Rachel began stirring in the opposite direction.

She later recalled, in spite of her initial exhilaration at the engagement, "I could see marriage suffocating me, and I really was not eager to rush into it." Not only did Jackie want the marriage, but Zellee Isum had also become one of his biggest backers. In frustration, she once consulted a psychic about Rachel, who advised, "Tell her to either marry a certain man or stop riding around in his Buick." Jackie, of course, happened to drive such a vehicle.

In early 1944, some persistent right ankle pain that had dated to a football injury sustained several years prior caused Robinson nagging trouble. He was eventually found to be physically disqualified for general military service but qualified for limited service. This finding—combined with the issues in his later court-martial—may have actually saved Robinson's life, as many of the men within his battalion were killed in Europe.

Around the same time, his issues with Rachel's independence came to a head. Rachel's half brother, Charles Williams, had been shot down over Europe, and was believed to have been captured. Meanwhile, she chafed at the inactivity of nursing at a civilian hospital during the chaos of the war. She wrote Jackie to advise that she had decided to join the Nurse Cadet Corps. To Robinson, this was tantamount to a betrayal.

Thinking of his beloved Rachel being ogled by other servicemen drove him into a rage.

Rachel's actual motives were much more benign. First, there was boredom. Second, there was money—the corps stipend of $20 per month was attractive to a broke college student. And third, Rachel recalled, she loved the heavy flannel coat that she would be given to use around San Francisco, where biting winds made such a garment attractive.

It had taken Jackie Robinson some time to realize how much he cared for Rachel Isum. But now that he knew he did, with no paternal example of his own to work from, he determined that he would tell her how things would be—she could leave the Corps or end their engagement. Robinson had much to learn. Rachel Isum was too wise, too intelligent, and too involved to allow herself to become arm candy for a great athlete. She returned his ring and bracelet by mail.

During this breakup, Robinson was transferred to Texas, faced court-martial, and by the fall of 1944 found himself on inactive status—on November 28th, he was honorably relieved from active duty by reason of physical disqualification. Thus, he was neither dishonorably discharged nor honorably discharged; he would later receive no veteran's benefits despite his two-and-a-half years in the army.

When he returned to Pasadena, he made no immediate step to reconcile with Rachel, but he found himself unable to stop thinking about her. Eventually, it was Mallie Robinson who convinced him to telephone her. A handful of words down a telephone receiver later, as Robinson would recall, "I set some sort of record getting to San Francisco." He continued, "Making up was almost as sweet as falling in love the first time."

Jackie offered his ring again, and Rachel accepted. She again was wary about an immediate marriage, in part because when she graduated in 1945, she was planning a trip to New York. For a woman who loved to travel, the voyage to the Big Apple seemed like a once-in-a-lifetime opportunity. Rachel would have never expected just how much time she would spend in New York.

For the time being, they were engaged and they were together. Robinson wrote that he had learned a lesson—"never again to allow misunderstanding to make us forget our deep, mutual love." Unwritten, but doubtlessly true, was that he had learned a couple of other lessons—not to call Rachel's bluff, and not to think of his fiancé as any less of a part of their relationship than himself.

One positive aspect of his military service was Jackie Robinson's chance meeting with a fellow soldier named Ted Alexander near the end of his service. Robinson saw Alexander throwing a sharp curveball and stopped to ask him about it. Alexander played for the Kansas City Monarchs of the Negro National League. He told Robinson that if he was interested in a career in black baseball, he should write to team owner Thomas Baird, which Robinson promptly did. After some back-and-forth, Robinson was invited to spring training in April 1945, with the promise of $400 per month if he made the Monarchs team.

In the meanwhile, finished with the military, hoping to make a few dollars and bide the time until Rachel would finish school and their wedding could finally be scheduled, Jackie found short-term employment as athletic director and basketball coach at tiny Samuel Huston College in Texas, working for his old mentor, Reverend Karl Downs. The money was minimal, but the chance to help an old friend was too good to pass up.

But when spring training came, life in the Negro Leagues beckoned, and that summer of 1945 does not seem to have been a particularly enjoyable one for Jackie Robinson. In later years, Robinson was quick to cite a litany of complaints with the leagues: poorly organized and run teams and leagues, harsh travel schedules, difficulty in finding decent or reliable meals or accommodation, and lengthy bus trips. He also would later recall two other issues. "I began to wonder why I should dedicate my life to a career where the boundaries for progress were set by racial discrimination," he wrote. "Even more serious was my growing fear that

I might lose Rae again. . . . She had been hoping I'd settle down in California to work out our future. The way I was traveling, we saw each other rarely. . . . [W]here could I go, what could I do to earn enough money to help my mother and to marry Rachel?"

Money was important, and Robinson kept slogging along through the Negro Leagues. Not only by temperament, but by habit, he wasn't always a good fit for the league. Biographer Arnold Rampersad noted, "Jack no doubt seemed priggish to some of his teammates. . . . [N]o doubt to the genuine bewilderment of some teammates, he showed little or no interest in easy sex on the road." Another player, Sammie Haynes, recalled Robinson's constant praise of Rachel, and one night, Haynes finally asked him, "Have you been to bed with the woman?" When Robinson admitted that he hadn't, Haynes continued, "Man, are you going to marry somebody that you haven't been to bed with? Are you crazy?" Haynes recalled Robinson answering, "Sammie, this is the lady for me. I don't have to go to bed with her."

Rachel had graduated from nursing school in June, presented with the Florence Nightingale Award as the outstanding clinical nurse in her graduating class. She returned home and took a job in the nursery at Los Angeles General Hospital, and saved money for her October trip to New York with her friend Janice Brooks. After that, she figured she would return home and prepare to settle down in California with her soon-to-be husband, despite the many questions that still surrounded his future.

⌒

When Branch Rickey hosted the August 1945 meeting with Jackie Robinson that would change both of their lives and the face of baseball forever, legend has it that his first question to Robinson was, "You got a girl?" There would be few things Rickey could have asked that would prove more prescient or better demonstrate his awareness of his hoped-for path for Robinson.

Before finalizing his conclusion that Robinson was the iconic figure needed to integrate baseball, Rickey wanted to feel him out on certain issues, but first among them apparently was his relationship status. For his part, Robinson reluctantly offered, "I don't know."

"What do you mean, you don't know?" asked Rickey. Robinson admitted the crux of his problem—that he indeed had a girl, but given the roving life of a Negro League ballplayer, he wasn't entirely sure if she recognized just how highly he valued her. Given the time in the military and in the Negro Leagues, Rachel would once tell an interviewer, "We were engaged about five years before we were married, but if we combined all the days we were together it wouldn't add up to two months." Perhaps this weighed on Robinson's mind as he hesitated in his answer to Rickey.

"Is she a fine girl, good family background, educated girl?" asked Rickey. Robinson unhesitatingly agreed on all fronts.

"Then you know doggone well you've got a girl," concluded Rickey. "When we get through today you may want to call her up, because there are times when a man needs a woman by his side."

To be sure, the Great Experiment of integration was one of those times. When Robinson fulfilled Rickey's final qualifications in his interview, he was sworn to near-complete secrecy on the project. Rickey apparently stipulated that Robinson would be signed by November 1st, and that in the interim, he did not want the plan scuttled by publicity. Robinson telephoned Rachel, but he was careful in the conversation. "[H]e would only tell me that something wonderful had happened that would affect us both," Rachel later remembered. Truer words were never spoken.

Shortly thereafter, Robinson left the Monarchs before their season ended. He returned to California and confided the entire business to an excited Rachel. This set off an eventful fall of 1945. Rachel left for her New York trip in early October, and on October 23rd, the official announcement of Jackie's signing with the Montreal Royals was released. He traveled to Venezuela on a winter barnstorming tour, but he also visited with Rachel often in New York both before and after that trip.

With the integration of baseball finally providing some vague definition to their future, the Robinsons enjoyed the time before their wedding. One biographer notes, "Rachel began to think of them as complementing one another. Her identity was fluid; his was a rock. He was impulsive, she was organized and practical. . . . What they needed was a chance, and this was what Rickey and white baseball were offering."

On February 10, 1946, Jackie and Rachel Robinson were wed by Reverend Karl Downs at Independent Church in Los Angeles. The ceremony was a relatively large and glamorous one, noted by Rachel as an attempt to accommodate the wishes of her mother rather than herself or Jackie. After some hijinks from the Pepper Street Gang, who apparently borrowed Robinson's getaway car for a few hours, the couple finally managed to get safely ensconced at a local hotel—the arrangement made more difficult because Jackie had forgotten to book a room. Rachel recalled "finally clos[ing] the door on the outer world" at the hotel as a newlywed couple with "all of my fears and doubts vanished." She continued, "It was a precious moment filled with feelings of completeness."

Those few first days as a married couple were made more precious when a fortnight later, the Robinsons headed for Florida and Jackie's first spring training. The trip through Dixieland was a nightmare—spanning two days, and subjecting the couple to several embarrassing instances of bigotry and hatred. Rachel recalled weeping quietly in the back seat of a segregated Florida bus as the couple completed their odyssey of a trip toward Daytona Beach and the Dodgers. She took solace that "we had the survivor's most crucial traits—resilience and indestructible hope." For his part, Jackie depended on Rachel's solidity, and carried her courage as motivation. Years later, he wrote of those difficult days getting to spring training and noted, "I could have lost my temper and ended up clobbered unconscious in some obscure Southern jail—or worse. Maybe this would have happened if it hadn't been for Rae. Acutely conscious of how much she was hurt by all the insults and the deprivations, I was also aware that she wanted me to keep a tight grip on myself. She wanted me to take what I had to take so I could survive to do the job ahead."

As the insults and deprivations continued throughout those first years in baseball, Rachel had to be a fount of that resilience and hope, and she assumed a multitude of roles in the new Robinson family. Having worked as long as she could remember, she found herself now accepting the role of housewife, although very much with its own unusual twist. As the Robinsons were bounced from multiple towns, as Jackie faced a new employer, new teammates and managers, a new position on the field, and the pressure of being baseball's first black player in six decades, Rachel was not only the woman who charged herself with providing Jackie with a positive and supportive homelife but also his confidant and best friend.

In the late 1950s, Rachel recalled in an interview, "We found that our marriage was cemented in the first year in a manner which made it indestructible. The first six weeks in Florida, where we spent hours and hours shut up in our tiny bedroom, reading together and talking, playing cards, and talking some more, worrying about the team and making the team, or not getting any hits." Those first days of marriage were definitive to the Robinsons' identity as a married couple. Rachel later wrote, "[M]y role had begun to unfold. It evolved and became more crucial over time. My most profound instinct as Jack's wife was to protect him—an impossible task. I could, however, be a consistent presence to witness and validate the realities, love him without reservation, share his thoughts and miseries, discover with him the humor in the ridiculous behavior against us, and, most of all, help maintain our fighting spirit." She continued, "I knew our only chance to survive was to be ourselves."

Rachel's role in the marriage was consistently validated by her husband. One biographer noted, "With this closeness, Jack began to think and talk, as many observers would note over the years, not in terms of 'I' but most often about 'we'—as in 'We hit a home run that day.' . . . [H]e found himself sharing more of his thoughts with her and starting to crave the experience. A sense of themselves as a couple, strong in unity and purpose, began to grow."

That sense of unity grew not only from ball game to ball game, but moreover with the spring revelation that Rachel was pregnant with their first child. She later recalled some initial disappointment, as she "had hoped for a year of travel and freedom," but Jackie was ecstatic, and his first letter to her after she had broken the news to him by mail during a road trip is full of the kind of sentiments that an over-the-moon father-to-be would experience. For at least a moment, integrating baseball and blazing new paths on the diamond took a back seat. "We can't miss," wrote Jackie. He later added, "We will always court each other as long as we live."

Pregnancy added an extra emotional dimension to the marriage, but it also complicated Rachel's daily life. She went on Jackie's Montreal road trips until it was almost impossible. She recalled later, "In Montreal, Jack would leave our apartment to go on the road, and he would say, primarily because I was pregnant, 'Now, I will not call you and ask you to join me on the road trip this time.' But by the second or third day, he would call, and I was equally eager to go, and I would take any accommodations I could get at a moment's notice on the train, and frequently horrify porters by climbing into upper berths—and I was huge with [the baby]."

She also underwent pregnancy complications that left her with soaring fevers and puzzled doctors. "I never told Jack about the fever," she admitted. "I couldn't risk upsetting him. He would call at night from the road and I would say, 'Everything's just fine.' When he got back, I would be better. I had to make the sacrifice, because I had begun to think that I was married to a man with a destiny, someone who had been chosen for a great task, and I couldn't let him down."

This sense of keeping one's troubles to herself pervaded Rachel's early approach to marriage. She told an interviewer in 1958 that in being the wife of an athlete, "[Y]ou try to be sensitive to every mood and aspect of their mental attitude. You rarely ask them to perform any tasks or chores at home, and never during the season do you confront them with problems of household matters of yourself. . . . In fact, there were things that happened in the summer that I would take up with Jack in the winter."

While some of Rachel's desire to take control of the domestic life of her young family was likely a reflection of the cultural norms of the time, some of it was also the acknowledgment of the fact that even in Robinson's golden 1946 season in Montreal, when he led the International League in batting average, tied for the league lead in runs scored, and was one of the top base stealers for the champion Royals, the day-to-day grind of being a pioneer was a draining task.

At one point late in the 1946 season, after suffering from difficulty sleeping and a loss of appetite, Robinson saw a doctor, who assessed him as being on the cusp of a nervous breakdown. The doctor ordered a period of rest away from baseball for 10 days, which the team lessened to 5 days. However, because of both his loyalty to the Royals and his fear that he would be accused of trying to back into the batting title, Robinson's actual rest break ended up being much shorter. Rachel recalled, "I managed to get in one outing, a picnic, before he felt compelled to return to the fray." Rachel indicated that the brief respite—and the knowledge that his issues were not due to some more immediately serious medical cause—were sufficient for Robinson to return to minor-league domination.

While it would not necessarily be the pinnacle of the Robinson marriage, 1946 was a significant year. They married, Jackie broke the color line of professional baseball, and he excelled in doing so. That excellence was always accompanied by him giving primary credit to Rachel, who despite living in a foreign country where many of her neighbors spoke French instead of English, despite being a new wife and with the days of motherhood bearing down on her, forged a brave new identity as part of a spousal team that already had and would continue to change the world. It was a year that culminated in the Royals winning the Little World Series and Jackie being carried off the field in triumph—bringing about the great line by Sam Maltin of the *Pittsburgh Courier*, who wrote of a mob of white fans running after a black man with love instead of lynching in their hearts. A month later in Los Angeles, Jackie Robinson Jr. was born, and the family of three looked forward to yet another year to remember in 1947.

If 1946 had been a marital trial by fire for Rachel Robinson, 1947 was scarcely easier. Given the Dodgers' decision to move spring training from Florida to Cuba—likely done to avoid some of the hardships of Jim Crow that Robinson had experienced—Jackie would have to depart to the most pivotal days of his young professional baseball career without Rachel. It was with a heavy heart that Jackie Robinson went to the airport to fly to Havana. In fact, it wasn't until his first flight was canceled and he got an impromptu pep talk from Rachel once he returned home that his heart was truly invested in the venture. But Jackie went, and made his way through the confusing and sometimes difficult spring that ended with his contract being purchased by the Brooklyn Dodgers on April 10th, five days before Opening Day of the 1947 season.

While Jackie's appearance in the big leagues signaled a victory to his on-field crusade, it just started another round of domestic chaos. Uncertain as to the long-term situation and lacking enough money to make any long-term plans, the Robinsons found themselves living in the Hotel McAlpin in Manhattan with a five-month-old baby. Rachel later recalled living in a single hotel room with Jackie Jr., who struggled early in the season both with a cold he caught from the unseasonable Brooklyn weather in April (certainly so compared with what he had experienced in California) and with diarrhea because of a change in the water, as "an utter nightmare."

She further remembered, "As if all this were not enough, we were plagued almost every hour by newspapermen rapping on our door. It would have been comical if it hadn't been such a burden on us to go through this constantly recurring ritual of pushing utensils under the bed and rushing to close the bathroom door so newspapermen would not see the diapers hanging over the shower rod." While the situation did improve slightly when the Robinsons shared an apartment, it was still far from ideal. At least they had a kitchen—at the McAlpin, they would take turns with Jackie Jr. while the other ate at a nearby cafeteria. Still, their only leisure pastimes were recalled as taking streetcar rides and pushing the baby carriage around the neighborhood at night. So much of that famous year centered, not surprisingly, on the ballpark.

This was something of a culture shock to Rachel, who did not grow up as a baseball fan. She later recalled learning the game initially during spring training of 1946, confessing in a 1951 magazine article, "Gradually I began to learn about the strategy which makes baseball interesting. . . . I am still not a rabid fan . . . [b]ut I don't see how any wife of a baseball player could help being vitally interested in her husband's team and particularly what her husband does." So complete was this interest that Rachel did not miss a home game in Brooklyn for all of 1947—just as she had not missed one in Montreal in 1946. She took Jackie Jr. with her—even on that electric Opening Day, when she had brought him to the ballpark in apparel more suited to California sun than Brooklyn clouds. While his father broke the big-league color barrier, Jackie Jr. was warmed inside Roy Campanella's mother-in-law's fur coat. His bottles were heated at the nearest hot dog stand, which did become a Robinson family tradition.

On the field, sportswriters observed the uniqueness of Jackie's position, and the cool aloofness he initially received throughout the game. Jimmy Cannon famously dubbed him the "loneliest man I have ever seen in sports." On the field, it may have looked that way. But off the field, Rachel did everything in her power to make sure the home front was very different. One biographer noted, "She spent most of her days housecleaning, toting the considerable amount of laundry generated by Jackie Jr., to the Laundromat, and rushing off to the ball games which she never missed." Rachel herself later recalled, "As we traveled back to McDonough Street from the ballpark, we discussed the day's events. We vented our anger and frustration and shared the joy and excitement of winning a game or a new supporter. By the time we got home, Jack could enter in relative peace." Another writer comments, "[S]he tried hard to make their home a haven. . . . Once at home, however, he felt both contentment and the usual irritations, which he understood only imperfectly. . . . Around the house, he helped a little, but only a little; he had a traditional attitude to what was man's work and woman's work."

One element that undoubtedly added to Robinson's stress was the hate mail that flooded in as he began tearing through the National

League. The Dodgers quickly began sorting his mail for him, pulling all but the most serious of the death threats and hateful letters. At least twice during his playing career, the FBI received serious enough intelligence to scout on Cincinnati's Crosley Field due to threats Robinson received before games at that stadium. On the home front, the hate mail made little impact. Rachel related, "[I]t wasn't in a period of kidnappings or things like that so we never worried about the baby being hurt, or our being accosted too much except by some crazy or irrational person who might shoot from the stands."

For all of the problems and difficulties of 1947, the Robinsons kept pushing on. Their mutual sanctuary away from the crazed chaos of celebrity kept them grounded, and the almost daily hatred and animosity that they battled at least became less significant as Robinson's consistently brilliant play marked him as a star instead of a sideshow in his rookie year in the National League. If a fringe minority was still given to hating him, many more embraced Robinson—a fact that was made crystal clear on September 23rd, when the Dodgers, after prompting by the *People's Voice* newspaper, staged "Jackie Robinson Day" at Ebbets Field.

The Robinsons were presented with many impressive gifts, including a set of cutlery, silverware, a television set, and a new Cadillac. Entertainer Bill "Bojangles" Robinson appeared at the event, dubbing Robinson "Ty Cobb in Technicolor." That week, Robinson was awarded *The Sporting News'* first annual Rookie of the Year award, and he was featured on the cover of *Time* magazine. Time, as well as *Time*, was figuratively and literally on the Robinsons' side, and while the constant ebb and flow of domestic life could complicate their lives, the difficulty of the first two years of marriage ended in a celebratory explosion. Brooklyn had won the pennant, Jackie Robinson was a star, and he and his family were more likely to be cheered as heroes than reviled by hatemongers. During that offseason, Jackie Jr. took his first steps, and the promise of better days lay ahead.

As the years of baseball passed by, the Robinsons' essential blueprint remained unchanged. Even as Jackie's situation became more settled, the social aspects of being a baseball wife were always rendered somewhat uncomfortable for Rachel. She later recalled of the early years of the marriage, "Though we shared a few fun evenings with Joan and Gil Hodges, whom we especially liked, there was little socializing with team members except at Dodger parties. . . . We enjoyed having a small circle of friends and relished spending time alone together in our attractive home with our child, music, and books. The team's monthly road trips were required separations to recover from and store up for." These recollections must have been accurate, as she had written in 1951, "Jack and I really don't need many friends. We do things together or not at all. . . . In California, where we have many old friends, we go out more. But here we have little social life." In the same article, Rachel admitted, "[I]t is hard to get genuinely close to the other girls [Dodger wives and girlfriends], because the competition is so terrific. . . . There is very little open bickering, but a great deal of tension."

Accordingly, the Robinsons cultivated friendships outside of baseball. A local African-American family, the Covingtons, became good friends, as did a nearby Jewish family, the Satlows. Sarah Satlow had trained to be a nurse, and became good friends with Rachel. Satlow later recalled that even early in the relationship the two women would swap off babysitting each other's children, although she recalled that at the time, she had three children and the Robinsons then had only one. "It was nothing to her," noted Satlow, "she was such a kind and efficient person."

Even decades later, Sarah Satlow's positive memories of Rachel Robinson were strong. "She was a very demanding person, both with herself and others," Satlow remembered. "Rachel dressed very well . . . she had fabulous taste. She was fastidious; she had class and dash about her. She could sew; she was a wonderful cook; she baked beautifully."

Jackie also grew fond of the Satlow family, even if that friendship once took a mildly comical turn. Jackie, concerned that the Satlows did not have a Christmas tree one winter, bought an extra one, and he and

Rachel decorated it and presented it as a gift. "In California, we knew nothing about Jewish culture," admitted Rachel years later. However, the Satlows, rather than being offended, decided to keep the gift and display it. "The children liked it," noted Satlow, "and Jack and Rachel meant well."

As the Robinsons had two more children, Sharon in 1950 and David in 1952, it soon was time for them to purchase the sort of permanent home that would serve as their private sanctuary. Jackie deferred to Rachel's lead on the decision, and then watched as she encountered her own horrific instances of prejudice and discrimination. As Rachel hunted houses in the periphery of the New York area, again and again, houses suddenly disappeared off the market when she became interested, or the prices elevated wildly. Jackie later wrote, "Sometimes it was hard to tell whether we were being subjected to color prejudice or celebrity prejudice or both."

Not unlike her husband's crusade a few years earlier, Rachel made use of both media pressure and a sympathetic insider to end the matter. The Bridgeport (Connecticut) *Herald* ran a series of articles on housing discrimination that highlighted Rachel's plight. Meanwhile, Andrea Simon, the wife of publisher Richard Simon (of Simon & Schuster fame) and a member of a local committee to fight housing bias, learned of the situation and telephoned Rachel. With Simon's help, Rachel found a large tract of land in Stanford, Connecticut. The Robinsons purchased the property in 1954, but the construction underwent numerous delays. So that the children could attend local schools, Simon offered temporary use of her own local home to the Robinson family.

Andrea Simon, by virtue of her assistance, became a favored friend to the family. Rachel later wrote, "The friendship Andrea and I shared crossed all boundaries of age, race, and culture, and we quietly congratulated ourselves on our ability to meet the challenges and protect the bond between us as the social changes and disruptions of the following decades tested us." Indeed, while the Robinsons may have been finally settled in a residential sense, there were still more challenges on the horizon.

Few people who observed the close dynamic between Jackie and Rachel were foolish enough to challenge it. One who did—but who quickly learned the error of his ways—was Dodger boss Walter O'Malley. O'Malley forced out Branch Rickey after the 1950 season, and his dislike of the man whom Jackie regarded as a second father was so great that he allegedly fined Dodger employees for mentioning Rickey's name.

During one of the later seasons in Robinson's career, probably 1952, O'Malley found himself at loggerheads with Robinson. Jackie had missed a couple of exhibition games due to injury. The year 1952 seems to best fit the narrative, because Robinson had spring injuries including a severe chest cold and a broken toe. O'Malley was angry that Robinson had missed the games, likely because, as a Cincinnati newspaper article from March 1952 noted, Robinson remained one of the best attendance draws in baseball. He decided to meet with Robinson, and for some reason that doesn't stand up to retroactive scrutiny, he apparently thought it would be a good idea to involve Rachel in the meeting.

O'Malley began the meeting by complaining about the missed games, indicating that it wasn't fair to fans. But then he upped the ante by also questioning Robinson as to his unhappiness at having to stay at another hotel from the rest of the team. Jackie recalled O'Malley saying, "That was good enough for you in 1947. Why do you have to make trouble now?"

This was an obvious sore spot for Jackie, as he indicated that he had paid his dues and then more. He later recalled telling O'Malley, "I happen to feel now . . . that there are a lot of insults being suffered by Negro ballplayers that wouldn't be necessary if the owners would show just a little bit more courage." Doubtlessly, Robinson was referring to the continued Jim Crow situation in Florida, which would not truly be rectified until after Jackie had retired.

Jackie also stood up for himself in regard to injuries, and accused O'Malley of being willing to risk regular season defeat in the interest of "a few extra dollars." This time, it was O'Malley's turn to be stung.

"You're behaving like a prima donna," he told Jackie, "and I don't like it a bit. Other ballplayers, great ballplayers, play day in and day out, and they don't become crybabies over a little sore leg or something like that."

Enter Rachel Robinson.

She had held her peace so far. Jackie admitted, "She had never become involved with matters concerning me and the team except for our own discussions at home." She was involved now. "I can't remember ever seeing her so infuriated," Jackie wrote.

Rachel began clearly but powerfully. "Of all the things Jackie Robinson is," she lectured, "the one thing he is not is a prima donna. I've seen him play with sore legs, a sore back, sore arms, even without other members of the team knowing about it, doing it not for praise, but because he was always thinking about his team. Nobody worries more about this club than Jackie Robinson, Mr. O'Malley." Considering the rapid physical decline of Robinson late in his baseball career and then post baseball, history certainly reflects that Rachel's claims bear up much better than O'Malley's.

With O'Malley feeling the wrath of a woman scorned, Rachel then really dug in. "You know, Mr. O'Malley," she continued, "bringing Jack into organized baseball was not the greatest thing Mr. Rickey did for him. In my opinion, it was this: having brought Jack in, he stuck by him to the very end. He understood Jack. He never listened to the ugly little rumors such as you mentioned today. . . . He would talk to Jack, and they would get to the heart of it like men with a mutual respect for the abilities and the feelings of each other."

Not only had Rachel brought up O'Malley's blood enemy by referencing Rickey and his role in Jackie's integration of baseball, but she had struck him exactly where time would prove her right. Rickey had been a trailblazer not only because he called on Jackie, but because he stood by him. O'Malley, by comparison, never truly understood Jackie, and never appreciated his excellence because O'Malley was fickle, listened to the rumor mill, and did inane things like expecting Rachel Robinson to be won to his side in his argument.

Over many years, Rachel had sat in the stands and listened to Jackie's manhood questioned, she had withstood Jim Crow accommodations, and she had tried to ignore biased sportswriters who misunderstood or misrepresented her husband. But when O'Malley tried to pile on, Rachel Robinson, the crisp, professional, usually pleasant lady, showed that she had the same internal fire as her celebrated husband. He protected teammates and pennants, and she protected him.

Having spent just over a decade leading the family behind the scenes, in the years after the children had reached school age and Jackie's active baseball days had come to a close, Rachel made another transition that challenged both her own self-image and Jackie's idea of her place within the family. After Jackie's 1956 retirement from baseball, he worked as a vice president of Chock Full o'Nuts, where company president William Black valued Jackie's unique skills and input enough that he basically crafted a job for him. Jackie also volunteered extensively for the NAACP, and wrote a weekly newspaper column for the *New York Post*.

But Rachel no longer felt fulfilled being a housewife. Many of the loose strands of her past demanded to be tied together. On some level, she must have still identified with her childhood days experiencing the thrill of her own earning power. She had not forgotten her academic excellence, and the joy of involvement in her intended profession of nursing. She wanted to return to the workforce, even though most women, particularly most married women—and almost certainly those women of a relatively well-heeled economic status—still tended not to do so. Her biggest opponent to her own battle against the tradition of her era might have been her crusader husband, whose progressive liberal ideas about race did not quite extend into gender.

"Jack experienced my move toward greater independence and individualism as a loss," wrote Rachel. "He felt confused and threatened by my ambitions—and furthermore, he felt I was breaking a premarital understanding that I would stay at home." Rachel recalled no such understanding, and while she understood Jackie's desire to be the family breadwinner, particularly in light of the unceasing hard work of Mallie Robinson that he had witnessed, she did not agree.

"We had created a true partnership, a heady 'us against the world' kind of thing," she recalled of their early marriage, "and had been privileged to find a special mission early on. My guess is that we both sensed that finding our way with more separate identities was going to be the most serious challenge of our marriage—and it was."

"I needed greater freedom to develop personally and professionally," she stated. "I was indeed buoyed by the changing role of women. I knew that what I wanted for myself wasn't aberrant and that women had the right to pursue their dreams."

She began taking classes at New York University's graduate school. The transition was not an easy one. On her first day, carrying an armload of books, she was confronted by a group of ebullient younger students, and she quickly dropped her books. She remembered "reducing myself to the stature I feared—a helpless and befuddled 'old lady.'" She needn't have worried. Between her own excellent credentials and the resilience she had learned in Jackie's trial by fire, Rachel was something near destined to succeed.

When Rachel had night classes, Jackie would wait for her at the closest Chock Full o'Nuts store, and they would drive home and discuss the day—the circumstances echoing those of Jackie's early days as a Dodger. "I felt we were close in a new way," remembered Rachel. "It seemed that he had accepted that it was his turn to support me, at least through the student phase. . . . I just loved the sight of him waiting patiently for me to arrive."

There were still challenges ahead for both Robinsons in this new age. Rachel completed her master's degree in 1960 and took a job as a psychiatric nurse in a research program conducted by the Albert Einstein College of Medicine Department of Social and Community Psychiatry. Rachel helped to plan and establish the first American day hospital for acutely ill psychiatric patients. She held this position for five years before further funding failed to extend her program beyond its initial run.

In 1965, she was appointed the director of nursing for the Connecticut Mental Health Center and also as an assistant professor of nursing at Yale University. This was intense work and included the development of new models and roles for nurses, and it placed the program as a forerunner in psychiatric care.

Rachel also played a role in the increasing number of political causes that Jackie supported with his time, money, and energy. A longtime music lover, she was instrumental in helping to establish the Afternoon of Jazz concert, which raised funds for a different humanitarian cause each year and which she and Jackie annually enjoyed.

With Jackie in the twilight of his public career and indeed his life, Rachel continued to shine the brighter as a capable, efficient, professional woman. Her mother, Zellee Isum, came to live with the family and helped out in domestic activities. As time went on, even Jackie Robinson was at least somewhat won over by his wife's reentry to the workforce.

Jackie wrote on the matter extensively near the end of his life. "To be very honest, if I had my way, Rachel would not have a job," he admitted. "But having my way would constitute selfishness as well as insensitivity to her needs as a person." Jackie was able to find humor in an incident when a coworker had asked Rachel if she was Jackie Robinson's wife and she had denied it. Jackie astutely noted, "Rachel realized that she didn't really want to deny that I was part of her life but that she wanted to be known and respected as an individual in her own right."

The pioneer who had changed people's view of the color barrier lived to admit that his wife changed his view of gender roles. "I am proud that my wife has had a successful career," he wrote. Jackie mentioned that Rachel liked to tease him for saying "we" when he was referring to himself. He explained their read on that habit: "Rachel has told me, 'You don't think of me as separate, and sometimes you have a hard time allowing me to be separate.' She's right about that."

Having spent their early marriage building a joint identity, it was at times difficult for the Robinsons to forge separate identities thereafter. But they always managed. Sadly, circumstance would mandate their separate identities much too soon.

The final years of Jackie Robinson's life were fraught with several difficulties. He found himself politically out of favor throughout the 1960s. He drew fire from many for his choice to support then–Vice President Richard Nixon in the 1960 presidential election, a decision he later came to regret. Within a few years, he found himself castigated by radicals like Malcolm X, who painted Robinson as an "Uncle Tom" who was lost without his great white benefactor, Branch Rickey (or William Black, in his postbaseball years).

Even more painfully, in April 1968, Jackie Jr., only a year past US Army service in Vietnam, was arrested on drug and weapons charges. A saddened Jackie faced the press near the police station and told them, "I've had more effect on other people's kids than my own." Jackie Jr. went on to fight addiction and ultimately triumphed in that battle. His parents were proud of his progress, and he worked for the Daytop Rehabilitation Program, the facility where he had undergone the treatment that had changed his life. He was still working there on the morning of June 17, 1971, when he had a single-vehicle crash on the Merritt Parkway near New York City, and he died at just 24 years old.

Meanwhile, Jackie's diabetes continued to grow worse. His legs and his vision were deteriorating—by 1972, he was almost completely blind and was likely facing amputation of a leg. Additionally, he suffered heart attacks in 1968 and 1970. None of this made life easier for Rachel, who was still grieving the loss of Jackie Jr., trying to maintain her work, and trying to guide Jackie through his difficult medical issues. Given all the difficulty in her life, she withdrew, becoming distant and silent. This wasn't lost on her family.

Sharon Robinson was visiting her parents one night and heard an odd noise as she passed the living room. Looking into the room, she saw Jackie sitting on the couch and crying. When she asked why he was crying, Jackie admitted, "First Mr. Rickey and my mother [Rickey died in 1965, Mallie in 1968], then your brother. Now I wonder if I am losing my wife." When Sharon immediately went and told Rachel of the conversation, Rachel hurried to comfort her husband. He would not lose her, but unfortunately, she was drawing closer to losing him.

On the morning of October 23, 1972, Rachel was preparing breakfast and Jackie was readying for a doctor's appointment. Suddenly, Rachel looked up to see Jackie rushing down the hall. She ran to him, and he put his arms around her, told her, "I love you," and fell to the floor. He was gone.

And yet, on some other level, he has never really been gone. Shortly after his passing, Rachel and some family and friends began the Jackie Robinson Foundation. The nonprofit organization was designed to provide educational and leadership development opportunities principally for minority youth. By the late 2010s, 1,500 Jackie Robinson Foundation scholars had attended more than 260 colleges and universities, with a 98 percent graduation rate. For more than four decades, Rachel has been the public face of the legacy of Jackie Robinson. She has performed brilliantly, maintaining a positive but honest outlook on the years of struggle that grow more and more distant.

In 2017, the National Baseball Hall of Fame presented Rachel with its Buck O'Neil Lifetime Achievement Award. At that ceremony, she told the assembled fans and media that she hoped to see them at the Jackie Robinson Museum, which is scheduled to open in 2019. "I don't know if I'll be there," she joked. "I just turned ninety-five."

Whether she is still alive and healthy or not, Rachel will be there in some sense at the celebration of Jackie Robinson. "I am one of the fortunate ones," she wrote in 1995, "granted a mission at the age of twenty-three, a great partner, and the spirit to prevail." That partner helped her to live the sort of rich and full life that served to reveal her own indomitable spirit.

"Jack and I had modest plans when we became engaged," she admitted in 1950. But in hitching her wagon to the young sports hero who she initially thought cocky, Rachel had defined not only her own life but also a large segment of American history. The modest plans were reserved for someone else. Rachel became one-half of one of the greatest "we" tandems in American history. Whether it was staring down Jim Crow, finding the courage to reinvent herself as a professional in midlife, or having the longevity to help define Jackie's legacy for decades after his passing, Rachel did it all.

She once wrote, "I feel that the legacy of Jackie Robinson has been carried forward in the hearts of the men and women whose lives he touched." She should know—she herself has carried the torch into a new century, into new endeavors, and into new generations of lives forever changed. Jackie Robinson was the pioneer who integrated baseball, but off the field, when life went beyond the box score, Rachel was there at every step and turn. Her devotion and constancy shaped Jackie Robinson as much as his intensity and focus shaped her—and together, they changed the world.

CHAPTER TWO

ATTENDANCE, JESUS, AND AMERICA: THE MOTIVATIONS OF BRANCH RICKEY

Years before he was a major-league catcher, or the man who redesigned baseball's minor leagues, or the architect of the plan to integrate Major League Baseball, Branch Rickey was a beleaguered farm boy in rural southern Ohio. Angry with a schoolteacher, he had abruptly announced his intention of quitting school and working the land with his father. But after three days of farm labor, Rickey had lost his delusions of agrarian grandeur. Many years later, he recalled, "I felt like I imagine a runner feels when he is finishing a marathon." Frank Rickey treated his son graciously and encouraged him to return to school.

A month later, Rickey's older brother, Orla, who was at the time a local schoolteacher, returned home with a new discovery for the boy. Orla Rickey developed into a fine left-handed pitcher, and his younger brother by happenstance became his catcher. And the season of life that had begun in self-doubt and discouragement ended in self-discovery. Baseball would forever be a major part of Branch Rickey's life. Sometimes even against his own wishes, the game had sustained him, served as a vessel for his shrewdness, his wisdom, and his unshakable moral determination to follow the precepts of the God who made him. Rickey would have no doubt years later that baseball was a game that could forever change the life of Jackie Robinson, and indeed, could forever change America—because it had first profoundly changed Rickey himself.

Many years and teams and jobs removed from being that farm boy, Rickey found himself sitting in a meeting of Major League Baseball owners in 1943. The very meeting was itself a sham designed to silence critics of baseball's vigilant policy of racial segregation. Rickey sat quietly and scribbled notes on a sheet of paper. At one point, he wrote, "Attendance," "Jesus," and "America." No one else could see the vision still forming in Branch Rickey's mind, but he intended it to be a triumph for the pockets of himself and the other owners of the Brooklyn Dodgers, for the fundamental worth of all persons under the Methodist doctrine that guided much of Rickey's life, and for the nation dedicated to the principle that all men are indeed created equal. Among the photos that lined the walls of Rickey's office when he and Robinson began the quest to integrate baseball was one of Abraham Lincoln. Before Rickey's career was over, he added a photograph of Jackie Robinson. While Lincoln inspired the type of legacy Rickey desired, Robinson—and the work he and Rickey brought about together—created that legacy.

Wesley Branch Rickey was born December 20, 1881, in a rural corner of either Pike or Scioto County, Ohio. (Rickey credited it as Pike County, but his descendants later indicated that they believed it was Scioto.) Indeed, his entrance into the world was so inauspicious that his birth certificate stated that he was born on the wrong date (either November 20th or December 6th, depending on who was telling the story), though Rickey himself always asserted the December 20th date as accurate. He was the middle of three children of Frank and Emily Rickey, who moved a few miles shortly after his birth to a farm of 102.8 acres in what was then known as Duck Run.

Rickey was an intelligent and curious boy, his destiny perhaps forever shaped when his father acquired a small library of a dozen volumes after a nearby fire sale. Rickey feasted upon the books, reading and rereading until he could recite passages from memory. From his mother he acquired a love of storytelling and an intense religious zeal. Branch would later recall that after a youthful transgression, Emily knelt in prayer beside her son, asking God to forgive her for failing to teach Branch better. "I felt as though I had hit her," he later recalled, "and I was thoroughly chastened."

While the Rickeys were intense people of faith, they were Methodists, which earmarked them as a people more inclined to pursue learning and intellectual pursuits than some of their more fire-breathing contemporary denominational friends. One of the most iconic informal creeds of Methodist thought came from founder John Wesley, and ran as follows, "Give all you can, without hurting yourself or your neighbor. Save all you can, waste nothing living or dying, on sin or folly. And then give all you can, or in other words, all you have to God." Rickey lived with these words, even many years and miles later.

After his brief flirtation with being a farmer, Rickey became a schoolteacher in the community of Turkey Creek. He did so at the age of 17, without the benefit of a high school diploma of his own. Again, though, he experienced a character-defining moment. He either hammered the class troublemaker in a fistfight, or as he preferred the story to be told, intimidated the boy into submission, and quickly won the respect of his students. When another school sought to hire Rickey after that first year at a salary increase of nearly double, he intended to leave. The townspeople of Turkey Creek gathered a petition, asking him to stay and offering him a much more meager salary increase, largely because they themselves could not fund more. When Rickey viewed "those Xs of poor people who wanted their children taught," he changed his mind and stayed another year.

By that time, he had fallen in love with Jane Moulton, whose father owned a store in Lucasville, Ohio. Jane was studying at Western College for Women in Oxford, Ohio, and Rickey made up his mind to attend Ohio Wesleyan University in nearby Delaware, Ohio. Rickey's father objected both on the grounds that college was not the appropriate place for a farmer's son and the fear of untold vices and temptations lurking on a college campus. Generally the dutiful son, Rickey prevailed against his father—so much so that the elder Rickey later mortgaged his farm so that he could help his son pay the expenses of college.

At Wesleyan, Rickey made his mark both as a good student and a great athlete. He starred for the football team, scoring the winning touchdown to knock off Ohio State, and also was an excellent baseball player. However, his college career was short-lived as Rickey inadvertently broke amateurism rules by playing for a local semipro baseball team. When the team's owner tried to deny the relationship, Rickey admitted that he had played for pay.

Rickey feared that with his athletic eligibility gone, he would have no place at Wesleyan, but the president took no disciplinary action beyond barring him from playing for the school's teams. Instead, in 1903, Rickey became the 21-year-old baseball coach of the Wesleyan squad. Rickey was something of a natural as a coach, but beyond his success on the field and his aptitude at maintaining his place as a student at Wesleyan and progressing toward graduation, the coaching job provided another definitive experience in Rickey's life.

The 1903 Ohio Wesleyan baseball team included an African-American player named Charles Thomas. Thomas was from nearby Zanesville, Ohio, and while Wesleyan did not bar black students as many schools then did, there were few of them on campus. Wesleyan had a game at Notre Dame in South Bend, Indiana, and the team prepared to check into the regal Oliver Hotel in South Bend. The Oliver was a grand and glorious hotel, and while its staff featured a number of African Americans, the hotel was not interested in housing Mr. Thomas as a guest.

Rickey was stupefied, explaining the situation to the desk clerk, who did not intend to yield. Eventually, Rickey asked if Thomas would be allowed to stay in his own room but not register. This sufficiently assuaged the sensibilities of the hotel, and Rickey sent Thomas up to the room they would share as he finalized the arrangements.

When Rickey came up to his room, he found Thomas in tears, scrubbing at his skin as if to remove the color that had precluded him from being treated the same as his teammates and fellow students. Various words have been assigned to Thomas in the multiple retellings of the story, but they all carried the same sense of frustration. As for Rickey, he would remember years later, "I never felt so helpless in my life." Rickey certainly remembered the story, as he would return to it time and again as an explanation of his motivation for pushing the integration of baseball. Thomas, who later became a dentist, verified the essential details of the story. Rickey's critics often noted that it was a long time between 1903, when Rickey was allegedly inspired to combat the evils of segregation, and 1945, when his crusade reached the stage of action. True as the criticism may ring, the 21-year old Rickey had his own livelihood to establish before he was ready to tilt at racial injustice.

⤏

Rickey continued to play minor-league baseball as he finished college. Once he graduated, he coached and taught at Allegheny College while he continued playing baseball. In 1904, his contract was purchased by the Cincinnati Reds. But before he could play in a game, Reds manager Joe Kelley overheard Rickey explaining that he would not be at the park for a Sunday game. This was a staple of Rickey's life—he kept the biblical Sabbath strictly, and he thought Reds management understood this scruple of his. Many sportswriters subsequently credited Rickey's refusal to play on Sundays as a pledge he made to his mother. There is no indication that Rickey ever actually made such a pledge, and in fact, his parents were upset by the report it was on their account that he had jeopardized his career. He wrote them of his sorrow at this misunderstanding, assuring them that his "convictions are not for sale." Actually, it was after some ridiculed Rickey for his literal application of scripture that he determined that he would never enter a ballpark on Sunday. He heard his mother defend him and determined that his not bending on the issue in question would be a link with her.

Reds owner Garry Herrmann did release Rickey, and he never played in a game for the Reds, although Herrmann expressed his sadness at the misunderstanding and paid Rickey a healthy severance salary. In 1905, Rickey was signed by the Chicago White Sox and then traded to the St. Louis Browns. He played in only one game for the Browns before he left to tend to his ill mother. While Emily recovered, Rickey began studying lawbooks, as he realized that his potential father-in-law,

Chandler Moulton, would likely always object to his courtship of Jane as long as Rickey played baseball for a living. Before the 1906 season, Rickey approached Moulton and indicated that he would give up baseball by the end of the 1907 season and then study law. In return, Moulton acquiesced to the wedding, which occurred on June 1, 1906.

Meanwhile, Rickey batted .284 with three home runs for the Browns in 1906. However, his career took a sharp decline in 1907, after he was traded to the New York Highlanders (who would one day be called the Yankees) when he suddenly was unable to throw. In the deadball era, a catcher who could not throw was a guarantee to be exploited, and Rickey was. On June 28, 1907, the Washington Senators stole 13 bases on Rickey, whose efforts to throw out runners were so woeful that by the end of the streak, he didn't even bother to try to throw.

Rickey played a few other positions, but in 1907, he batted just .182, and generally played his way out of major-league baseball. He returned to Wesleyan to teach and coach, and also took night law classes at Ohio State. Burning the candle at both ends, Rickey experienced a severe decline in health and a loss of weight. He was diagnosed with tuberculosis and sent to upstate New York for care. In the Adirondack Mountains, Rickey slowly returned to health, even drinking glasses of beer under the direction of the medical staff, which did conflict with his generally teetotaling nature. He was eventually discharged from the tuberculosis sanitarium and admitted to the University of Michigan law school.

Rickey finished his legal studies, but he always kept a toe in coaching baseball. In 1911, he and Jane moved west to Idaho, where he intended to focus on practicing law. When the firm he joined had virtually no business, Rickey was excited to hear that Michigan had not hired a replacement baseball coach. His law partners encouraged him to return, and he did. After 1912, St. Louis Browns owner Robert Hedges sought out Rickey and offered him a job as the business manager of his Kansas City minor-league team. Rickey held Hedges at bay while he returned to Idaho for another summer of diminishing returns in the practice of law. Later that summer, Hedges contacted him again—this time asking him to run the Browns instead of a minor-league team. Rickey was torn, as one writer noted, recognizing the "tremendous sense of intellectual challenge and physical excitement, and . . . prospects for considerable financial reward," but also knowing "it wasn't the respectable life of law that the Moultons expected of their son-in-law." With Jane's blessing, baseball won out, and Rickey never looked back.

~

Rickey led the Browns and then the crosstown rival St. Louis Cardinals, and he always found himself running baseball teams under circumstances that left him without the financial means to recklessly lavish cash on the best available talent. Rickey spent almost a decade as a field manager for the bereft Browns and Cardinals, amassing a career record of 597-664. However, while his managing was generally mediocre, during the early 1920s, Rickey struck gold as a business manager—the modern equivalent of a general manager.

Rickey had sent one of his best scouts, Charley Barrett, to Texas to sign some promising young players. When other, more profitable franchises frustrated the plan by outbidding the Cardinals, Rickey had a stroke of inspiration. He sent Barrett a telegram saying, "Pack up and come home—we'll develop our own players."

Cardinal owner Sam Breadon assented to Rickey's new plan, so Rickey directed him to buy a majority interest in a minor-league team in Fort Smith, Arkansas. Next came the Houston Buffaloes of the Texas League. An affiliation with a team in Syracuse, New York, soon followed. The elements of the plan were simple, as one biographer noted: "Buy raw talent inexpensively, watch it develop under the best managers, coaches, and instructors, and patiently wait to reap the profit from the finished product while trading away the surplus players for cash and maybe other prospects." Rickey termed the activity as gaining young players and keeping an eye on them until they could "ripen into money."

The pattern continued throughout the 1920s, even as Rickey finished his career as a manager in 1925. Breadon told him, "In time . . . you will see that I am doing you a great favor. You can now devote yourself fully to player development and scouting." By the end of the 1920s, the Cardinals owned eight minor-league teams and had agreements regarding player acquisition with several others. In the late '30s, the farm system had grown to over 700 players and some interest in more than 30 teams.

Rickey also extended the grasp of the farm system by introducing widespread tryout camps, which helped the Cardinals get an early glance at literally thousands of unknown young players. By the late '20s, Rickey had expanded the reach of the tryouts beyond St. Louis to neighboring territories such as Illinois and Oklahoma.

The effect in St. Louis was palpable. In 1926, the year after Rickey was relieved as manager, the Cardinals won the World Series. The Cardinal farm system had produced a full 15 of the 25 players on that 1926 team's roster. As the farm system grew in size and significance, it continued to become the backbone of a Cardinal team that had gone from second-division staple to perennial contender.

Between 1926 and 1942, when he left St. Louis, the farm system resulted in six pennants and four World Series titles—and in even more, if one considers the excellent Cardinal squads of the first few years after Rickey's departure, which were largely a product of the farm system. But there was a dark side to Rickey's sudden reputation as the father of the farm system. For one, some within baseball, most likely the opposing owners who had once sat back and outbid Rickey for prime talent, felt that the farm system was monopolistic and could wreak havoc on the minor leagues. It is important to remember that unlike the modern minor leagues, those early leagues had been very much independent of Major League Baseball, and were run with an eye toward competition and profit above improving young talent for future baseball development. The critics of Rickey's farm system had a powerful ally in Commissioner Kenesaw Mountain Landis.

Landis was baseball's first commissioner, and on the strength of his agreement to come and help clean up the Black Sox scandal in 1921, he wielded authoritarian power in baseball. That power was perhaps most significant when he utilized it to help keep baseball's unwritten code of segregation intact. But Landis was not a man who avoided conflict, and what he saw in the Cardinals' control of a massive number of young minor leaguers concerned him. He did not intend to dispatch advice and sit idly by.

In fact, one of Landis's first rulings as commissioner was to take a minor leaguer, Phil Todt, from Rickey's Cardinal organization because Rickey had "covered up" his interest in Todt via his minor-league team in Texas. Landis frequently threw barbs in Rickey's direction regarding the farm system, which some in the media dubbed "the chain gang." Perhaps the most dramatic confrontation came at baseball's 1929 winter meetings, when Landis railed against the system and indicated his intention to destroy it. When Sam Breadon protested, and indicated that he had statements from several minor leaguers in favor of his and Rickey's system, Landis exploded. "You are both guilty of raping the minors," he fumed.

It took a few years for him to complete his destruction plan, but in 1938, Landis finally zeroed in on the farm system. He specifically focused on the fact that Rickey controlled multiple teams in the Three-I League (named for teams from Illinois, Indiana, and Iowa). Rickey admitted that his control of multiple teams would allow him to dictate whether each team could claim players for itself or not. Landis pushed Rickey to admit that the connection between his teams was "as big as a house." When Rickey declined to agree, Landis asserted that the connection was "as big as the universe." The commissioner voiced concern for the competitive integrity of the minor leagues, should they be subject to Rickey's whims rather than the competitive fight for a championship. Eventually, Landis dropped the hammer by allowing somewhere between 74 and 91 Cardinal minor leaguers to become free agents.

Rickey defended his system in part based on the economic necessity of the Depression and post-Depression era. Frustrated that Landis would criticize the existing system without offering any meaningful alternative, Rickey made his viewpoint clear. At a meeting of major-league owners in 1930, he had lectured on the number of minor leagues shutting down and admitted, "The farm system is not an ideal system, but when people are hungry, they eat food which may or may not be ideally cooked and served."

Aside from the constant rebuffs from the commissioner of baseball (and the loss of an estimated $200,000 worth of players in Landis's 1938 decision), the other negative aspect of the farm system was that it enhanced Rickey's already present reputation for frugality. His contract with Sam Breadon (like his later contract with the Dodgers) paid him an unnamed bonus for any sums of money obtained in trades of players. The logic went that Rickey was monopolizing cheap labor, and when the players actually were worth any money, he promptly sold them to the highest bidder and skimmed a chunk of the purchase into his own pocket.

It was, of course, true. Baseball had always operated on a financial system that ranged somewhere between monopoly and fiefdom. The reserve clause bound players to a one-sided financial arrangement, and given the multitude of replacement players always available to him, Rickey's natural inclination to trade a player a year early rather than a year late was doubtlessly enhanced by the money coming back into his own pocket.

However, as Rickey's career continued, his stinginess developed a reputation perhaps even greater than that of his baseball wisdom. After the 1942 season, Cardinals owner Sam Breadon grew tired of paying a high salary (and likely losing a fair amount of the credit for the Cardinals) to Rickey, and so he allowed his contract to expire. It was in Rickey's next stop, Brooklyn, where the media so thoroughly established the man's reputation as a skinflint. In the fall of 1942, Rickey signed a contract similar to the one he had maintained in St. Louis—which also included the bonus return from the sale of every Brooklyn major or minor leaguer.

Then as now, the New York sports press was hardly less than formidable. But it was Jimmy Powers of the *Daily News* who absolutely made Rickey's blood boil. Powers dubbed Rickey "El Cheapo," a nickname so good that he relied upon it, again and again. One biographer noted that over a six-month period in 1946, no fewer than 80 of Powers's columns contained shots at Rickey. Another noted that 74 of the 180 columns mentioned the "El Cheapo" nickname. At one point, Powers began a campaign to have Rickey fired, writing to ask readers whether he should be sent over Niagara Falls in a barrel, before ultimately determining that fans should each donate a $20 bill and "perhaps Rickey's desire for milking money out of the franchise will be satisfied and he will pack his carpet bags and go away to another town and run his coolie payroll there."

Rickey was so frustrated with the injustice of Powers's crusade that he ordered his staff to prepare a rebuttal document, which ran to some 37 pages and which he circulated to fellow Dodger brass, asking about the possibility of filing suit against Powers. The document ultimately concluded that Powers's charges were "poisonous smokescreens, personal vilifications, innuendos, colored exaggerations, half-truths, untruths, flat lies, a disgrace to the sports writing profession." Ultimately, cooler heads prevailed as the Dodgers would prefer to neither alienate the New York media or to have to open their account books to a thorough analysis.

At some point, much to Rickey's frustration, whether he actually was cheap or not became more or less irrelevant. The reputation became the reality. Carl Erskine, who played for Rickey's Dodgers, later recalled that due to some irregularities with his initial signing, he actually collected a bonus from Rickey on signing, and then another to resign after the Commissioner of Baseball voided his contract. Erskine told the story to Dizzy Dean, who played under Rickey's leadership in St. Louis. At the time, Erskine was about to be interviewed on television by Dean after pitching his second career no-hitter. When Erskine shared the story, Dean told the television viewers, "Folks, this young man deserves to be in the Hall of Fame. Not because he pitched two no-hitters. He got two bonuses from Branch Rickey."

For much of Rickey's career, this was how he was defined. He was an aging tycoon who built the Cardinals into a near dynasty by monopolizing control of the minor leagues. He was an excellent talent scout, but a blowhard. He was a wise businessman, but a penny-pincher. He developed young baseball talent, but always with a hand in his own pocket. He was a passionate Christian who still refused to go to the ballpark on Sunday, but he never refused his share of Sunday-game gate receipts.

Had Rickey retired from baseball in 1942 instead of moving to Brooklyn and soon changing the sport forever, he still would have been a respected baseball mind. He probably would not have been a Hall of Famer, and his critics would have an answer for every accomplishment he had compiled. But the legacy of Branch Rickey was still being written, and there was a pivotal chapter about to unfold.

When exactly did Branch Rickey begin contemplating the integration of baseball? He loved to tell the story of Charles Thomas back in 1904, to the point that one of his own daughters later recalled that the Thomas story was something "we got at the table" in the Rickey family. But the Thomas story contravenes the more practical birth of Rickey's masterstroke. As was noted before, while Rickey doubtlessly felt bad for poor Thomas, he didn't rush out and integrate the St. Louis Browns or Cardinals. In Rickey's defense, as one biographer noted, not only was St. Louis the southernmost city in the major leagues, and a place where the local media commonly referred to blacks as "darkies" in print, but until May 1944, even Sportsman's Park, where the Cardinals played, was segregated. This led to an awkward moment when Charles Thomas came to see Rickey in St. Louis, apparently during the '30s, and Rickey kept him in his office, opining that one day racial discrimination in the United States would no longer exist. For all of Rickey's belief in the future of America, in the present day of St. Louis, he could not sit with Thomas to watch that afternoon's baseball game.

The plan to integrate must have come soon after Rickey's late 1942 move to Brooklyn. Of course, after two decades of feasting on minor-league talent, Rickey doubtlessly looked around and saw that his ever-present source of future help had been left behind in the Show-Me State. It was then that he realized that the existent Negro Leagues were a fertile source of available talent that he could tap, and that he could do a great thing for American society by integrating the game carefully and thoughtfully. Or maybe it was the other way around. Rickey was not above making clear that he was signing Robinson only based on competitive motives. He wrote to one sportswriter, "I don't mean to be a crusader. My only purpose is to be fair to all people and my selfish objective is to win baseball games."

However, on other occasions, particularly as the years rolled along and the long-term success of the "Great Experiment" of baseball integration was long since assured, Rickey felt more freedom to tip his hand as to other reasons for his actions. For instance, in 1955, he wrote in a letter, "When I hired Jackie Robinson, I gave as the salient reason simply the fact that I wanted to win a pennant in Brooklyn; that I didn't care whether the man had long horns and a forked tail or not. . . . That was a good reason and a sufficient reason. However, it was not really a statement of the whole truth." This was the explanation that had roots in Charles Thomas's painful story, that had Rickey telling others that he had wanted to include black players on the Cardinals in the '30s. The injustice of segregation had weighed on him, he later insisted. Ultimately, there is no reason to doubt either version of events.

Whatever Rickey's motivations and the proportion thereof, he was never a man to go into a pivotal venture without a well-thought-out plan. One of Rickey's much-relied-upon anecdotes was the story of an old couple taking their first railroad trip. Seeing cliffs ahead, the old couple—or sometimes, the wife, the story could vary—moaned and complained of "trouble ahead, trouble ahead." Of course, the old couple completed the trip without incident, their handwringing all in vain over borrowed trouble. Rickey loved the story so much that he told it to Robinson in their famous first meeting on August 28, 1945, culminating the story with its moral—"That's the way it is with most trouble ahead in this world, Jackie—if we use the common sense and courage God gave us. But you've got to study the hazards and build wisely."

For Rickey, building wisely resulted in a six-part plan to integrate baseball. First, he had to secure the blessing of the Dodgers' owners and stockholders. Next, he had to identify the game-changing baseball talent who could change the game. Third, he had to make sure that this player was also of sufficient character and reserve to handle the nonbaseball aspects of the quest. Fourth, Rickey needed positive reaction from the fans and media. Fifth, he sought support—but a thoughtful, nonabrasive support—from African Americans so as to build up Robinson without creating ill will from white fans, media, and others. Finally, he wanted the player in question to be fully accepted by his teammates as part of the Dodgers.

To the extent that Rickey's plan can be accurately dated, it appears to have certainly been in place by the beginning of 1943. In January of that year, Rickey met with George V. McLaughlin of the Brooklyn Trust Company. McLaughlin's bank controlled the Ebbets' family stock, and thus, the ownership of the Dodgers. The meeting was fairly routine, with Rickey reviewing the previous season and discussing some plans for the next season. Casually, almost slyly, he mentioned to McLaughlin that he would be scouting for new talent. "We are hoping to beat the bushes," Rickey said, "and that might include a Negro player or two."

If McLaughlin was the guinea pig for the entire idea—and he probably was—he didn't budge. "If you're doing this to improve the ball club," he told Rickey, "go ahead. But if you're doing it for the emancipation of the Negro, then forget it." Good enough for Rickey, at least in early 1943. A full meeting of the board of directors was planned for the following week, and they concurred in McLaughlin's cautious affirmation of this plan.

Indeed, Rickey may well not have intended for the first player to break the color line to be African American. Rickey asked Jose Seda, the athletic director of the University of Puerto Rico, to watch for prospects, which Seda did at home and in Mexico. Professor Robert Haig scouted Cuba on Rickey's behalf. Finally, Rickey allegedly sent Walter O'Malley to Cuba with instructions to sign Silvio Garcia, who had been drafted into the Cuban army, and thus was not available to make baseball history. This anecdote apparently springs from O'Malley, who was always eager to embellish his own credentials in the integration of baseball. A more generally accepted version of events is that the Dodgers did not try to sign Garcia, but did scout him via Tom Greenwade, the legendary scout who discovered Mickey Mantle, among other baseball diamonds. Garcia, the other version of the story goes, did not impress Greenwade.

Signing a Latin player would have raised its own set of complications, as the slow advancement of such players ultimately proved. Perhaps Rickey realized that breaking a culture barrier and a language barrier both would be difficult for anyone to bear. Latin pioneers like Vic Power spoke to the truth of this difficulty. Or maybe a Latin player simply would not have been a full measure of integration. Baseball did have a history of light-skinned Latin players disguising or lying about their heritage and gaining occasional grudging entry into Major League Baseball. Whatever the reasons, Rickey ultimately decided that his pioneer would be African American.

Or perhaps that decision was made for him as his legion of scouts and contacts homed in on Jackie Robinson, whose name seemed to keep coming up. After a potentially game-changing scouting visit, Clyde Sukeforth brought Robinson to Brooklyn to meet Rickey. When Sukeforth attested that Robinson passed the on-the-field test, it was time for Rickey to determine the fiber of his character.

There were three people present in Rickey's Montague Street office on August 28, 1945, when the decision to integrate baseball took a massive step from theory to reality. Robinson had temporarily abandoned the Kansas City Monarchs and traveled to Brooklyn with Sukeforth to meet with Rickey. Unlike virtually every aspect of the Robinson biography, all three versions of the events of that meeting are relatively consistent. Of course, no one had a tape recorder, so any dialogue reported should probably be taken with a grain of salt, but each of the three persons present for the meeting confirm the same basic conversation.

Rickey asked Robinson whether he had a girl. Jane Moulton Rickey had been the backbone to her husband's tossed-about life. Rickey could hardly fail to appreciate the significance of a spouse who had been a soul mate, and Robinson quickly established his own bona fides on that score.

Rickey asked Robinson about his religious faith. Again, Robinson satisfied his future boss on that point. Both men were Methodists, and Robinson's life lessons learned from Reverend Karl Downs were probably mentioned. Both men were generally abstainers from alcohol, another point that probably came out in conversation.

Everyone recalled Rickey asking Robinson if he was under contract to the Kansas City Monarchs. Doubtlessly, Rickey had good reason to anticipate a legal battle for poaching a signed player, but here again, Robinson set his mind at ease, confirming that he had no signed contract or even any oral understanding beyond a payday-to-payday agreement between himself and the team.

Through Sukeforth, Tom Greenwade, Wid Matthews, George Sisler, Wendell Smith, and a variety of other sources, Rickey had scouted Robinson well. The man known as "The Mahatma" (nicknamed after a newspaper description of Gandhi that had described the Indian leader as "part your grandfather, part Tammany Hall") held forth on his research. Robinson later recalled, "In ten minutes he covered practically every highlight of my career. He knew my mother's first name, the fact that my older brother had been killed in a motorcycle accident, that I had a tendency to hit to left field, that I was a 'holler guy' who argued with umpires."

In fact, this last point was an issue for Rickey. His research had included Robinson's Texas court-martial during the war, and he had heard from several sources that Robinson could be more than slightly assertive in the name of competition. This concerned Rickey enough that he asked Wendell Smith about Robinson's temper. Smith later admitted, "I didn't want to tell Mr. Rickey, 'Yes, he's tough to get along with.'" However, the more he investigated, the more Rickey saw that the issue was not surprising. Rickey, said one biographer, "understood that what might be called an 'uppity' attitude in black players would be praised as admirable aggressiveness in white players."

But it was Robinson's attitude that Rickey had truly invited him to Brooklyn to test. He revealed to Robinson that he had brought him to Brooklyn not to discuss playing for the Brown Dodgers of the new

Negro League that Rickey had discussed openly for months as a smoke-screen for his true intention. He wanted to sign Robinson for Brooklyn, perhaps place him in Montreal. "I know you're a good ballplayer," Rickey is reputed to have said. "What I don't know is whether you have the guts."

Rickey the aged baseball general manager now took a back seat to Rickey the amateur thespian. He imitated baserunners sliding into Robinson, waiters or hotel clerks who would not serve him, railroad conductors who would not acknowledge him, and gave Robinson a veritable preview of the life that would be ahead if he proved himself to have sufficient guts to satisfy Rickey. He cursed, he name-called, at one point, he even swung his fist dangerously close to Robinson.

The dramatics concluded, Rickey picked up a copy of Giovanni Papini's *The Life of Christ* (or may have handed it to Robinson to read for himself). Having verified a religious touchstone with Robinson minutes earlier, Rickey now went to it immediately. He quoted Christ, "Ye have heard that it hath been said, an eye for an eye, and a tooth for a tooth: But I say unto you, That ye resist not evil: But whosoever shall smite thee on thy cheek, turn to him the other also."

Robinson, thoughtful and quiet throughout Rickey's interrogation and performance, now said only, "I have two cheeks, Mr. Rickey. Is that it?"

That was indeed it. Other versions of the story have Robinson reacting to the dramatics by asking Rickey if he wanted a player without the guts to fight back. In that version, Rickey answers, "I'm looking for a ballplayer with guts enough not to fight back."

There was more to the conversation, elements generally redacted from the big-screen versions featured in 1950's *The Jackie Robinson Story* and 2013's *42*. Rickey emphasized to Robinson that they would not have many allies in the quest. "No army, no owners, virtually nobody on our side," Robinson recalled him saying. He emphasized the importance that Robinson be equal to the task. Clyde Sukeforth recalled Rickey bringing up Prohibition and the 18th Amendment, and how even the right decision, if poorly handled, could backfire. Sukeforth told Rickey in 1950 that he recalled that he "pointed out that an incident could set back the cause of the negro race, and therefore you and he would be carrying a tremendous load."

Listening to Rickey's presentation, Robinson had made up his mind to carry that load. "I had to do it for several reasons," he later wrote. "For black youth, for my mother, for Rae, for myself. I had already begun to feel that I had to do it for Branch Rickey."

Near the end of the meeting, Robinson reassured him. "If you want to take this gamble, I will promise you there will be no incident."

Sukeforth later recalled that when Robinson made this promise, "I thought the old man was going to kiss him."

After the signing of Robinson became public in October 1945, Rickey—at least mostly—had the positive reaction from the fans and media that made up the fourth stage of his plan. Dan Parker in the New York *Daily Mirror* noted, "Why a good respectable Negro athlete shouldn't fit just as well into organized baseball as he does college football, basketball, boxing and cricket is something I have never been able to figure out." More boldly, Elmer Ferguson of the *Montreal Herald* approvingly stated, "Those who were good enough to fight and die by the side of the whites are plenty good enough to play by the side of the whites!"

Of course, no message carries universal approval. On March 12, 1946, Rickey's old enemy Jimmy Powers was back at it with the *Daily News*, trying to figure out where to bury the sword. Not only did Powers state his belief that "we don't believe Jackie Robinson . . . will ever play in the big leagues," but he went on to cite Rickey's penchant for paying low salaries, concluding, "We find it awfully hard to believe that Branch Rickey is kind, generous, and full of good will to all men." Plenty of others questioned both Robinson's skill and Rickey's motives, but Rickey knew that with every base hit and stolen base, Robinson would tilt the totals in their favor.

Rickey hired Wendell Smith so as to both facilitate better interactions for Robinson with the otherwise white world and to keep a bold pen in the African-American press carrying his message, thus looking after the fifth prong of the plan. Rickey was not above carrying that banner himself. In early 1947, after Robinson's successful season in Montreal but before his promotion to the Dodgers was a fait accompli, Rickey summoned many local African-American community leaders to the Brooklyn YMCA. There he shocked the assembled minor dignitaries, telling them that if he chose to promote Robinson, "the biggest threat to his success—the one enemy most likely to ruin that success—is the Negro people themselves." He continued, lashing out at the type of treatment he was imagining. "You'll strut. You'll wear badges. You'll hold Jackie Robinson Days . . . and Jackie Robinson Nights. You'll get drunk. You'll fight. You'll be arrested. You'll wine and dine the player until he is fat and futile. You'll symbolize his importance into a national comedy . . . and an ultimate tragedy—yes, tragedy."

Reaching the crescendo of his remarks, Rickey told his audience, "If any individual, group, or segment of Negro society sees the advancement of Jackie Robinson in baseball as a symbol of social 'ism' or schism, a triumph of race over race, I will curse the day I ever signed him to a contract, and I will personally see that baseball is never so abused and misrepresented again!"

His message delivered, and backed up by Wendell Smith, Sam Lacy, and others close enough to the story to see the wisdom beneath the bitter taste of the comments delivered, Rickey set out doing everything in his power to make Robinson's story a triumph.

⌁

The Dodgers were preparing for spring training in Daytona Beach, Florida, where Rickey had already been laying the groundwork to try to assure a peaceful spring for Robinson and his fellow African-American signee, pitcher John Wright. While Rickey apparently did engineer the situation so that Robinson and Wright were accepted in Daytona Beach, he was not as successful in selling progressive politics to the neighboring Jim Crow Florida towns, resulting in canceled games and hard feelings.

Rickey supported Robinson when he struggled. When Robinson developed a sore arm early in camp, Rickey told him that he would have to play through the pain. "You can't afford to miss a single day," he told Robinson. "They'll say you're dogging it, that you are pretending your arm is sore." However, at the same time, Rickey apparently engineered for Robinson to work out at first base, where his sore arm would cause less of an issue.

Additionally, Rickey tried to encourage Robinson to be himself on the bases. "Be more daring," he would yell, or "Gamble. Take a bigger lead." It was this sense of "adventure" that had sold Rickey on Robinson as a player. In his talent-scouting soul, Rickey doubtlessly recognized that while Robinson was a sore-armed player in an unfamiliar position, his base running would give him a chance to shine.

Rickey also reminded Robinson of the need to avoid fighting violence with violence. In a spring scrimmage, Robinson was spiked by Eddie Stanky, one of the more combative Dodgers who was less than enthralled at Robinson's presence in spring training. Some accounts indicate that Robinson retaliated by tagging Stanky in the testicles, although whatever the exact exchange, Rickey apparently felt it necessary to warn Robinson to control himself, and Robinson assured him that he would.

While Rickey could not provide equality in accommodations or in the sentiment of the locals for Robinson, he could do everything within his power to give him an equal chance on the field. Mississippi-born Clay Hopper was assigned to manage Robinson. Hopper reportedly begged Rickey not to make him manage a Negro player. For his part, Rickey was unabashed in his reply. "You can manage correctly, or you can be unemployed," he told Hopper. He further elucidated, "You manage this fellow the way I want him managed, and you figure out how I want him managed."

Ultimately, Rickey merely wanted Robinson to have a full and complete opportunity. In pondering his six-point plan, he realized the final key, acceptance by fellow players, lay in the text of Alexander Pope's *Essay on Man*:

> Vice is a monster of so frightful mien
> As to be hated, needs but to be seen;
> Yet seen too oft, familiar with her face,
> We first endure, then pity, then embrace.

Within those words, Rickey found his ultimate aim. Robinson's teammates, he said, would endure him, then pity him, and then embrace him. If that first Florida spring training did nothing except move past endurance into pity, it was a worthwhile part of the integration of baseball.

The 1946 season moved past pity to embracing. Hopper, the same manager who had begged not to have to manage Robinson, shook his hand at the end of the year and called him a great ballplayer and a fine gentleman. He practically begged Rickey to have Robinson back for 1947, should the Dodgers not need him. Teammates and baseball personnel watched as Robinson dodged insults and catcalls, and played even better the more he was heckled. By the end of 1946, Rickey believed Robinson would be ready.

As the Dodgers prepared for 1947, Rickey moved ahead with promoting the final hurdle of the goal. Aware that word of team turmoil was sweeping the clubhouse, down to rumors of a petition circulating against Robinson, Rickey took matters into his own hands. Sussing out which Dodgers felt strongest against playing with Robinson, Rickey met individually with each. The players whom he could convince as to the error of their ways, like Carl Furillo, he did so. Rickey is alleged to have asked Furillo, an Italian from Pennsylvania, how long it had been since his father immigrated. After he answered, Rickey asked him what Furillo's own life would have been like if "a few idiots got together and made up another petition to send him back to Sicily." Point taken.

When other players, like Bobby Bragan or Dixie Walker, were not as receptive to the message of unity that Rickey was selling, he made arrangements for them to move on—some immediately, some with a bit more deliberation. However, there was no question where the Dodgers' loyalty stood.

Rickey was not above putting the rest of organized baseball in its place. When Phillies general manager Herb Pennock called to ask him not to bring Robinson on the Dodgers' upcoming road trip to Philadelphia, Rickey assured him that Robinson would be there, and that Brooklyn would happily accept forfeit victories if Philadelphia did not deign it appropriate to meet their challenge on the field.

To be certain, Rickey did not always intervene. When Phillies manager Ben Chapman led his team in a vicious verbal assault on Robinson, Rickey sat back and watched. Not that he enjoyed it, but because he knew what it meant to the Dodger team. "When he poured out that string of unconscionable abuse," noted Rickey later, "he solidified and unified thirty men, not one of whom was willing to sit by and see someone kick around a man who had his hands tied behind his back." They would endure Robinson, then pity him, and then embrace him.

By the end of 1947, even many of those initially opposed to Robinson were changing their tune. J. Taylor Spink of *The Sporting News*, which had taken virtually every opportunity to belittle Robinson and turn its nose up at the integration of baseball, named him Rookie of the Year. The decision, Spink assured his readers, was based only on his on-field exploits. "The sociological experiment that Robinson represented, the trail blazing that he did, the barriers he broke down, did not enter into the decision," wrote Spink. Robinson was a success, and he would forever be tied to Rickey.

After a slow-starting 1948 season, Robinson returned to top form the following year. He turned 30 years old just before the 1949 season started, and enjoyed his finest season in organized baseball, culminating with winning the National League Most Valuable Player award and leading the Dodgers to their second pennant in his first three seasons.

The year 1949 was significant because of Robinson's breathtaking play, as he set career highs in batting average (a league-leading .342), RBI (124), and stolen bases (37). But arguably more important than how well he played was how he played. According to many accounts, 1949 is accepted as the season that Rickey removed the last social shackles from Robinson. On or about the initial August 1945 meeting, Rickey allegedly extracted a pledge for three seasons of meek tolerance from Robinson before he could play the game as he fully wished. But is this consistent with who Rickey or Robinson were, or is this, like Rickey's mother extracting a fictitious pledge to abstain from Sunday baseball, a case where the story fit the facts, and so it was erroneously determined to be true?

There are several sources who believe the three seasons of turning the other cheek were mandated. Rickey biographer Murray Polner has Rickey saying to Robinson in their initial meeting, "You will have to promise that for the first three years in baseball you will turn your other cheek. I know that you are naturally combative. But for three years— three years—you will have to do it the only way it can be done. Three years—can you do it?" Similarly, Red Barber attested, "I've heard Rickey say, 'For three years—that was the agreement—this man was to turn the other cheek.'"

Frankly, the conversation reported by Polner feels stilted. Even given Rickey's love of planning, to have determined an exact amount of time that Robinson must deny his natural inclinations before it would suddenly be acceptable seems quite a stretch. Certainly, Rickey discussed during that fateful afternoon that it would be incumbent on Robinson to avoid some sort of embarrassing incident that could scuttle the entire project of baseball integration. Clyde Sukeforth recalled Robinson saying, "Mr. Rickey, I think I can play ball, but I will promise you that I will do the second part of the job. I won't be involved in an incident." Nowhere did Sukeforth mention three years.

Nowhere did Robinson ever mention three years, either. Despite penning several accounts of the meeting, Robinson never discussed a time line for him to be turned loose on the rest of baseball. What is discussed is a much more humane, intellectual conversation between Rickey and Robinson before 1949. Rickey recalled, "All along I had known that the point would come when my almost-filial relationship with Jackie would break with ill feeling if I did not issue an emancipation proclamation for him. I could see that for two years the tensions had built up. . . . I also knew that whereas the wisest choice for Robinson overall for those first two years was to turn the other cheek, not to fight back, there were many in baseball and out of it who . . . would not understand. . . . So I told Robinson that he was on his own."

Robinson later recalled Rickey calling him into his office and simply saying, "Jackie, you're on your own now. You can be yourself now."

However, lest too much be made of this conversation, many close to both parties have expressed reservation that the formality of Rickey's proclamation was sought or needed. Rickey's grandson, Branch B. Rickey, stated, "The idea that Branch Rickey had kept Jackie Robinson from exploding is nonsense. Branch Rickey was not on the field when someone spiked or hit Jackie. Jackie was not on a leash. It was Jackie Robinson who kept Jackie Robinson from exploding. He had given a pledge he believed in and he stuck by it—that's all."

Rachel Robinson wrote, "Some have made it seem as if Rickey granted Jack permission to be himself. I would say that Jack had already made that decision on his own, and that Rickey agreed and released him." Similarly, author Jules Tygiel noted, "In reality, Robinson had removed the matter from Rickey's hands; the Mahatma simply recognized and approved the change."

This matter came to a head (and probably to public attention) in 1949 because Robinson had an altercation with a minor-league pitcher named Chris Van Cuyk during spring training. Robinson had drawn some insults from minor leaguers after misplaying a ground ball, and then had a few critical remarks for Van Cuyk, who had reacted by brushing him back. Robinson supposedly told Van Cuyk, "If you had hit me, I would have punched you."

The day before, Robinson had told a writer that opposing players "better be rough on me, because I'm going to be rough on them." That comment, reported *after* the Van Cuyk incident, got Robinson a meeting with Commissioner Chandler. Robinson argued that he was misquoted and—accurately—that the comment was printed out of context.

It is quite a stretch to go from Robinson having a spring training tussle with a teammate to assuming that he had somehow been liberated by Branch Rickey from a set period of some sort of sociological servitude. The relationship between the two men ran much too deep for that sort of staged theatrics. Admittedly, Rickey would allow some latitude to those who wished to credit him with Robinson's success. But the actions and words of Robinson himself speak sufficiently on that front.

Rickey and Robinson had only one more season together, and 1950 ended in disappointment for all. The Dodgers came up short on the last day of the season in a game to try to force a playoff for the National League pennant, and Rickey was squeezed out of ownership by Walter O'Malley following the season. Considering the extent to which Rickey and Robinson changed the face of baseball forever, it's hard to believe that they were together in Brooklyn for only four seasons.

Rickey's exodus was brought about by the death of chemist John Smith in July 1950. Smith, like Rickey, had owned 25 percent of the Dodgers. O'Malley quickly moved to control the voting rights of Smith's share, which gave him a 50 percent interest. This left the Dodgers torn, with Jim and Ann Mulvey (whose daughter later married Dodger pitcher Ralph Branca) controlling 25 percent, Rickey 25 percent, and O'Malley 50 percent. With no love lost between Rickey and O'Malley, Rickey decided he would try to sell his stock.

O'Malley offered to buy Rickey's stock for the price at which it had been purchased, roughly $350,000. As the Dodgers ran a surplus of roughly $2.5 million, this didn't seem right to Rickey. Behind the scenes, Rickey cooked up a scheme by which William Zeckendorf, a friend of Pittsburgh Pirates owner John Galbreath, offered $1 million for the stock. O'Malley was skeptical of the legitimacy of the offer, but he had to either match it or risk failing to gain ultimate control of the Dodgers. He did match the offer, and paid an additional $50,000 fee, as a result of tying up Zeckendorf's funds during his bid for the Dodgers. Ultimately, Rickey sold for the $1,000,000 price, Zeckendorf ended up giving the extra $50,000 to Rickey, and Walter O'Malley had about 700,000 new reasons to dislike Branch Rickey.

None of this was exactly pleasing to Jackie Robinson. He loved Rickey and came to despise O'Malley. One man had been his benefactor, and the other seemed to scramble to try to attach himself to anything meritorious from Robinson, including the very idea of integrating baseball.

Robinson was not fooled. In a surviving letter to Rickey after the 1950 season, Robinson wrote:

> It is certainly tough on everyone in Brooklyn to have you leave the organization, but to me its [sic] much worse and I don't mind saying we (my family) hate to see you go but realize that baseball is like that and anything can happen. It has been the finest experience I have had being associated with you and I want to thank you very much for all you have meant not only to me and my family but to the entire country and particularly the members of our race. I am glad for your sake that I had a small part to do with the success of your efforts and must admit it was your constant guidance that enabled me to do it. Regardless of what happens to me in the future it all can be placed on what you have done and believe me, I appreciate it.

While the end of their time with the Dodgers had come, nothing changed the affection within the friendship. Rickey's grandson admitted, "Sometimes my family believed that my grandfather really had two sons—my father and Jackie. We all accepted it as a fact of our lives; we knew that my grandfather loved Jackie, and we all respected Jackie. My own father knew how much Jackie meant to my grandfather and he was careful not to be resentful."

The relationship of Rickey and Robinson took on significant overtones. To Robinson, whatever else Rickey did, he would always be the man who had believed in him to accomplish a feat that few believed possible. It is not an overstatement to concur with the assessment above—that in many senses, Robinson, who was fatherless from the beginning of his memory, found his father figure in Rickey. For Rickey's side of things, Robinson always remembered and emphasized his best qualities. He would never be "El Cheapo" to Robinson (who in fact expressly denied these charges in print multiple times). He was never a baseball robber baron or exploiter of talent. Whatever benefits, financial or historical, he derived from Jackie Robinson's successes, Rickey had put in his own time in the trenches planning and supporting his prodigy's triumph.

A less ambitious man than Rickey probably would have been done with baseball after his time with the Dodgers. At nearly 70 years old, with a growing family, he had every excuse to slowly edge out of baseball. But if Rickey hadn't possessed the energy and intellectual curiosity that made that impossible, then he probably wouldn't have accomplished enough to establish the legacy that some wished he would protect.

Instead of retiring, Rickey moved on to Pittsburgh, where the Pirates had been the garbage dump of the National League for several years. Unfortunately, things did not go any better during Rickey's time in Pittsburgh. Sometimes, his reputation as a brilliant executive with superb talent evaluation skills was justified, as when he led the Pirates to select a young Puerto Rican outfielder from the Dodgers farm system in the 1954 minor-league draft. Roberto Clemente had appealed to Rickey not just because of his on-field talent, but because of a Robinsonesque interview in which he told the executive that he loved baseball more than eating.

Unfortunately, for every Clemente, there was a Ron Necciai. Necciai was a talented young pitcher whom Rickey deemed as one of two young pitchers he had seen who were destined for greatness. The other was Dizzy Dean, and Rickey told reporters that Necciai was harder to hit. In a 1952 minor-league game, Necciai proved Rickey right, striking out 27 batters. In the major leagues, however, no one seemed to have much trouble hitting him. Necciai was 1-6 with a 7.08 ERA in 54⅔ major-league innings.

Rickey did quietly assemble some excellent young talent, but much of it was buried beneath inexperience. He was removed as general manager of the Pirates after the 1955 season, although he remained in an executive capacity for the team until 1959. In his wake, Rickey left behind many of the pieces that led the team to claim a World Series title in 1960.

Perhaps Rickey's boldest post-Dodgers adventure was his stint as president of the Continental League. With Walter O'Malley and Horace Stoneham's money-driven moves of the Dodgers and Giants from New York to the West Coast, Rickey found himself among those who believed New York deserved another major-league team, sooner rather than later. The Continental League was to be a full third major league, the necessity of which Rickey was convinced. So convinced was he that he led a movement toward legislation that would greatly curtail baseball's famous reserve clause. Yes, Branch Rickey, infamously rendered "El Cheapo," pinned much of his hopes for the Continental League on a pro-player end to baseball's antitrust exemption.

While history may consign the Continental League to the same scrap pile as the 1970s White Sox uniform of short pants and the 1970s Oakland A's attempts to use fluorescent-colored baseballs, even though the league never played a game, it provides a legitimate claim for yet another significant baseball brainchild of Branch Rickey. The threat of the Continental League scared Major League Baseball ownership into expansion, which was probably overdue. After 57 years of two eight-team leagues, new franchises were added in Houston, New York, Minneapolis–Saint Paul, and Los Angeles. The major-league owners also announced that they had voted to add four more franchises at a later time. In a sense, Rickey was not only the father of integrated modern baseball, but of the Astros, Mets, Twins, and Angels.

By the early '60s, Rickey had moved full circle, working for the Cardinals in an advisory capacity under owner August Busch Jr. Rickey was not terribly popular in his last stop in St. Louis. He advised management to trade Stan Musial, which was both sacrilege to Cardinal fans and entirely consistent with Rickey's theory of trading a player a year early rather than a year late. However, never again after the halcyon days in Brooklyn did Rickey find himself atop the baseball world. His late-career exploits, while they aligned with his desire for "adventure," never challenged the primacy of his legacy. The crowning of that legacy certified that.

In 1962, Jackie Robinson was inducted into the Baseball Hall of Fame in his first year of eligibility on the ballot. An exuberant Robinson invited three people critical to his success to join him on the dais—his mother, Mallie; his wife, Rachel; and Branch Rickey. Robinson credited Rickey as "a man who has been like a father to me."

As Robinson's health began to fail, the two icons kept in close contact. A couple years later, Robinson was hospitalized with a heart attack and a staph infection. Rickey was 82 years old, but he traveled to New York to visit Robinson. As Rickey aged, he also had numerous health problems. Doctor after doctor throughout Rickey's life had counseled rest and reduced activity, but Rickey never listened.

In his later years, Rickey favored an anecdote regarding his own father, who had lived 86 years. The elder Rickey still planted new peach and apple trees on his farm well into his old age. At some point, Branch asked him who would take care of the fruit. "That's not important," said Frank Rickey. "I just want to live every day as if I were going to live forever."

In November 1965, Rickey checked out of the local hospital after a short stay to go and give a speech at his induction into the Missouri

Sports Hall of Fame. His speech was on courage, and his text that night, which one of his daughters recalled was a Rickey favorite, was on Zacchaeus, the biblical proof of a man whose reputation could change profoundly with a single brave midlife course of action. Rickey never completed the speech, suffering a heart attack during its delivery that sent him into a coma. He never regained consciousness and died on December 9, 1965.

Robinson lived seven years longer, long enough to write, "As I mourned for him, I realized how much our relationship had deepened after I left baseball. It was that later relationship that made me feel almost as if I had lost my other father. Branch Rickey, especially after I was no longer in the sports spotlight, treated me like a son."

Two years after Rickey passed away, he was posthumously inducted into the Baseball Hall of Fame, where his plaque is only a few feet away from Robinson's. His biography on that plaque, which seeks to reduce a life of 83 years to four sentences, begins by crediting him with the invention of the farm system. But it ends, "Brought Jackie Robinson to Brooklyn in 1947."

That last sentence separates Rickey from Charlie Comiskey or Cap Anson or any of a legion of baseball legends who were great business-men. Rickey was a great baseball executive, a decent player, a solid man-ager, an exemplary talent scout, and a shrewd trader. But then he brought Jackie Robinson to Brooklyn and changed baseball, and indeed America, forever.

CHAPTER THREE

TRICKY NAVIGATION: HAPPY CHANDLER, JIM CROW, AND JACKIE ROBINSON

Unlike most key moments of the Robinson triumph, the two moments alleged to pivotally involve Commissioner A. B. "Happy" Chandler are both shrouded in mystery—and perhaps, in myth. First, there's a major-league owners' meeting. A typically smoke-filled room brings forth a report on the feasibility of integration. This report is probably prepared after Branch Rickey had already signed Jackie Robinson for the Montreal Royals. The report says what one would imagine a contemporary report by a major-league owner not named Branch Rickey (or perhaps Bill Veeck) would say about integration—that it's a terrible idea, that it will cripple black and white baseball, and that it should not be undertaken. There's a vote—although nobody is terribly clear whether the vote was for some sort of definite action or just to affirm the conclusions of the report. It's 15-1, and while nobody can remember the details of the vote, they all remember that the 15-1 vote was against integration. The vote is just Rickey (or perhaps his representative, as he may not have even been there) against the rest of baseball. But Rickey has a silent ally.

Soon thereafter, Rickey travels to Versailles, Kentucky. And in a cabin on the back of A. B. "Happy" Chandler's farm, the commissioner of baseball and the owner bent on integrating baseball discuss the problem. Chandler knows he's important, reminds Rickey that integration can't happen without him. But when he's convinced of Robinson's bona fides, he agrees to support Rickey. Integration rolls forward.

Except that none of this—or all of this—may have happened. And the details of the stories are pivotal. And the fact that 70 years on, no one can pin down the details of the role—or the lack of the role—of Commissioner Chandler speaks volumes.

Unlike most everyone else involved in the Robinson triumph, Chandler was not primarily a baseball man. Sure, he had played the game, and followed the game, and became Major League Baseball's second ever commissioner. But Chandler was a politician—a governor, a US senator, even a legitimate candidate for the presidency of the United States. And as would befit a politician, Chandler's activities and even attitude can be difficult to pin down. Was he a major part of Robinson's triumph? A reluctant bit player? A little of both? Untangling the truth is almost impossible, and that impossibility is befitting of a Jim Crow Democratic politician who was sometimes revered as progressive on racial issues, and sometimes condemned as backward on them.

In his famous August 1945 meeting with Robinson, Branch Rickey had looked forward to a day when a baseball box score—at-bats, hits, runs, errors—would be all that mattered. But it was never that simple, and the political question of race and baseball requires political analysis, particularly to try to understand the unique political creature at its center.

There was very little in the early life of Albert Benjamin Chandler to suggest that he would find himself at the center of any significant political issue. Born on April 18, 1898, Chandler was the son of a rural Kentucky farmer and his much younger wife, who had grown up in an orphanage. When Chandler was four years old, his mother left the family. His father, Joseph, asked if she wanted the children. She expressed interest in taking Albert's little brother, Robert, but said that Albert looked too much like Joseph. Joseph would not allow her to take one child and not the other, so both boys stayed with him in rural Corydon, Kentucky, which Chandler later described as "just a wide place in the road."

Chandler remembered his father as a workaholic, noting that this was "the foremost and most satisfying characteristic that I inherited from him." Albert grew up working on the family's 50-acre farm, and he ultimately became some combination of Huey Long and a Horatio Alger hero. This isn't to say that Chandler's rise was merely fortunate or was speedy. He recalled spending the summer before he finished high school working with a local African-American man, dumping 100-pound sacks of corn into a freight car. He wrote, "Every day we filled and dumped into the railroad car 880 sacks—440 each. Our pay was not bad, a dollar and a quarter a day."

When Chandler was 16, his brother Robert fell out of a tree and died a few days later of a broken neck. Chandler buried himself in work, graduating as valedictorian of his high school class. Joseph didn't want Albert to attend college, but a chance encounter with the chancellor of a nearby standout liberal arts college, Transylvania University, resulted in Chandler being promised both a tuition scholarship and help finding sufficient work to pay the rest of his bills.

Chandler would later announce in his stump speeches that he had arrived at Transylvania with a red sweater, a $5 bill, and a smile. That ubiquitous smile earned him his lifelong nickname, bestowed on a freshman Chandler by a senior student who observed him walking to class, smiling and whistling. Chandler himself laconically noted, "Thank God he didn't dub me 'Stinky.'"

It was at Transylvania that the happy farm boy began to grow into the political machine. Chandler played baseball, basketball, and football. The highlight of his baseball days came when he pitched Transylvania to a 10-4 victory over the much larger University of Tennessee. He would later briefly play semipro baseball for the Lexington Rios, where he was a teammate of future Yankee star Earle Combs. Off the field, Chandler loved to sing, and his fine tenor voice was a point of pride throughout his life.

He graduated from Transylvania and headed to Harvard University for law school. Chandler enjoyed a year at Harvard, but then left, later saying that his grades had been good, but "trying to scrape by in Cambridge on odd jobs was just too rugged." He transferred back to the University of Kentucky for law school, where he proceeded to attend law classes in the morning and then to teach two history classes and coach football at nearby Versailles High School for the princely sum of $80 per month.

From there, much of the rest of Chandler's life—at least, as he told it in his 1989 autobiography *Heroes, Plain Folks, and Skunks*—seems to consist of various people falling under the spell of his charm, work ethic, and general small-town decency. In 1925, he married Mildred Watkins, a teacher whom he met at an amateur theater group at which they sang together. He was immediately smitten, but she told him that he sang too loud. He won her over and soon married her, later adopting her daughter from a previous marriage. Chandler called Mildred "Mama," and she was a natural force in his upcoming political career, which she aided and abetted for the 65 years of their marriage.

Chandler got into politics via the Kentucky State Senate, but after two years there, he was elected lieutenant governor under the wonderfully named Ruby Lafoon. Ever the populist, Chandler soon split with Lafoon over the governor's imposition of Kentucky's first state sales tax. Displaying the sort of political maneuvering that would serve him well for decades to come, Chandler waited until Lafoon traveled to Washington to consult with President Roosevelt. As Kentucky law made him active governor while Lafoon was out of the state, he immediately convened the legislature and railroaded through a bill establishing primary elections in Kentucky. Chandler promptly won the first such election, and in 1935, he was elected governor of Kentucky.

Kentucky law mandated until the 1980s that a governor could not serve consecutive four-year terms. So in 1938, the year before Chandler's term as governor ended, he set his sights on the US Senate, where fellow Kentucky Democrat Alben Barkley had become a fixture.

Chandler never got on well with Barkley. For that matter, he was a most unconventional Democrat. In the last years of his life, when penning his autobiography, he scarcely had a positive word for Franklin D. Roosevelt or Harry Truman, but at one point, he went out of his way to heap praise on Richard Nixon.

Chandler lost his election for the Senate in 1938, as President Roosevelt came to Kentucky to campaign for Barkley. However, the following year, two months before Chandler's term as governor ended, Kentucky's other senator, Marvel Mills Logan, suddenly died. Chandler promptly resigned as governor, and his successor, Lieutenant Governor Keen Johnson, then appointed Chandler to Logan's Senate seat.

Chandler completed Logan's term and in 1942, he was elected to a full term of his own in the Senate. His political career in the Senate earned him some critics, however, including the NAACP's Louisville chapter, which noted that Chandler had failed to support an antilynching bill (Chandler stated that he was against lynching, but that the penalties imposed by the bill on local government were too severe) and a repeal of a poll tax. Eternally upwardly mobile, Chandler eyed his next promotion from the Senate.

Chandler hoped to be chosen as Franklin D. Roosevelt's vice president in FDR's fourth-term bid in 1944. However, some within the Kentucky delegation would not support his candidacy, and Roosevelt instead chose a senator from the neighboring state of Missouri, Harry Truman. Thus, it was Truman and not Chandler who was elevated to the White House by Roosevelt's sudden death in April 1945. However, Chandler again did find himself making a career change prompted by a sudden death—in this case, that of the major-league commissioner Kenesaw Mountain Landis—only weeks after Roosevelt won his fourth term in 1944. Once again, good fortune seemed to be on Chandler's side.

After Landis's death in November 1944, baseball's owners set about to choose a replacement. Many names were considered, perhaps most notably then–National League president Ford Frick. But no consensus had emerged from multiple meetings of the nominating committee, and the voting was at something of a stalemate at the owners' meeting of April 24, 1945. At that point, Yankee owner Larry MacPhail began to push for Chandler. MacPhail asked for an informal straw poll, and Chandler received 11 of 16 first-place votes. The voting then began again, and on the second ballot, Chandler secured the ¾ majority needed to win, with a third ballot making the vote unanimous.

The election of Chandler was seen as a smooth power transition, from one agent of baseball's status quo to another. One particularly interesting column, printed in the New York *Mirror* on the day after Chandler's election, was headlined, "Few Problems Face New Czar Chandler."

Columnist Charles Segar speculated, "Chandler's biggest problem will be the returning ball players from the armed services." A few lines later, he noted, "There are other problems, but none too serious."

The (white) press seemed gleefully unaware of a storm that had long been brewing, in America at large, but especially in baseball. Chandler would face several controversies, but the most significant one was nearing at a speed that only a very few would have guessed.

In baseball, unlike most of American society, there was no open and acknowledged legal basis for racial discrimination. The policy separating blacks and whites had evolved entirely unwritten, never sanctioned by the official rules. On the other hand, Chandler had spent all of his political career and life within the purview of the Jim Crow laws that not only countenanced strict racial segregation but also mandated it. As such, he seemed an unlikely ally for Jackie Robinson, Branch Rickey, or anyone who wished to counter the racial status quo of the era.

The Jim Crow laws of the American South were a high-water mark of shame for the democratic legislatures of a free America. In the years following the Civil War, with the slaveholding states forced to contemplate anew the possibility that persons held as property were in fact persons, those states had to determine a way to both legally recognize black people as people while still confining them securely to a lower tier of the established social hierarchy than white citizens.

Enter Jim Crow. In the immediate aftermath of the Civil War, Northern reconstruction Republicans held control of the Southern governments for a brief period in which African Americans were actually afforded many political freedoms and something vaguely resembling equality. But both pragmatically and politically, Northern control of Southern governments could not endure, and when Republican Rutherford B. Hayes and Democrat Samuel J. Tilden were in a deadlock for the 1876 presidential election, the freedom of self-government for the white, Democratic Southern states became the bargaining chip that the

Republicans surrendered in exchange for the presidency being handed to Hayes.

And so beginning in or around 1877, Southern legislatures reverted to self-rule, and almost immediately, they began passing laws that mandated strict racial segregation, or, alternately, punished any attempted integration. If African Americans had to be treated as people, the thinking behind Jim Crow legislation clearly ran, they didn't have to be treated the same as white people.

It took the US Supreme Court to legitimize Jim Crow and prescribe it a life that lasted nearly a century. In Louisiana, the legislature had passed the Separate Car Act, which required separate railway cars for blacks and whites. A group of concerned citizens chose Homer Plessy, who was born a free man and was actually one eighth African American, to test the legality of the act. A similar law from Pennsylvania was also under fire. However, in 1896, the Supreme Court held that the laws were constitutional. Justice Henry Billings Brown wrote for the majority, "We consider the underlying fallacy of the plaintiff's argument to consist in the assumption that the enforced separation of the two races stamps the colored race with a badge of inferiority. If this be so, it is not by reason of anything found in the act, but solely because the colored race chooses to put that construction upon it." *Plessy v. Ferguson* gave popularity to the phrase *separate but equal*, the legal distinction that the Court had drawn to allow blacks to be treated as second-class citizens in terms of public transportation, public schooling, and a variety of other public accommodations.

Ultimately, Jim Crow culminated in poll taxes or literacy tests that operated to disenfranchise African-American or poor white voters. Stripped of the right to vote, subjected to second-class accommodation in hotels, restaurants, theaters, and swimming pools, African Americans had long been made to understand that any objective opportunity at influence was held at the mercy of white legislatures, many of whom were governed by men still carrying grudges over lives lost at Gettysburg or Antietam.

Kentucky had been a border state during the Civil War. However, Jim Crow laws gained a foothold during the post-Reconstruction period and were a staple of the state when Chandler was governor and then senator from Kentucky. Attempts to enforce some semblance of equality in Kentucky were wildly unsuccessful. For instance, in 1908, Berea College had a case before the US Supreme Court. At issue was a Kentucky law that criminalized a university admitting black and white students—unless their classes were at least 25 miles apart. As a private school, Berea cited the religious aspect of its education, and claimed that denying blacks and whites the ability to experience the same education violated their freedom of religion. The Supreme Court did not agree, and upheld the Kentucky law.

Other Kentucky laws regulated intermarriage, public education, railroad cars, railroad waiting rooms, streetcars, circuses and shows, and residence in apartment buildings.

In light of the fact that Chandler was a southern Democratic politician from a Jim Crow state, his appointment to baseball's highest position seemed likely to continue the game's unwritten but very tangible color barrier well into the future. Even an optimist on the issue, like *Pittsburgh Courier* star reporter Wendell Smith, noted after questioning several Kentucky blacks on Chandler's racial attitudes, "The general trend seemed to indicate that he had been well liked as Governor, but there was some doubt as to how he might react about the abolition of racial lines." A more common opinion might come from *Baltimore Evening Sun* editor Paul Menton, who stated, "I doubt if Chandler will change very much despite the problems he will be called on to solve as the years unfold."

However, few counted on the effect that World War II could have on an unconventional politician like Chandler. When he was first named commissioner, a group of African-American journalists went to see Chandler. One of them recalled him telling the group, "I'm for the Four Freedoms. If a black boy can make it on Okinawa and Guadalcanal, hell, he can make it in baseball." Of course, even Landis would occasionally comment to writers on the absence of any prohibition on teams signing blacks, so the writers were somewhat skeptical. Chandler countered that by saying, "Once I tell you something, brother, I never change. You can count on me."

On that front, Chandler would be tested. Because what he had just told the journalists contradicted not only their expectations and the established political bent of the era, it contradicted the long-established, albeit unwritten political leanings of baseball.

~

Professional baseball's color barrier was venerable, completely off the written books, and the product of a power structure in which the sport was governed by a single hegemonic despot. In baseball's earliest days, there was no ban on black players. Moses Fleetwood Walker and Weldy Walker both had brief major-league experience with Toledo's American Association squad in 1884. The Walkers met resistance when their squad played Cap Anson's National League Chicago White Stockings. Anson, one of the greatest players of the 19th century, was an avowed racist, and he threatened to refuse to play Toledo if Moses Walker played. It was pure bluff, and Walker played.

However, by 1887, Anson's stature and sway had continued to grow. Faced with a game against black pitcher George Stovey, Anson pulled the same stunt, but this time, Stovey did not play. Moses Fleetwood Walker struggled on for a few more years, although one of his own teammates noted, "He was the best catcher I ever worked with, but I disliked a Negro and whenever I had to pitch to him I used anything I wanted without looking at his signals."

Within a few years, the final handful of black players had slowly been driven from organized baseball, a trend of exclusion that would last for about half a century. Unfortunately, the years of baseball's greatest development and gain in popularity happened to coincide with the years during which America as a whole was segregating itself with vigilance.

Had baseball been otherwise inclined to change in this perspective, a change in the sport's governance took care of any such tendencies. In the early years of the modern two-league major leagues, big-league baseball was governed by a national commission made up of three men—the presidents of the American and National League, and a supposedly neutral third party. However, the neutral third party was Cincinnati owner Garry Herrmann, who was such a good friend of AL president Ban Johnson that he slanted most decisions toward that league. Accordingly, disputes like the one between NL pennant-winning New York Giants manager John McGraw and AL president Johnson, which resulted in the cancellation of the 1904 World Series, were not only possible but almost inevitable. Each league prospered, but there was no central governing body.

Many things around baseball changed in the wake of the Black Sox scandal of 1920. The Chicago White Sox had conspired with gamblers to throw the previous year's World Series to the Cincinnati Reds. While it was the largest scandal that baseball faced, it was hardly the only one. That said, it was the type of scandal that required action—and specifically, the type of bold action that might restore public confidence in a sport that had been very publicly established as corrupt.

In actuality, the National Commission had dissolved even before the Black Sox scandal, but especially in light of the scandal, baseball ownership needed the sort of strong leader who would and could clean up baseball's house. They decided on federal judge Kenesaw Mountain Landis, who had drawn public attention by fining Standard Oil $29 million in a landmark case. Landis had perhaps endeared himself to ownership by sitting on the Federal League's pending antitrust suit against the other two major leagues until the suit was rendered moot by the dissolution of the challenging league.

Landis demanded absolute authority and a pledge of loyalty from the owners, who thus vowed that they would not publicly criticize the commissioner or his decisions. He was hired as baseball's first commissioner, and he soon used his powers to ban the eight Chicago White Sox players who were involved in the World Series fixing. Landis was an imposing, silver-haired jurist, always looking gruff and prepared to dispense some authoritative ruling. He had fixed himself well on the bad side of Branch Rickey with his rulings against the propriety of the Cardinals' extensive minor-league holdings.

Landis also, in the quietest way possible, kept the major leagues segregated. There was no official statement from Landis regarding segregation. Indeed, in 1943, after a minor controversy when Dodger manager Leo Durocher's past comments about desiring to sign black players had been published in a news article, Landis called Durocher to his office, with the latter deciding after their meeting that he had been misquoted. Landis made headlines by proclaiming that there was not, nor had there ever been, any rule barring black players, and that owners could sign a roster full, if they so desired. Of course, no one did. Meanwhile, misled writers offered headlines like "Landis Steps to Bat for Negro Ball Players." If Landis ever did so, he spent 23 years as commissioner preparing to step into the batter's box.

Bill Veeck, who would go on to own the Cleveland Indians, offered more immediate evidence of Landis's segregationist tendencies. In 1944, the Philadelphia Phillies were for sale. Veeck planned to join forces with Abe Saperstein, the owner of basketball's Harlem Globetrotters, to buy the moribund franchise and stock it with African-American talent. Veeck's error was telling Landis of his plan. Landis offered no immediate reaction, but the team was promptly turned over by owner Garry Nugent to the National League, from whence it was sold to William Cox, a lumber dealer who had no such plans to integrate the sport. Veeck alleges that the sales price was one-half of what he had offered. Veeck was careful to say that he could not prove that Landis had blocked his purchase of the team, but the telling of the episode certainly revealed his suspicions. The story is not enhanced by the fact that Cox was banned from baseball a year later for gambling. Of course, a great many have suggested that Veeck's entire story was revisionist history lacking any real basis in truth.

Landis ruled baseball with an iron fist from 1921 to 1944, when he passed away. While he was careful to never make any explicit statement on his sport's color barrier, it is clear that he certainly did nothing to change it, and it appears as though he was often the architect of its preservation. In light of what had gone before him, Happy Chandler would not have an easy path if he did want to break with tradition and encourage the integration of baseball. It was a path that Chandler later said cost him his job as commissioner.

When Branch Rickey signed Robinson to a Montreal contract in October 1945, reaction from the commissioner's office was muted. It was not until March 1946 when Chandler made any comment on the Robinson signing. At that point, he told Wendell Smith, "[I]t's nice to know that everything is working out okay and that they're getting a fair chance. That's the way it should be. That's the American way." Publicly, Chandler was tepidly polite about Robinson, and had little to say that was incendiary to anyone.

It may be that Chandler himself was still figuring out where he stood on the issue of Robinson as a major-league player. A civil rights moderate at best, Chandler found himself quickly at loggerheads with other owners, who wasted no time trying to wrestle away much of the power that Landis had claimed for the office of commissioner. Larry MacPhail, who was allegedly Chandler's champion in the procurement of the position of commissioner, was vociferously against the integration of big-league baseball. It may be that the pivotal event in making clear Chandler's path is the one that is among the most disputed occurrences in the entire Robinson story.

There was a meeting of major-league owners on August 28, 1946, in Chicago. What is alleged to have transpired at this meeting was not revealed by anyone for roughly a year and a half. Early in 1948, Branch Rickey told an audience at Wilberforce University, a black college in Ohio, about this meeting. Rickey told his audience that day that a report had been circulated that had been critical of Rickey's efforts in integrating baseball. He told his audience that day in 1948 that the report said, among other things, "However well intentioned, the use of Negro players would hazard all physical properties of baseball."

Rickey went on to say that National League president Ford Frick had carefully taken back all copies of the report after it had been reviewed, discussed, and then voted upon. Exactly what was being voted upon was never entirely clear, but Rickey was clear that it was a 15-1 vote, with every other owner in the room opposing his stance.

Several other owners made contemporary denials of the existence of any such document. MacPhail called Rickey's allegations "false and inflammatory," Phillies owner Bob Carpenter called them "ridiculous," and Clark Griffith denied the general tenor of Rickey's remarks. The two league presidents and Commissioner Chandler were unavailable for comment. As Rickey could not provide the document in question, many in the sporting press cited it as another example of Rickey's penchant for creating a windmill against which to tilt. And so the meeting and the vote remained shrouded in mystery for years.

By the time Chandler got around to telling the tale, the meeting took place in New York in January 1947. He sometimes recalled the meeting being "for the purpose of letting the other owners know what Rickey was planning to do," and on other occasions stated that the Robinson matter was not on the agenda for the meeting but was brought up anyway. Chandler sometimes explained away the lack of data regarding the meeting by noting that no minutes were taken at the meeting. He recalled Rickey speaking in favor of Robinson and seeking a resolution of support of his action, which was then voted down by a 15-1 margin. The discussion was spirited, with Chandler recalling that one of the opposing owners "flat out said if we let Robinson play, they'd burn down the Polo Grounds the first time the Dodgers came in there for a series." Chandler didn't discuss this meeting publicly until 1972, seven years after Rickey's death. Given the wealth of details that contradicted the only real evidence in favor of the meeting, which was Rickey's own account, again the entire matter looked doubtful.

In fact, Chandler and Rickey were both probably right. While Chandler's memory didn't corroborate Rickey's details, his papers did. National League president Ford Frick may have destroyed the other copies of the report for submission to the National and American Leagues on August 27, 1946, but he missed the one held by A. B. Chandler, Commissioner. The report, which lists as authors a committee of league presidents Frick and William Harridge and owners Sam Breadon, Philip Wrigley, Larry MacPhail, and Tom Yawkey, supports the general tenor of what Rickey had told Wilberforce students in 1948.

The report lists and discusses six problems adjudged to be then facing baseball—with "race question" being the fifth of the six. That fifth section draws heavily on a report MacPhail had authored for the mayor of New York in 1945 as La Guardia considered the Ives-Quinn antidiscrimination law, and which he had sent Chandler on October 25, 1945, exactly two days after Rickey first signed Robinson.

Still, the three pages of the report constituting the "Race Question" discussion are incredible. In one breath, MacPhail and/or his cohorts single out "certain groups . . . including political and social-minded drum-beaters" who are "not primarily interested in professional baseball." Two paragraphs later, the document astoundingly notes, "The thousands of Negro boys of ability who aspire to careers in professional baseball should have a better opportunity. . . . Signing a few Negro players . . . would contribute little or nothing toward a solution of the real problem."

MacPhail or his abhorrent coauthors went on to distort a comment by Sam Lacy, African-American sportswriter, to argue that "few good young Negro players are being developed." The report next points out that the destruction of the Negro Leagues, and the loss of stadium rental money to big-league teams, would be calamitous. The report concludes by noting that "there are many factors in this problem . . . which will have to be solved before any generally satisfactory solution can be worked out." It then points a broad finger at Rickey, saying, "The individual action of any one Club may exert tremendous pressures upon the whole structure of Professional Baseball, and could conceivably result in lessening the value of several Major League franchises."

Rickey plainly was not manufacturing outrage when he discussed this event a year and a half later. The only part missing is the 15-1 vote, which is the one aspect both men concurred on. It is certainly plausible that the vote did happen in August 1946, although exactly what the import of the vote would have been is very much unclear. That said, the points where Chandler's recollections differed from Rickey's do not necessarily constitute error on his part.

In 1997, Buzzie Bavasi wrote of a meeting of owners 50 years earlier. He believed that the meeting was on January 27, 1947, at the Waldorf Astoria in New York. Bavasi recalled the meeting because Branch Rickey had experienced an attack of vertigo "and wanted me to go along with him in case he lost his balance." Bavasi recalled the meeting being positive, with Bill Veeck mentioning his intention to promote a player who was better than Robinson, apparently referencing Larry Doby. He also indicated that Philip Wrigley indicated that "the Robinson matter" was "a Dodger problem and not a league or baseball problem," but that the Dodgers had his approval whatever their course. Horace Stoneham allegedly stated that he hoped the Dodgers would bring up Robinson because it would help attendance at his stadium.

So Bavasi's recollection of the existence of a meeting, the timing of a meeting, and the location of a meeting square with Chandler's memory. Rickey had lifelong problems with Ménière's disease, an inner-ear issue that is indeed very similar to vertigo. He was not always well during the offseason of 1946–1947, and he was not present in Montreal because of health problems some two months prior to the alleged meeting when the signing of Jackie Robinson was announced. But the one aspect that cannot be squared with either Chandler's or Rickey's memories are the statements of at least lukewarm approbation. Bavasi's memories certainly do not sound consistent with a meeting where a 15-1 vote condemning Rickey's course of action or refusing to endorse it would have taken place. And yet, the 15-1 vote is the one particular detail that both Rickey and Chandler recalled.

However, the track to clearing up the meeting, report, and vote is positively clean and clear compared with the second act of the Chandler/Rickey drama. According to Chandler, shortly after the January 1947 meeting, Rickey came to see him at his home in Versailles, Kentucky. The two discussed the problem, with Chandler recalling Rickey being "as emotional as I had ever seen him."

According to Chandler, Rickey told him, "I can't do this without I'm assured of your complete cooperation."

Chandler recalled saying, "[T]hat fifteen to one turndown your partners gave you at the Waldorf meeting—I think that was supposed to be mainly for my guidance, wouldn't you say?" Rickey agreed. Chandler continued, "I am the only person on earth who can approve the transfer of that contract from Montreal to Brooklyn. Nobody else. You still want to go ahead and go through with it?" Rickey assented that he did, and assured Chandler that he believed Robinson to be of major-league caliber.

Chandler told Rickey he had been pondering "this whole racial situation," and then brought up the war service of African-American troops. "You know, Branch," he continued, "I'm going to have to meet my Maker some day and if He asks me why I didn't let this boy play and I say it's because he's black that might not be a satisfactory answer."

Chandler continued, "If the Lord made some people black, and some white, and some red or yellow, he must have had a pretty good reason. It isn't my job to decide which colors can play big league baseball. It is my job to see that the game is fairly played and that everybody has an equal chance. I think if I do that, I can face my Maker with a clear conscience. So bring him in. Transfer Robinson. And we'll make the fight."

It is a phenomenal story, such a good one that the scriptwriters for *42* used the dialogue about meeting God for a Branch Rickey conversation with Phillies GM Herb Pennock. It neatly paints a picture of Robinson's two benevolent, conservative, white benefactors. The only problem is that there is absolutely no evidence supporting the occurrence of this Kentucky meeting beyond Chandler's own recollection, which arrived many years after the fact and once it was clear that it was glory and not blame that could be shifted regarding the institution of Jackie Robinson in Brooklyn.

The first public reference by Chandler to the Kentucky meeting came in early 1965, when he discussed it with a writer from *The Sporting News*. At the time, Rickey was still alive, so the disclosure is a bit less suspicious than it would have been had it waited until the only other party was no longer around to contradict the account. Historian John Paul Hill argues that the meeting "would not have fit Rickey's behavior pattern" and disputes Chandler's alleged claim that only he could approve Robinson's contract, as it was NL President Frick who actually did approve it. However, Hill does admit that Chandler would have had the power to void the contract, which is a difference perhaps without a distinction as far as the story is told.

Rickey's behavior pattern could also look very different to different sets of eyes. His daughter, Jane Jones, told a historian, "Dad would say to someone, 'You're the only person I've told this to, and I don't want you to repeat it to another soul,' and then he'd proceed to say the same thing three different times on the same day to three different people—and they'd all wind up thinking that they were the only one." Indeed, Rickey's actions from 1945 to 1947 consistently indicate what historian David Falkner terms his "uncanny ability to make people believe that he was confiding in them."

From financier George V. McLaughlin to broadcaster Red Barber to even Dodger player Clyde King, several have spoken out regarding Rickey's initial confidences to each in regard to his desire to sign first a black player or, later, Robinson in particular. In early February 1947, Rickey had his infamous YMCA meeting in Brooklyn where he hammered African-American community leaders with their responsibilities to Robinson's well-being as a potential major leaguer. It seems hardly implausible that, realizing that Chandler could scuttle the entire matter, that Rickey could well have come to see him, have buttered him up on the proposition of Robinson, and left once Chandler assured himself of his own wise decision in lending his support to the entire venture.

All of this said, whether the meeting happened exactly as Chandler recalled, or somewhat differently, or not at all, Chandler did make actual and tangible steps to support Robinson, which on their own justify his classification as one of Robinson's baseball defenders.

Chandler had already taken significant steps to support Robinson before 1947. During the 1946 Little World Series, there were fears that the Louisville Colonels would encourage racial animosity toward Robinson and his Montreal teammates. While Chandler could not take action on the fans, he did send someone to advise the Colonels to control their behavior.

A season later, when Phillies manager Ben Chapman was making himself notorious for his consistent and hateful bench jockeying of Robinson, it was Chandler who contacted Phillies general manager Herb Pennock to warn him that Chapman and his players could not continue this course, and that if they did, they would be subject to punishment from the league.

Indeed, Chandler was so protective of Robinson that he later recalled that he contacted a fellow Kentuckian, John DeMoisey, once an All-American basketball player at the University of Kentucky, and had DeMoisey trail Robinson in 1947, not to observe him, but to protect him. Of course, Robinson was never made aware of the situation, so DeMoisey's activities were not contemporaneously documented, but given the lifelong association of the two men, the presence of DeMoisey is hardly implausible.

Less certain is whether Chandler deserves any direct praise for condemning the potential St. Louis Cardinals player strike in May 1947. Of course, one of the central questions is whether the strike was ever a going concern. But reports surfaced from Stanley Woodward of the *New York Tribune* on May 9, 1947, that the Cardinals had planned to strike as a political statement against the presence of Robinson. Woodward reported that Frick had told the Cardinals, "This is the United States of America and one citizen has as much right to play as another. The National League will go down the line with Robinson whatever the consequences. You will find if you go through with your intention that you have been guilty of complete madness."

Immediately on the appearance of Woodward's column, yelps of protest sprang up from St. Louis that the story was completely untrue. Frick himself was very vague in substantiating that there had been some talk of a strike, but that he believed the talk had passed. Even Dodger manager Burt Shotton commented at the time that he didn't believe the rumors. Moreover, Frick expressly told reporters that he had not consulted with Chandler in regard to the possible strike. Chandler, however, made clear where his loyalties stood. "Baseball is an American game," he told reporters. "It is open for all Americans, regardless of race, creed, or color, with equal opportunity for all."

Chandler further indirectly assisted the integration movement—although also the cause of major-league owners—when he handled the iffy question of compensation for Negro League owners whose stars were poached by the big leagues. Rickey was careful to emphasize that Jackie Robinson had reported to him that he had no contract, written or verbal, with the Kansas City Monarchs. But a letter from Cumberland Posey, secretary of the Negro National League, to Landis on November 1, 1945, included a form Negro National League contract and a statement that the Negro Leagues were not protesting that Robinson was signed, but "the manner in which he was signed."

Admittedly, the Negro Leagues apparently had contracts but rarely bothered with the formality of signing them. For his part, Chandler was thoroughly in his element, and working all angles. After Effa Manley wrote him to protest a lack of compensation after one of her players was poached, Chandler awkwardly replied with a letter to "Mr." Effa Manley, directing that person to lodge his complaint through the commissioner of the Negro National League. He greeted another letter with a request for the reserve list of the Negro League squads, presumably so he could alert owners not to sign players with contracts. But ultimately, the tone of his letters went from grave to relatively flippant. As a politician, Chandler doubtlessly sensed that doing nothing would appease big-league owners and aspiring African-American players, and if he had to hurt the feelings of a handful of Negro League owners to do so, so be it.

Many historians do not react kindly to suggestions of Chandler's importance in the integration of baseball. Historian Jules Tygiel critically noted, "At best, one can describe Chandler's role as endorsement by abstinence." The actual record is much more complicated. As one journalist noted, days after Robinson was first signed by Montreal, "Chandler is political minded, and his Southern constituents back home will remember. Happy needs the wisdom of a Solomon." As a politician, Chandler had spent his entire professional career building consensus, and in the America of the Robinson era, there was a fair amount of difficulty in reconciling opposing constituencies under the same political banner. It was a lesson that Chandler had learned time and again, and one that Robinson would certainly learn as well.

Unfortunately, the prophecy that Chandler would face few difficulties in office was a completely erroneous one. Where he had built majorities around his opinions consistently as a governor and senator, he failed to do so as baseball commissioner. Of course, no small part of the problem was that as a politician, Chandler was working for a plurality or a simple majority, but as the high lord of baseball, he needed to keep in the good graces of no fewer than three quarters of the major-league owners. While Chandler handled many difficult issues, and generally handled them well, he alienated his fair share of critics.

Players coming back from war never became much of an issue. Those who were good enough went back and gained their spots, and those who weren't did not. However, a much more dangerous enemy emerged with a raid on talent from the Mexican League. Team owner Jorge Pasquel waved substantial money under the noses of some minor and major big-league stars, and many of them jumped. Recognizing that any other league opening up on MLB talent would create potential for a war around the infamous reserve clause that was the backbone of baseball's (admittedly horrifically uneven) economy, Chandler struck quickly, fining St. Louis Cardinal owner Sam Breadon for trying to deal with Pasquel himself, and banning 18 former MLB players for five years for jumping to the Mexican League. Chandler ended up withdrawing the ban after three years, but he exacted a steep price for disloyalty.

A much thornier issue concerned Brooklyn manager Leo Durocher. Durocher had a multitude of off-field problems, any of which would have been a headache, but the confluence of several rendered him as a problem child Branch Rickey could not control. It was Durocher's association with several big-time gamblers that finally launched Chandler into action, although a burst of negative publicity for Leo's home-wrecking marriage to divorced actress Laraine Day did little to help his cause. The Catholic League had threatened Rickey with a boycott, and in desperation, he turned to Chandler for help, expecting the commissioner to perhaps scare Durocher into a more prudent course of conduct. Meanwhile, Durocher and Yankee owner Larry MacPhail ended up at loggerheads after Durocher had been warned off several gamblers by

Chandler, only for one of them to turn up in MacPhail's box at a spring training game. Irate over the double standard, Durocher, through ghost-writer Harold Parrott, made some negative comments in a newspaper column. Ultimately, the matter received a full-blown hearing, and while Durocher and MacPhail could shake hands and put the matter to rest, Chandler ultimately decided to suspend Durocher from baseball for a year, and to mete out a few other small penalties at Dodger and Yankee personnel. Oddly, MacPhail was one of the parties most critical of the decision.

Chandler made an enemy of St. Louis Cardinals owner Fred Saigh when he had Saigh investigated for his off-field ties. In Chandler's defense, Saigh later was convicted and sent to prison on tax evasion charges. He was forced to sell the Cardinals in 1953. Less fruitful was Chandler's investigation into new Yankee owner Del Webb, who was part of a group that replaced Larry MacPhail. Chandler also voided the sale of player Dick Wakefield from Webb's Yankees to the White Sox, a move that he later said had left the Yankees "out to get my job, and I guess they did." Chandler ruled against the Pirates for trying to hide prospect Danny Lynch from the bonus rule by signing his father as a scout, despite the senior Lynch working full time with a bus company and not apparently scouting anything. He angered the Braves by making pitcher Jack Lohrke a free agent after Boston violated the option rule of the time.

Chandler said loudly and frequently that it was his backing of Jackie Robinson that ultimately cost him his job as commissioner. There is little record to support that assertion, beyond the fact that multiple baseball owners were clearly against integration in the years leading up to Robinson's signing. That said, many of Chandler's biggest backers in his time as commissioner were some of the same men who had either publicly or privately dragged their feet on integration—like Connie Mack and Clark Griffith, to name a pair. More accurately, it was probably his conflicts with owners like Saigh and MacPhail, who, after all, would need only three more votes to assure Chandler's defeat in a second term as commissioner.

Chandler's unpopularity was more likely tied to his desire for auton-
omy. Coming on the heels of Landis, baseball's ownership doubtlessly
hoped for a commissioner who would support the game's power structure. At times, Chandler was both a bold leader and very farsighted. The
Robinson incident aside, Chandler also foresaw the future of television
rights as a significant baseball issue. He negotiated the first deal with
Gillette to televise the World Series and All-Star Game. He also carefully funneled the majority of the money earned into a players' pension
fund, as he recalled seeing older baseball legends not supported in their
hours of need.

But whatever the reasons for Chandler's opposition, in December
1950, ownership voted 9-7 in favor of renewing his seven-year contract,
which was up in mid-1952. Of course, a dozen votes were needed to
approve the reelection. A few months later, in Miami Beach, another
vote was held, and the results were the same. Chandler allegedly complained to his wife, "If Jesus Christ were baseball commissioner, I'm not
sure he could carry twelve votes." In any case, the writing was on the wall,
and Chandler resigned effective mid-1951. He took his severance pay
and returned to Kentucky, back to the life he knew so well.

Back in Kentucky, Chandler applied the lessons he had learned of the
changing tides on racial integration. He ran for governor again in 1955,
and he was promptly elected to a second term. The political tide that
had helped sweep Robinson into baseball resulted in the *Brown v. Board
of Education* decision by the US Supreme Court desegregating public
education. In states throughout the South, governors such as George
Wallace and Orval Faubus used their influence to condemn the federal
government as outside agitators, and blocked the doorways of public
schools to physically prevent African-American students from enrolling
or attending. Not so with Chandler.

Kentucky's challenge came in 1956, when tensions ran high at Sturgis High School in Union County, near Chandler's old hometown, and a

nearby elementary school in Clay, Kentucky. Chandler recalled that the mayor of Clay angrily told him on the telephone that "no nigger [was] going to school down here." Chandler replied, "I don't know whether they are or not, but if they show up they are! You own that town and you are the mayor and you got certain powers that you can exercise but I'm going to take charge."

Chandler called in the National Guard, with instructions to make sure the school was open for whoever wanted to attend it. "The tank had to sit in Clay for a while," Chandler wrote, "But finally the situation simmered down, and I was able to withdraw the troops."

Interestingly, a month later, Chandler wrote to Jackie Robinson after the World Series to congratulate him on his outstanding play. Robinson replied with a letter in which he noted, "I will never forget your part in the so called Rickey experiment." In another speech nine years later, Robinson told an audience, "I had everybody in high places on my side in the middle '40s—Mr. Rickey, Ford Frick, Happy Chandler, everybody."

Robinson would struggle to keep everybody on his side as the years rolled along.

Once Robinson retired from baseball after the 1956 season, he became much more heavily involved in politics. He worked as vice president for Chock Full O'Nuts, where the company president, William Black, was a liberal who encouraged Robinson to take the time and trouble to be involved politically. For a time, Robinson was a shining star of the NAACP, acclimating quickly to life as a stump-speaking fund-raiser. He was named to the organization's National Board of Directors in late 1957. However, as time went by, Robinson found himself drawn to Dr. Martin Luther King Jr. and the Southern Christian Leadership Conference, which doubtlessly made him some enemies within the factionalized NAACP circles.

Robinson also took up the pen to express his own views on a range of topics, but much more often related to politics than baseball. The

New York Post gave him a weekly column, and Robinson's political views tended toward conservative.

In that vein, Robinson decided to support Richard Nixon's presidential bid in 1960. Given Chandler's own positive comments (and support of Nixon), it's easy to see the parallel between both political figures, each trying to blaze a trail of moderation, and both leery of Kennedy's youth and inexperience—Chandler of his inexperience in politics, and Robinson of his inexperience with African Americans. Still, Robinson's open endorsement of Nixon cost him his newspaper column, and in later years, it would cost him dearly in credibility within the African-American community.

After Nixon lost to Kennedy, Robinson next attached himself to Governor Nelson Rockefeller of New York. An attractively moderate candidate with relatively enlightened views on civil rights, Rockefeller became not only a friend of Robinson but also ultimately hired him in an advisory capacity in 1964.

Slowly, Robinson's conservative politics and his willingness to align himself with Republican politicians drew him a negative reputation in an increasingly militant African-American political community. Robinson found himself arguing with Malcolm X, who was only too willing to open up some painful black-on-black image battling. In an open letter following a critical newspaper column from Robinson, Malcolm X ripped Robinson for everything from his dependence on his "white boss [who had] lifted you to the major leagues" to trying "to 'mislead' Negros into Nixon's camp during the last president election."

Robinson occasionally found himself at loggerheads with Dr. King, especially on Vietnam, where Robinson allowed his oldest son to fight just as Dr. King was turning public opinion against the war. The tone of dialogue between Robinson and King was more measured and civil, but the results may have been just as devastating in public opinion.

Just as baseball had forced Robinson to try to moderate paths between being the "cringing, obsequious fellow" he had told Rickey in 1945 that he could not be and the biggest gun of black militancy in a battle for on-field equality, politics was a constant balancing act. It was not kind to Robinson, and sometimes, it was not even kind to a wily professional like Happy Chandler.

⌒

When Chandler's second term as governor ended in 1959, he was 61 years old. He had aspirations toward the presidency, and might have made a more logical running mate for John F. Kennedy than the vice-presidential choice of Lyndon B. Johnson. But Chandler never conducted a successful campaign after 1959, and the Civil Rights Act of 1964 rendered Chandler's political compromise even more tenuous than it had been. In fact, in 1968, States-Rights Dixiecrat George Wallace considered Chandler as a potential running mate, but he went a different direction, Chandler indicating that the move was because of differences over civil rights, which subsequently was rendered a public opinion feather in Chandler's cap.

Despite three additional unsuccessful runs for the governorship, Chandler did find himself well appreciated as an elder statesman. He was a fervent supporter of the University of Kentucky and its legendary and purportedly bigoted basketball coach Adolph Rupp. While Ford Frick had not appreciated Chandler, Commissioner Bowie Kuhn openly expressed his admiration and support of Chandler, and led a successful move to have Chandler elected to the Baseball Hall of Fame in 1982, an honor that delighted Chandler.

Still active in politics, he helped an obscure gubernatorial candidate named Wallace Wilkinson win the Kentucky race in 1987. Wilkinson responded by awarding Chandler voting rights on the University of Kentucky Board of Trustees, whereas he had previously held an honorary spot in that role.

In 1988, the 89-year-old Chandler caused a furor when he remarked, during a Board of Trustees discussion of a project in Zimbabwe, "You know, Zimbabwe's all nigger now. There aren't any whites." Chandler apologized, but qualified his apology by noting that in his youth, he had grown up around blacks who were called "niggers" and in his opinion, they didn't dislike this name. The Kentucky football team threatened to boycott its upcoming Blue-White scrimmage game, and students asked Governor Wilkinson to remove Chandler from the Board of Trustees. He did not.

It was a sad final act in Chandler's story. He passed away in 1991, a month shy of his 93rd birthday. He was recalled by historian Tom Clark as the man who could "slap more backs, kiss more babies, and hug more mamas than any other politician in Kentucky." Chandler insisted on the significance of his own role in the integration of baseball. As befits a politician who spent his life trying to please opposing constituencies, the record on that front is far from clear. But while Chandler may not have devoted himself single-heartedly to promoting Robinson's cause, he clearly defended it in good faith, and relied on that experience to help him integrate Kentucky schools in an era when many other southern governors not only did not help integration but also defied its tide. Chandler's legacy is complicated, but then, politics is complicated, and in his own brushes with it, Jackie Robinson could have certainly affirmed that fact.

CHAPTER FOUR

WENDELL SMITH AND THE POWER OF THE PRESS

The young pitcher rocked and fired, and the hitters were hopelessly off balance. Fastballs blew past and breaking pitches ducked around bats, turning would-be line drives into harmless pop-ups. The young man on the mound got scant support from his teammates, only a single run in this American Legion championship game. But he was as determined as he was skilled, and when the game ended, the crafty young pitcher had a 1-0 victory, and his team won the championship.

It wasn't the game that changed the pitcher's life, though. It was what happened after the game.

In the crowd at that Midwestern ballpark was a venerable link to baseball's past. Aloysius "Wish" Egan had reached the athletic pinnacle of which these young American Legion players dreamed—he had pitched briefly for the Detroit Tigers and St. Louis Cardinals between 1902 and 1906. After his brief playing career was over, Egan became one of the legendary scouts of baseball's predraft era. Without the amateur draft (which wouldn't appear until 1966), major-league teams still relied on traveling evaluators of young baseball talent. Egan was one of those, a man noted to wash dishes with a prospect's mother or descend into a mine shaft to better connect with a prospect's father. His discoveries included Jim Bunning, Hal Newhouser, and Dizzy Trout.

Also in the park was a link to baseball's future—that young pitcher who won the game, 1-0. Egan approached the excited young prospect. He didn't beat around the bush.

"I wish I could sign you, kid," he told the pitcher, "But I can't."

Even in Michigan, where the young pitcher grew up and competed in integrated youth baseball leagues, there was no way of turning a blind eye to reality. It was 1933. Wendell Smith was an African American. Neither the Tigers nor any other major-league team could sign him.

"That broke me up," recalled Smith, decades later. "It was then that I made a vow that I would dedicate myself and do something on behalf of the Negro ballplayers."

Smith was simply born too early to do anything about it on the baseball field. He was 33 years old when the color barrier was broken in the major leagues. By that time, he had long since moved on from the pitcher's mound—but not from his crusade to make major-league ballparks a place where other African Americans could play.

~

Wendell Smith was born in 1914 in Detroit, Michigan, to a Canadian father who worked his way up the household staff of auto magnate Henry Ford, eventually becoming Ford's cook. His experience in and around the Ford mansion showed Smith that there was another very different world out there than normal middle-class life—and that many of the doors to that something else were closed to him because of his color.

Smith grew up in a white neighborhood, and was the only black student at Detroit's Southeastern High. His brush with organized racism on the ballfield aside, Smith recalled few racial difficulties in his youth. He learned to adroitly handle two worlds—one in which black and white could informally cooperate, and one in which the division of races was arbitrary, structured, and well enforced.

Smith's path to his role in changing baseball history wound through West Virginia State College. After his high school graduation, Smith headed South to continue his education and to figure out how to enact his vow to help Negro ballplayers. Institute, West Virginia, seems like an unlikely destination for a young man of Smith's intellect and social upbringing. The land itself had once belonged to George Washington, part of his reward for service to the British Crown in the years before the Revolutionary War. It became a slave plantation before it was purchased by Samuel Cabell, whose father had been an early governor of Virginia. Cabell married one of his own slaves and proceeded to sire 13 children by her—all of whom he freed from slavery and some of whom he sent to

Ohio for education not then available to blacks in the local area. After Mr. Cabell's death, Mrs. Cabell eventually sold the land to the state of West Virginia to be utilized as the grounds for the West Virginia Colored Institute, under which auspices it opened in 1891.

Obscure origins aside, the school was a trailblazer in African-American education. By 1927, WVSC, then known as "State," became the first land-grant school to be accredited by the North Central Association of Colleges and Schools, and only the fourth black college to be so recognized. For that matter, it was the first university of any kind in the state of West Virginia to be granted such status. And it was into this impressive academic arena that Wendell Smith took his inquisitive young mind to find the outlet for his own quest to change the world.

Smith didn't give up on sports—in fact, he attended State on an athletic scholarship and played baseball and basketball there. Smith has tenuously been credited as the inventor of the jump shot (and thus could be stakeholder in the cultural evolution of both Jackie Robinson *and* Michael Jordan). But a bigger discovery awaited him at State—journalism. He became the sports editor of the school newspaper, and if the professional ranks of baseball and the murkier ranks of basketball were not welcoming to Smith, journalism was a different matter.

⸺

In the "separate but equal" world of early 20th-century Jim Crow culture, journalism was one of the areas in which not only success but also prestige was attainable for African Americans. African-American newspapers had a proud history, not only thriving in the early 20th century but also fanning the initial flames that brought about the Civil War itself.

The African-American press is generally considered to have begun in 1827 with *Freedom's Journal*, a New York publication started by a Presbyterian minister and an astute businessman. After two years, the businessman relocated to Liberia, but from the humble origins of *Freedom's Journal* came much greater things. Several other newspapers had brief periods of success, but it was Frederick Douglass's paper, *The North Star*, founded in 1847, that played a significant role in history.

Douglass pulled no punches, admitting in his first issue that his paper would exist "to attack slavery in all its forms and aspects, advocate Universal Emancipation; exact the standard of public morality; promote the moral and intellectual improvement of the colored people; and to hasten the day of freedom to our three million enslaved fellow countrymen."

With such an immediate and overtly political focus, it is hardly difficult to understand that African-American newspapers like *The North Star* set a very different standard than much of modern journalism. Their beat was not news, as that was already reliably covered. Their beat was how the news mattered to African Americans, and implicit in that was an editorial focus on improving the functions of their society. Accordingly, when Douglass's stated aims were either met or greatly advanced by the North's victory in the Civil War, it wasn't a matter of changing the style of African-American journalism—just a matter of changing focus.

In the post-Reconstruction South, many of the bravest voices for a move away from Jim Crow came from African-American newspapers. Editor Ida B. Wells ran Memphis's *Free Speech and Headlight* beginning in 1889. Opposing lynching and the worst political injustices of the era, Wells was so militant that she focused her ire on anyone she found wanting—even fellow Civil Rights crusaders like Booker T. Washington. When she told the people of Memphis that she had given up hope on living conditions in Memphis and that they should leave, many did.

Into the 20th century, African-American newspapers continued to become more numerous and more productive. World War I presented a significant moral quandary, as African-American newspapers generally made a reluctant decision to encourage African Americans to fight in the war, despite the lack of equal rights provided by their own government. The kaiser of Germany was considered unlikely to represent a more benevolent ruler.

The Chicago Defender took hold during this era, encouraging the Great Migration of southern blacks to the North, and facilitating superb writing from young contributors such as Langston Hughes and

Gwendolyn Brooks. A few years later, *The Pittsburgh Courier* emerged as another leading light in the African-American press.

By 1919, an equivalent to the Associated Press emerged, as African-American stringers covered news in every major American city. African-American newspapers, freed of having to span far and near on news coverage, used their extra space and energy to dig deeper in editorial content, speaking up for labor rights (via the Brotherhood of Sleeping Car Porters) and educational and employment opportunities. In 1932, Robert Lee Vann, the editor of *The Pittsburgh Courier*, told his readership to vote Democratic, advising them to "go home and turn Lincoln's picture to the wall."

As a development of this era, one of the most sympathetic supporters of the black press's work in favor of racial integration was the Communist press. Sports editor Lester Rodney of the widely circulating *Daily Worker* was politically aligned with the cause of integration, and he wasn't shy about saying so. In later years, the Red Scare and the fallout from World War II caused most writers in the African-American press to distance themselves from their Communist brethren, but in the initial push for equal rights, the odd alliance of blacks and Communists packed a solid one-two literary punch.

This was the world that Wendell Smith encountered when he graduated from West Virginia State College in 1937. He took a post with the *Pittsburgh Courier*, which had just bypassed the Baltimore *Afro-American* and *The Chicago Defender* for highest-circulation African-American daily paper. Smith was employed first as a sports columnist, but within a year he became sports editor of the burgeoning paper. A photograph of Smith taken in April 1938 captures him at Pittsburgh's Loendi Club, in a gathering of incredibly successful African Americans. Around the table are beautiful women and successful men including Joe Louis, a few months away from regaining the heavyweight crown, and Cab Calloway, with his million-watt smile. Smith, while only 24 years old, is smiling comfortably in the picture. He looks like a young man who is exactly where he should be. He looks like he's biding his time while figuring out how he would change the world, blissfully unaware of the struggles to come.

Smith did not wait long to start taking on the integration of baseball as a familiar theme. It was hardly an isolated topic, as the African-American papers took on a variety of employment issues with an eye toward curtailing Jim Crow one triumph at a time. As the sports editor, Smith's step happened to be on the baseball diamond. He was writing in favor of the integration of baseball as early as May 1938, and his initial approach reveals the naivete of youth. Surely, Smith seems to have thought, what we have here is a failure to communicate. Smith had a feeling that he could corner men in organized baseball and put them on the record that the vast majority of them would at least grudgingly accede to integration. Once that was a fait accompli, how could the powers that be fail to follow? If they could be shown that the players and managers would not rebel, surely the opportunity to sign cheap and untapped wells of talent would be too much to avoid.

Smith was proven right on his first point but misread the situation completely on the second. He polled several dozen players and managers in the National League (the National League was selected since Pittsburgh housed the Pirates, but not an American League franchise). He put these men on notice that their position would be reported, and tried to budge any who equivocated on the issue. The vast majority of these players and managers indicated that they had no issue with blacks playing Major League Baseball.

But rather than this triumph hastening a shift in the attitudes of the owners and executives toward integration of the major leagues, Smith was dismayed to see that it apparently had no affect at all. Much of the preemptory dismissal of black baseball players stemmed from Commissioner Kenesaw Mountain Landis. Landis, most biographers agree, played a dual game. One author noted that Landis "upheld baseball's unwritten ban on black players and did nothing to push owners toward integration."

Of course, Bill Veeck's claims that Landis barred him from purchasing the Phillies because of his plan of integration would place Landis solidly in the camp not only of not accommodating integration but also actively pushing for segregation. Meanwhile, from the other side of his mouth, Landis claimed in 1942, "Negroes are not barred from organized baseball by the commissioner and never have been in the 21 years I have served. There is no rule in organized baseball prohibiting their participation and never has been to my knowledge. If [Leo] Durocher, or if any other manager, or all of them, want to sign one, or twenty-five Negro players, it is all right with me. That is the business of the managers and the club owners."

Whether or not Landis was applying heat privately, the majority of big-league owners and executives continued to show absolutely no interest in integrating their teams. Philip Wrigley indicated in 1943 that the Cubs had no objection to signing black players, could accommodate black players, but would do so only when public demand required such a change. Wrigley took another decade to integrate the Cubs.

Perhaps more candid, if even more wrongheaded, was some of the coverage from the press. The *Sporting News* asserted in November 1945 that "Col. Larry MacPhail of the Yankees . . . and [Branch] Rickey himself admit there is not a single Negro player with major league possibilities for 1946." In another masterstroke of shaky journalism, *TSN* also twisted the words of famous black newspaperman Sam Lacy to claim that the number of blacks who could hold their own in multiple phases of baseball was "virtually nil."

A consistent grilling in the world of public opinion and a complete lack of forward motion would have sidetracked a less determined journalist. But Smith, emboldened by the attitudes he saw within baseball as well as by the Double-V campaign of the era (co-opted from African-American soldiers who fought for freedom overseas and at home in World War II), would not be denied.

Smith's perseverance was pivotal, because he had yet to undergo his own personal humiliation in the crusade to integrate baseball. For years, Smith wrote columns that were either disputed or ignored by the powers that be. But that was nothing compared to the fateful events when the door appeared to be cracked open to him, and to integration.

In late 1943, African-American sportswriter Sam Lacy had finagled a meeting with Commissioner Landis and extracted a promise that Lacy could address the owners at their annual owners' meeting in New York City. Lacy approached a group of other newspapermen who ended up dispatching a delegation that included not Lacy but Wendell Smith, as well as actor Paul Robeson. Lacy was so furious that he switched newspapers in part due to the breach of etiquette.

Still, the unheard issue of segregation would at last be discussed by the owners. Opening the meeting on December 3, Robeson spoke at length in favor of integration. Writer Ira Lewis refuted Landis's recitation that there was no rule against integration, saying that he believed there was a gentleman's rule against it, and urging that owners "undo this wrong." Another writer, Howard H. Murphy, outlined a four-point plan of integration.

When the meeting ended, the presentation received applause. No owner offered a single question or comment.

"I guess that's all, gentlemen," exclaimed Landis, and promptly showed his guests to the door.

Worse than being ignored was being patronized, and that was the sum total of the reaction of Major League Baseball to the newspaper group's presentation. Smith's great crusade could not even inspire the ire of the owners. One source cited Landis telling the owners before the meeting, "Don't interrupt Robeson. Let's not get into any discussion with him."

Smith (and his writer counterparts) had come to New York with high hopes, but in the end, they couldn't even get a discussion. It was back to the drawing board.

A greater indignity came two years later. In the early spring of 1945, a Boston city council leader named Isadore Muchnick decided it was time to take a step for integration. The Boston city council had the ability to provide (or to deny) a permit for Sunday baseball to be played in their fair city. Muchnick decided that Sunday baseball might not hold much attraction for him if the major leagues continued to fail to even consider, much less to hire, black players.

Smith understood what this might mean and made contact with Muchnick, assuring him that he could provide legitimate black prospects who would like to try out for either or both the Boston Red Sox or Boston Braves. Phony tryouts were nothing new—the Pirates had publicly indicated that they would hold a tryout in 1942, only for the tryout to fail to actually materialize. Similarly in early 1945, a sportswriter named Joe Bostic had showed up at the Brooklyn Dodgers spring training camp with a pair of Negro Leaguers seeking a tryout. Branch Rickey had grudgingly allowed Terris McDuffie and Dave Thomas a 45-minute "tryout" and summarily dismissed the prospects without any interest. Bostic concluded that Rickey had no interest in integration.

Meanwhile, a few days later in Boston, on April 14 and 15, 1945, Smith showed up at Fenway Park with three players—outfielder Sam Jethroe, who led the Negro Leagues in hitting in 1944, and infielders Marvin Williams and Jackie Robinson. The tryouts were postponed on both days, earning a stinging rebuke from white columnist Dave Egan in the Boston *Daily Record*. Perhaps, Egan postulated, Red Sox general manager Eddie Collins should be reminded that he was "living in anno domini 1945 and not the dust-covered year 1865" and was "residing in the city of Boston . . . and not in the city of Mobile."

Accordingly, on April 16th, a tryout of sorts finally occurred. No Red Sox players were present and neither was manager Joe Cronin. The players shagged fly balls and took batting practice, and an elderly flunky told them, "You boys look like pretty good players. I hope you enjoyed the workout." By far the most memorable moment of the tryout—if those who remember it are correct—was an unknown voice heard loudly yelling "Get those niggers off the field."

The players never heard a word from the Red Sox. Jethroe told Smith, "We'll hear from the Red Sox like we'll hear from Adolf Hitler." When

Smith finally got in touch with Eddie Collins of the Red Sox, Collins "explained" that Cronin had broken his leg shortly out of the tryout that "threw everything out of gear." Collins also expressed fears of haggles from the Negro Leagues should he try to interfere with contracts he assumed each player had there.

Interestingly, Cronin much later recalled telling "them" (Cronin's peculiar identifier is utilized both to point out his objectification and because it wasn't clear whom he was referring to) that the only spots open were in Louisville and that the Red Sox doubted the players would be interested in playing there. None of the principals involved recall even the possibility of Louisville being mentioned. Obviously, given subsequent events, it is unlikely that the players would have turned down an opportunity of any kind in professional baseball, had it even been offered.

Meanwhile, in the sort of bad luck that could only underline the futility of Smith's conquest, President Roosevelt passed away, so any momentum gained in the major daily media was lost to coverage of his death and funeral and the assumption of the presidency by Harry S. Truman. Once again, Smith had been gamed with an allegedly fair opportunity that was never an opportunity at all. Once again, Smith had to go back to square one, or at least close to it.

⌐⌐

The biggest question of Wendell Smith's affiliation with Jackie Robinson might simply be why and how Smith found the strength and intensity to wholeheartedly support Robinson when he had seen previous possibilities dry up like so many raisins in the sun. In some ways, Smith's support of Jackie Robinson as the great integrator of baseball seems like a given. He had been beating the drum for the cause of integration for the better part of a decade before Robinson emerged as a likely candidate to step forward. In many ways, Smith (and his fellow writers) somewhat created Robinson. Their ceaseless support of allowing black players opened a sort of cultural vacuum into which Robinson stepped.

But while Smith had campaigned for a black ballplayer, there was still the question of whether it should be *this* black ballplayer. Certainly, Robinson was not the best pure baseball prospect available in the Negro Leagues. Monte Irvin was both younger and capable of a higher ceiling of performance. The inclusion of Sam Jethroe in the Boston tryout was equally legitimate. Satchel Paige, however old he was, had demonstrated time and again that he could handle big-league hitters. Roy Campanella would soon show that he had the skills and the companionable nature to make the jump into white baseball.

Smith, as with Rickey, Chandler, and everyone else tangentially involved with Robinson's promotion, recognized clearly the risk that Robinson would be subjected to. This was no simple matter of a young ballplayer who could be called up to sit on the bench or be sent back down to the minor leagues for more seasoning. If Smith chose to support Robinson, he was certainly putting most of his credibility in that particular basket.

Furthermore, Smith could not be ignorant of what Robinson would mean in the African-American community if he made it. Certainly, an expansive glass ceiling of exclusion would be forever shattered. But at the same time, how many players from the Negro Leagues would be allowed to move into white baseball? Certainly, Robinson would be exposed to a trial period before other teams would follow suit. Once they did, it seemed unlikely that teams would construct a significant portion of their roster from African-American recruits.

Meanwhile, the livelihood of hundreds of other African Americans playing in the Negro Leagues would be jeopardized deeply. If blacks could watch Robinson, would they still flock to ballparks to see Satchel Paige or Cool Papa Bell? While the Negro Leagues were often declaimed by Smith and many others, there was no getting around the fact that a subpar living in uneven leagues was better than being stuck in baseball purgatory while waiting on the world to change.

In addition, there was another issue that even Smith may not have been considering. If Robinson made the major leagues and other blacks followed, clearly the writers who had covered them for years would have an easier, more functional relationship with these athletes. How long could the black and white press exist side by side as separate but equal? Mainstream readership would demand the sort of insight that Smith would have . . . and if more money and a wider audience to show his skills was attractive to Jackie Robinson, how could it not also be attractive to Wendell Smith?

But like Robinson, if Smith chose to follow more money, more prestige, and a greater viewership, how would African-American traditional newspapers expect to keep up? If black fans wouldn't go to games to see second-rate black talent while the best of the best were playing in the National or American League, would black readers still pick up papers if those games were covered by second-tier sportswriters? Or was breaking through old prejudices merely creating a second set of problems for those who lived and worked and dwelled in the shadow of those prejudices?

Finally, not only did Smith have to weigh the selection of Robinson as his player to back, not only did he have to weigh the possible societal costs to the Negro Leagues and the black press, but finally, he had to determine just how deeply he intended to be involved with Robinson's quest. It was one thing to sit far from the action and write columns prescribing how everyone should act. It was another thing entirely to be in the thick of the business of integration itself.

⁓

Soon after the Boston debacle, Smith received a call from Branch Rickey, who asked him to stop by. Smith duly recounted the undertaking he and the players had received in Boston, and Rickey seemed suitably perturbed. When Smith was naming the players taken, he mentioned Robinson. Rickey's ears perked up. "I knew he was an all-American football player and an all-American basketball player. But I didn't know he was a baseball player," Rickey said.

"He's quite a baseball player," replied Smith.

Rickey called Smith a week later, and reported that he was sending Clyde Sukeforth for a look at Robinson. No rookie to the big-league song and dance, Smith cut the conversation to the quick and asked Rickey if there was any chance of Robinson ever becoming a Brooklyn Dodger. When Rickey hedged his answer and did not deny it, Smith recognized that this could be different territory.

Not long after Rickey signed Robinson, he also signed Smith, who was listed in the official club directory as a scout. Smith received $50 a week from the Dodgers, which equaled his salary from the *Courier*. For his wages, he would sometimes scout players. In a December 19, 1945, letter to Rickey, Smith recommended Kenny Washington as a possible teammate for Robinson, noting, "I understand that he is a much better ballplayer than Robinson."

In the same letter, Smith confirmed that he intended to attend spring training in 1946 at Daytona Beach. He asked if any "provisions have been made with respect to where Robinson will stay." In his reply, shortly after the New Year, Rickey wrote that he would indeed have another African-American player at spring training, then continued, "I hope very much that you can arrange to be in Daytona Beach ahead of time to see to it that satisfactory living accommodations are arranged for these boys." In this regard, Smith crossed the threshold of being an observer and instead became a participant.

When newlyweds Jackie and Rachel Robinson spent two days on a miserable trip from Los Angeles to Daytona Beach at the end of February and beginning of March 1946, the depths of the hostility they would face became clear. Bumped from flights, ordered to the back of a Greyhound bus, the Robinsons saw firsthand that the world they sought to change was not a very friendly place—at least until they arrived in Daytona Beach, already angry, tired and dirty. There to meet them at the bus station was Wendell Smith and a colleague, African-American journalist Billy Rowe.

"Well, I finally made it," Robinson told Smith. "But I never want another trip like this one."

Robinson was so upset that he felt he would not receive a fair shake from the Dodgers, and he considered leaving immediately to return to the Negro Leagues. For perhaps the first time, but not the last, Smith (accompanied by Rowe) was the voice of reason. It was all part of the price to be paid. And Robinson would not pay it alone.

In short order, Robinson and his lone African-American teammate, pitcher John Wright, traveled from Daytona Beach to Sanford, where the Dodgers held their earliest training exercises. This was where Smith became essential. He had arranged for Robinson and Wright, who were barred from the Mayfair Hotel where the rest of the Dodgers stayed, to temporarily board with a prominent African-American doctor, David Brock.

At the end of the second day, Smith's significance became clearer. Rickey had an informer who relayed the message that the white city fathers of Sanford, Florida, regardless of how hospitable the Dodgers were, did not intend to entertain Messrs. Robinson and Wright. After some frantic phone calls, Robinson, Wright, Smith, Rowe, and Rachel Robinson removed themselves back to Daytona Beach immediately. Robinson again was angry, expecting that the Dodgers were giving up on integration already. The truth was soon laid bare for him, if not for the general public. Smith later admitted that the Dodgers kept the story quiet for fear that Daytona Beach might follow in kind if word of Sanford's peculiar vigilante antitourism surfaced.

Smith again busied himself attempting to locate suitable accommodation for the Robinsons and Wright. This time, the lodgings—a tiny room in the home of a black pharmacist, Joe Harris—were not as elaborate or spacious as with Dr. Brock's family, but they would do, at least for the short term.

On the field, tensions were nearly as high. Robinson integrated Daytona Beach in a Dodgers/Montreal Royals scrimmage game on March 17th without significant incident. Six days later, neighboring Jacksonville asked the Dodgers to leave Robinson and Wright behind before Montreal traveled there to play the Jersey City Giants. When Rickey would not comply, the game was canceled. Three more games were similarly canceled, and a game scheduled for DeLand had to be moved to Daytona Beach, allegedly because of an issue with the stadium lights, which was clearly illusory as the scheduled contest was a day game.

Most embarrassing, in a game at Sanford against the St. Paul Saints, Robinson singled and scored a run in the second inning. When he prepared to take the field for the third inning, the local chief of police demanded that he be removed from the game. Manager Clay Hopper capitulated, and Smith could only complain in his column about "vicious old man Jim Crow."

Meanwhile, even when he could remain on the field, Robinson struggled. He injured his arm trying to impress, and struggled to hit. Robinson later told Smith he could hear the cheers of black fans and that accordingly "I wanted to produce so much that I was tense and over-anxious." His play was bad enough that a Montreal sportswriter confidently reported that pitcher Wright (who ended up pitching six innings for Montreal before spending the rest of his lone season in white baseball at a lower minor league) was the superior prospect. Another white sportswriter was heard to say of Robinson, "If he was white they'd have booted him out of this camp long ago."

Such were the headaches of Wendell Smith's spring of 1946—arranging Robinson's housing and meals, reporting on his every step on the field for the *Courier*, and trying to help Rickey head off any ugly incidents that could jeopardize the cause of integration. Although Rickey credited his philosophy of life to the prophet who had famously decried that man could not follow two masters, Rickey had no compunction about pulling Smith every which way. Part travel agent, part sportswriter, part political go-between, Wendell Smith was not merely reporting on the first spring of baseball integration, he was smack in the middle of it.

On one level, once Jackie was finally formalized as a Montreal Royal, life became easier. He and Rachel found an apartment, and the two of them enjoyed Montreal and found the city to be welcoming and tolerant of the new player and his wife. Freed of insecurity concerning whether he would be allowed to play, Robinson promptly went 4-for-5 with a home run in his first game as a Montreal Royal, stealing two more bases and scoring four runs in a 14-1 win. More significantly, he was mobbed afterward by excited Royals fans who were thrilled by the young hero.

But for every day like that, there were others that went a different direction, especially on the road. Smith traveled with the Royals, both covering Robinson as a journalist and obtaining lodging for him when it proved tricky. Sometimes, the road life was relatively calm. Buffalo was one city that welcomed Robinson enthusiastically. On the other hand, in his first trip to Baltimore, a mob waited for Robinson in the Royals locker room after the game and heckled him until three other Montreal players waited out the mob with Robinson and then escorted him back to his hotel on a city bus.

Robinson did his best to remain stoic. Sometimes, his sense of mischief crept through, despite his vow to Rickey to avoid making trouble. Robinson remembered a Syracuse player tossing a black cat onto the field from his dugout and yelling, "Hey Jackie, there's your cousin." After Robinson doubled and scored, he passed the Syracuse dugout and wryly observed, "I guess my cousin's pretty happy now."

Robinson's mythical cousin may have been happy, but he wasn't. Smith knew this, but protected both the Brooklyn organization and Robinson by refusing to reveal much of the detail. In early 1947, he wrote that Robinson, on the cusp of a nervous breakdown, had seen a doctor during the previous season, who asked him to take some time away from baseball and rest. Robinson was supposed to take a period of 5 or 10 days away from the game, but after a couple of losses, Robinson ignored the medical advice and dove back into the crucible of his crazy season.

But mostly, Robinson just dominated the game. He gave Smith plenty of good news to report in Pittsburgh—enough that some wondered if he would get a late-season call-up from the Dodgers, who were in the midst of a pennant race. Robinson did not get called up, but he gave a major-league performance even in the minor leagues. He finished the season hitting .349, with 25 doubles, 40 stolen bases, and 66 RBIs. He helped Montreal win the Little World Series—the AAA championship—and afterward the Mississippi-born manager Clay Hopper shook his hand and told him, "You're a great ballplayer and a fine gentleman. It's been wonderful having you on the team." This from a man who during spring training asked Rickey, "Do you really think a nigra is a human being?"

But if Robinson handled the on-field proof of his humanity, Smith had to transmit it to an audience that was far removed from Montreal, if not from Robinson's plight. Working for both the *Courier* and the Dodgers, his aims were essentially the same—to create a picture of Robinson as a thoughtful, careful man who did not speak out against ill-treatment and who was less interested in waging a crusade than he was in winning the next ball game.

The reality did not always equate with the picture that Smith chose to paint. Early on, he coached Robinson, pointing out the questions that other writers would ask and directing Robinson to choose the high road, even when Robinson's inner competitive spirit might make him veer toward another path. Smith's wife, Wyonella, recalled in 2014, "Wendell would always say, if you flared up, nothing good would come of it. When Mr. Rickey would worry that Jackie would be too hot tempered, Wendell would always say, 'No, no, he'll be just fine.'"

Smith's certainty was based partially on the fact that he would be Robinson's predominant mouthpiece to the world, and partially on his own friendship with Robinson. In those early days, when Robinson's quest was at its most lonely, Smith was following a parallel track. "Jackie needed somebody he could trust and Wendell was there," recalled Don Newcombe. Smith's responsibilities, professional and personal, led him to spin Robinson's thoughts and reactions in a way more equivalent to a White House press secretary than a sportswriter. He was, of course, not only involved but also dedicated.

Indeed, Smith's own path was far from smooth. He was not always welcome in press boxes in the same way that Robinson was not always welcome in hotels and restaurants. There were no black writers in the Baseball Writers' Association of America. Even if there were, facilities like Crosley Field in Cincinnati and Sportsman's Park in St. Louis would likely be less than welcoming to Smith. The film *42* depicts Smith plonking away on his manual typewriter from a seat in the bleachers. Newcombe recalled the reality decades later, saying, "They wouldn't even let him in the press box, it was worse than you could ever imagine. Everything we went through, Wendell went through the same thing."

If Smith endured the same hardships, he also felt the same thrill at Robinson's success. The first stage in Branch Rickey's experiment had been a smashing triumph. But Montreal is a long way from Brooklyn, and all the success in the world in the minor leagues could not have prepared either Robinson or Smith for the maelstrom of 1947.

Red Barber called 1947 "the year all Hell broke loose in baseball," and the year's beginning lived up to that name for Robinson and, to some extent, Smith. Due to the poor treatment that Robinson had received in Florida the previous year, the Dodgers decided to move their spring training south—to Havana. And while John Wright had departed the Dodger ranks to return to the Negro Leagues, Rickey, perhaps encouraged by Robinson's success, now included African Americans Roy Campanella, Don Newcome, and Roy Partlow in the Dodger camp.

For Smith, on one hand, Havana meant not facing down Jim Crow in Florida; on the other hand, it meant complete unfamiliarity. He explained to Rickey that he had no connections in Cuba, and that he would thus defer to the Dodger boss to figure out accommodations. He also leaned on Rickey to indicate whether Robinson would return to Montreal for another season (as Smith privately suspected) or might be called up to Brooklyn. As usual, Rickey had no intention of tipping his hand, if he was even certain of its eventual contents.

The Dodgers stayed at the Hotel Nacional, quite a step up from small-town Florida accommodations. The players destined for Montreal were housed at the Havana Military Academy, which was a prep school for the privileged offspring of government officials. But Robinson and the other dark-skinned Dodgers were placed in the Hotel Boston in the old part of Havana—a decidedly third-rate lodging alternative. This time, Jim Crow hadn't legislated the accommodations—Rickey had, presumably aware that he would have to quell internal rebellions within the Dodgers now that Robinson was a threat to star not in another country, but on the same field.

Playing in Havana did at least avoid the types of cancellations that had plagued the Dodgers in Florida. The question that remained was where Robinson would play in 1947, and a few days before the season began, Rickey quietly circulated a release through the press box announcing that the Dodgers had purchased his contract from Montreal. Once again, Wendell Smith's life got more complicated.

While the Dodgers' other African-American prospects were central to the team's future—in fact, so much so that the Nashua team was built from scratch to try to provide a smooth transition for Newcombe, Campanella, and Partlow into the white baseball infrastructure—Robinson was, of course, the only African-American player who was called up to the major leagues. Accordingly, Smith found himself back in the role of roommate, sometimes also collaborating with traveling secretary Harold Parrett to help Robinson find some reasonable lodging in the cities where his staying with the other Dodgers constituted a faux pas to the local social structure.

Moreover, as Robinson would go from being the most famous black athlete in America to perhaps the most famous African American of any profession, Smith, and his bosses at the *Courier*, recognized that their close connection to Robinson could yield some unique access. Accordingly, Robinson began contributing a weekly column to the *Courier*, ghostwritten by Smith, giving those readers his own insights into the transition into major-league baseball.

While Smith's friendship, support, and triparty facilitation among Robinson, Rickey, and the rest of the world was probably his lasting contribution to the "great experiment," the contribution that was more significant to the mass public was his work as the voice of Robinson. Again, Smith found himself tasked with giving the minutiae of Robinson's difficult quest a positive, winning spin that would make the average fan inclined not to regard Robinson's difficulties, but his winning attitude and his ability to persevere in the face of tribulation.

So when Phillies manager Ben Chapman led a verbal crusade to lambaste Robinson with every crude racial insult he or his players could imagine, it was Smith who gave voice to Robinson's Rickey-approved game plan of turning the other cheek. "The things the Phillies shouted at me from their bench have been shouted at me from other benches and I am not worried about it," Smith wrote as Robinson. "They sound just the same in the big league as they did in the minor league."

One recent writer, looking back at Smith's columns written as Robinson, noted, "[T]he column was really designed to emphasize that Robinson, a man of consummate dignity, met several white people of goodwill on his journey, and that the American spirit of fairness and fair play would not be stopped by what he pretended was a small number of racists. *If I can take it,* he seemed to say, *you can, too.*"

Moreover, Smith had another crucial role. In the frenzy over Robinson's apparent success, Smith had to be the voice of reason and patience to the African-American fan base. Rickey had long ago cautioned the African-American leaders within Brooklyn and surrounding environs that their work in governing expectations and behavior among their constituents would be an integral part of Robinson's quest. Smith was hardly alone in recasting that message, but he and his colleagues at the *Courier* mattered plenty.

Robinson's importance to blacks was such that on the road, he was as big of a drawing card as he was at home. And if there was one thing more likely to inflame white tempers than ballparks suddenly full of cheering black faces that hadn't been there before, it was when those cheering faces were rooting against the hometown team. Smith and other sportswriters like him found themselves talking less about balls and strikes and more about fan etiquette.

For instance, in the same issue of the *Courier* where Smith could proudly announce Robinson's promotion to Brooklyn, fellow scribe Billy Rowe took up the pen and (doubtlessly under the influence of sports editor Smith) wrote:

> [N]ot only is [Robinson] the test horse for every Negro player good enough for the majors, but the yard stick by which beige fans will also be weighed and judged. We know that a lot of those balls are going to look like strikes when he's [playing] first and many of those strikes are going to look like balls when he's at bat, but, by gosh, let's take it. Jackie has proven that he can and that's why today it's Jackie Robinson of the Brooklyn Dodgers. As fans, we have gotta help keep him there and open wider the door in which he is now the wedge and let others in. Our job is as big as his, if not bigger, so don't let us go forgetting it.

Smith and the other scribes provided words of wisdom in terms of everything from arriving early to dressing well to being polite to other players and umpires. There was no aspect too small to micromanage via the power of the pen. From Rickey to Smith to Robinson, the same game plan and united front was presented to the public, and if Robinson's dogged determination became the public face of the cause, Smith's private wisdom and sage counseling of patience both to Robinson and the fans who came to cheer for him provided a solid backbone of support to fortify the long-term success of the "Great Experiment."

The halcyon days of 1947, with Robinson devastating the National League and Smith chronicling his every move, forever ensured the success of baseball integration. Many of the foreseeable results of this success came to fruition in short order. Because of the success of Robinson, the Indians signed Larry Doby and Satchel Paige, the Dodgers prepared to bring up Campanella and Newcombe in 1948, and the raid for top African-American baseball talent was on.

Accordingly, the Negro Leagues suffered both in quality of play and in fan interest. With the struggles to keep top talent, the leagues ended up using more young talent, who ended up being even more desirable to major-league scouts. Willie Mays, Hank Aaron, and Ernie Banks might have spent more time working up through the bush leagues of black baseball. But with the run on talent, they came up earlier, gained experience faster, and were even more valuable when ultimately nabbed by the major leagues.

Not only were the rosters decimated, but fans no longer flocked to see the players who were often either too old or too mediocre to be immediately attractive to big-league clubs. At Yankee Stadium, attendance for black baseball dropped by more than half in 1947. A nearly equal rate of decline was noted in Newark. Smith wrote of "considerable apprehension" within black baseball "because they fear that Organized Baseball is going to take their stars and subsequently kill Negro baseball altogether." Smith's tone was not entirely sympathetic as he opined that if the Negro Leagues promoted and played games in a "dignified and business-like manner" they would have a better opportunity to retain their fans.

This didn't mean that Smith was uncaring. Privately, he still strove to try to preserve something of the Negro Leagues. In a June 1948 letter to Rickey, he wrote of conversations with J. B. Martin of the Chicago American Giants, indicating that Martin would be agreeable to allowing Rickey to stow some African-American players there for seasoning. A year later, Smith again wrote to Rickey. By that time, the Negro National League had folded, and the Negro American League was struggling. "It would be wise," Smith wrote, "for Brooklyn to subsidize one of the present operating clubs or form an independent club that would tour the country."

All the good intentions in the world could not restore the prestige of the Negro Leagues. Within the next year or two, the Negro American

League would cease organized operations. Some teams would continue to subsist for a decade and a half, barnstorming or playing some half-clowning baseball intended to approximate the Harlem Globetrotters of basketball.

Smith's top competitor Sam Lacy once noted, "The Negro Leagues were an institution, but they were the very thing we wanted to get rid of because they were a symbol of segregation."

⁓

The success of Robinson—and the access of Smith—only stoked the demand for Smith's own work. With more black teammates, Robinson would no longer need a card-playing sportswriter for a roommate. Smith still wrote for the *Courier* but supplemented that weekly income with daily work for the *Chicago Herald-American*, a white daily newspaper. The Baseball Writers' Association of American admitted Smith for the 1948 season—the official cover story was that now that he was writing for a daily, rather than a weekly paper, he no longer violated any policies that had kept him out. Ironically, positive media coverage of Smith's quest for recognition had probably helped pave the way to his admission.

With white papers now carrying more and more information on African-American news—and with Smith and other columnists beginning to slowly integrate many of those papers—the black press began a slow descent of its own. The *Courier* went from a circulation of 357,000 in 1947 to 250,000 by 1953. The *Courier* closed in 1966, although it reopened a year later as the *New Pittsburgh Courier*. Meanwhile, much of the readership of the paper slowly faded away. By 2012, the circulation of the *New Pittsburgh Courier* dipped below 3,500 per week—less than 1 percent of its heyday 65 years prior.

⁓

In 1948, Robinson's autobiography, *Jackie Robinson: My Own Story*, was rushed into print. Smith ghostwrote the book, but in his haste, he made significant errors, like misstating the actual names of both Jackie and Jackie's mother, Mallie.

Robinson, continuing to grow bolder with each passing day, eventually became a target for Smith's ire. In a March 1949 column in the *Courier*, after Robinson complained about coverage of a spring training scrap with a teammate, Smith noted, "This, it seems, is time for some one to remind Mr. Robinson that the press has been especially fair to him throughout his career. . . . If it had not been for the press, Mr. Robinson would have been just another athlete insofar as the public is concerned. If it had not been for the press, Mr. Robinson would not have been in the majors today." In those last two sentences, the reader might as well substitute "Wendell Smith" for "the press," so clear is the personal tone of the writing.

The remarks stung, and the relationship became increasingly distant. Smith spent more and more time covering boxing for the *American*, and Robinson developed an increasingly fractious relationship with the daily press who covered Dodger baseball. Dick Young of the *New York Times* contrasted Robinson's increasingly assertive behavior with Roy Campanella's more peaceable accommodation. "When I talk to Campy, I almost never think of him as a Negro," he told Robinson. "Any time I talk to you, I'm acutely aware of the fact that you're a Negro." Robinson may have been stung by the criticism, but he didn't intend to change who he was. The simplicity of the days when Wendell Smith had been his friend and his mouthpiece would not return.

As Smith was crusading to integrate the major leagues more than a decade before the idea gained significant traction, one may wonder whether his experiences with Jackie Robinson changed his path, or merely appeared as the fulfillment of Smith's ideal conqueror of segregation. Ultimately, it is the former rather than the latter.

Smith, like Robinson, had to determine whether he was willing to help in a social quest that would decimate African-American institutions.

It was one thing to crusade for a black player in the major leagues; it was another to clear the path for the destruction of the Negro Leagues. Because of Robinson's success, mainstream news media also eclipsed the African-American papers that had given Smith his start. Would he have found the courage to persevere had Robinson not come along?

On a more practical level, the lessons that Smith learned from Robinson stayed with him. Perhaps his last great social crusade was an exposé on the horrific state of segregated spring training facilities in 1961. Robinson was long retired, but those difficult days in Daytona in 1946 had never left Smith, and his writing once again made the plight crystal clear and helped end another vestige of Jim Crow. Within the year, the segregationist policies of Florida cities crumbled under the weight of public opinion, as led by Smith.

Finally, by following Robinson, Smith grew comfortable in his role as both crusader of a new age—and in his final days, as a protector of the better aspects of the past. Smith was chosen for a panel that would consider the Negro Leagues afresh for the Baseball Hall of Fame. For Smith, to be the historical caretaker for an institution that he had freely criticized and ultimately helped to bring down on some level completed the circle of his own career. In 1971, Smith helped elect Satchel Paige to the Hall of Fame. The following year, he was part of a movement that added Josh Gibson and Buck Leonard to the Hall.

⌒

Of course, Robinson was already in the Hall of Fame, with no regard to his Negro League Days. Time had softened his relationship with Smith, and, as he aged, Robinson freely admitted Smith's significance, acknowledging in his later, more candid autobiography, *I Never Had It Made*, that he was forever indebted to Smith for his initial assessment of Robinson's skill to Branch Rickey, which had started the entire "great experiment."

The two men kept in touch, and when Robinson passed away on October 24, 1972, Smith himself was too ill with the final stages of pancreatic cancer to attend the funeral. Instead, he paid tribute to Robinson

CHAPTER FIVE

CLYDE SUKEFORTH AND THE RESIDUE OF DESIGN

Baseball has long adhered to the military policy that loose lips sink ships—or pennant chances or scouting departments. If there is a department of baseball where the vaults of secrecy remain not only closed but also tightly locked, it is scouting. Today, teams have vast scouting networks, both domestically and internationally, which check and cross-check prospects, their own players, and opposing players. It is as close to a distilled science as talent evaluation can be, and the inside information of its trade can be the difference in winning pennants or getting a front office fired. Within the Baseball Hall of Fame's library materials on scouting, a handful of old manuals and memoranda reside. One of those, from the Dodger organization, is headlined with a Branch Rickeyism, "Luck is the residue of design." The motivational memorandum begins by asking, "What is it that makes a person lucky or unlucky? How much of our luck do we actually create ourselves? Does our good fortune depend wholly on being in the right place . . . Or is the old adage true— 'The harder we work, the luckier we get'?"

History tells us that Clyde Sukeforth, the Dodger scout who was assigned to investigate the baseball bona fides of Jackie Robinson and then arrange for Robinson to meet Branch Rickey, was lucky. A baseball lifer, Sukeforth had an unremarkable playing career, and while he spent many of his later years scouting, coaching, managing, and generally living with the game of baseball, there was nothing that marked him as a distinctive person who would be the third man in the room with Robinson and Rickey on August 28, 1945, when the decision to integrate baseball went from talk to something beginning to approach reality.

But Sukeforth was an intelligent and able baseball veteran. He intuited Robinson's character and perseverance, taught the inexperienced prospect many of the finer points of baseball, and unfailingly stood by both his young charge and his veteran boss in their desire to change baseball. Sukeforth found himself not only involved in Robinson's discovery but also fortunate enough to be the first man to write the name of Jackie Robinson on a big-league lineup card. Sukeforth's intelligence, character, and work ethic were not lost on Robinson, who credited Sukeforth as an instrumental part of his success both after this rookie year in Brooklyn and again in the weeks leading up to his death in 1972. History suggests that Clyde Sukeforth was lucky to have his somewhat ordinary life touched by Robinson's exceptional journey. But when the matter is examined a bit more carefully, perhaps Jackie Robinson was just as lucky to have had Clyde Sukeforth in his corner.

—

Clyde Leroy Sukeforth was born on November 30, 1901, in Washington, Maine, a town of just over 1,000 people on the state's southern coastline. Sukeforth later recalled a very rural childhood—noting that he and his older sister walked 3½ miles each way to a one-room schoolhouse. Sukeforth's most memorable education came in the town's public library, where the *Boston Post* was delivered daily by stagecoach, carrying tales of the faraway Boston Red Sox, who in Clyde's infancy were one of the best organizations in Major League Baseball.

Baseball was always a part of Clyde Sukeforth's life. He recalled playing "seven days a week," but also noted "[t]here was no organization to it." Given the scarcity of summer weather in Maine, Sukeforth noted, "two full months, we'd be out there and play all seven days a week." When questioned about how he had gotten into baseball, Sukeforth matter-of-factly replied, "Oh, growing up in that atmosphere, there was nothing else to do. I mean, there were two things you could do, you could take your ball and glove and play pass with the neighbor's kids, or you could dig a can of worms and go fishing in the trout brook, that was it!" Fortunately, fishing was not much of a temptation for Sukeforth.

Sukeforth finished high school at the Coburn Classical Institute in Waterville. Heavy industry had taken hold in Maine, and after graduation, Sukeforth found himself playing baseball for the Great Northern

Paper Company in Millinocket, Maine. With two years of semipro base-ball under his belt, he matriculated for a time to Georgetown University. But it was baseball that provided Sukeforth with the ultimate education that he needed in life.

⌒

As a player, Sukeforth was a left-handed hitting catcher, although he was a short, thin man by the standards of modern players. With an affable face and a pair of large ears, the young Sukeforth exuded a kind of boy-ish earnestness that he needed to navigate a fairly unremarkable playing career in baseball.

After hitting .363 in the minor leagues in 1926, Sukeforth earned an appearance with the big-league Cincinnati Reds that season. He struck out in his only at-bat and was promptly sent back to Nashua, which seemed a harbinger of the life of a backup catcher. In 1926–1928, Sukeforth managed only 112 total at-bats with the Reds. Years later, he recalled the effect that these seasons of irregular play had on his hitting. "[W]hen I'd get to hit once a week, I'd hit a ball fairly good, but I got tired of seeing that batting average at .140 or .150," remembered Suke-forth. And so, he adapted. "I took a big heavy bat and choked up on it, and . . . I legged a few," he continued.

That adaptation—and finally getting the chance to play in Cin-cinnati—led to Sukeforth's best big-league season. In 1929, he batted .354, although he did so in only 237 at-bats, and even managed one of his two major-league home runs. Sukeforth parlayed that success into two more seasons of playing well in relatively frequent appearances—batting .284 in 296 at-bats in 1930, and .256 in a career-high 351 at-bats in 1931.

But just when Sukeforth had made his place as a regular catcher for the Reds, he sustained the injury that would prematurely end his playing days. On November 16, 1931, Sukeforth had gone rabbit hunting near Cincinnati, when a companion on the hunting trip accidentally shot him in the right eye and face. A piece of birdshot went through the corner of his right eye, and doctors initially feared that he would lose his sight entirely in that eye.

He did not, but the career that had *The Sporting News* referring to him as "one of the best catchers in the National League" would never be the same. Sukeforth was released from the hospital after a couple of weeks, and in later years, he would only complain that he "couldn't read too well without squinting."

Sukeforth's vision difficulties were substantial enough that the Reds decided to ship him to the Brooklyn Dodgers during spring training of 1932. The trade brought the Reds catcher Ernie Lombardi, who would help them win back-to-back pennants in 1939 and 1940. Sukeforth's Brooklyn career spanned only three seasons, ending in 1934, with him having accrued just 190 total at-bats with the Dodgers.

The Dodgers sent him to Toledo in 1934, but Sukeforth didn't wish to play there in 1935. Instead, he hung around Maine, playing semipro ball. He had married Helen Miller after the 1933 season, and it looked as if Sukeforth might settle down to a quiet life in Maine. However, he merely changed directions.

Sukeforth took over managing Brooklyn's farm team in Draper, North Carolina, in 1936. He would occasionally play catcher, but he found an aptitude for working with young players—at least, when he could avoid controversy, such as an incident in July when Sukeforth insulted the integrity of the Bi-State League president so severely that he was suspended indefinitely and fined $20.

On the whole, managing fit Sukeforth well, as he went from a third-place season in Draper to a first-place finish in Clinton, Iowa, in 1937. Two years in Elmira followed, with his team winning the league championship in 1938. As a manager, Sukeforth's longest stop was his next, in Montreal, where he managed the Royals for three seasons, finishing second in the league in each of the last two years.

Following that final season of 1942, Larry MacPhail had left the Dodgers to fight in World War II, and the team was run by new general manager Branch Rickey, who utilized Sukeforth within his circle of baseball insiders. Sukeforth left the minor leagues behind and became a coach for Brooklyn. He later recalled that being a big-league manager "wasn't my ambition at all. I never really prepared myself for that." His minor-league boss in Montreal was noted to have criticized Sukeforth at one point for being "too good a fellow" to make a top manager.

That suited Rickey fine. Rather than settling into a managing job, Sukeforth began a career journey as a jack-of-all-trades—coach, scout, consultant, even player for a brief stretch in 1945, when he hit .294 in 51 at-bats for a war-torn Dodger squad. But Rickey had a job to fill that was much bigger than serving as a backup catcher for a few innings, and Sukeforth ended up being just the right fit for it.

Once Rickey resolved to scout darker-skinned players, he had several trusted scouts working on the assignment. In addition to Robert Haig in South America and José Seda in Puerto Rico, several of Rickey's friends and trusted baseball men were scouting other players who were not welcome in the established major-league hierarchy. Tom Greenwade, Wid Matthews, and George Sisler were three of the scouts who had all followed Robinson with interest. In fact, Greenwade, who is perhaps best known as the scout who signed Mickey Mantle, was noted in *The Sporting News* to have been "the only scout used on the Jackie Robinson job." While this is a misstatement, Greenwade did relate that he saw Robinson play "about 20 times."

Still, while several people scouted Robinson, Rickey was playing his cards close to the vest in regard to his reasoning. Early in 1945, he attacked the Negro Leagues and announced the forthcoming United States League. Rickey told reporters that he would run the Brooklyn Brown Dodgers, which not only never existed but also were most likely never intended to exist. The Brown Dodgers were a cover for Rickey's real mission.

Matthews, a Southerner who might have been most likely to reject his assignment had its true nature been revealed, was one of Robinson's champions. While he did opine that Robinson was "strictly the showboat type," he also credited him as "one of the best two-strike hitters he had seen in a long time." Greenwade was taken with his bunting ability, but he had reservations about his throwing arm. Sisler also had concerns about Robinson's arm, and so, when Rickey called in Sukeforth, he was clear on the one issue he had in mind.

Sukeforth said in January 1950 that August 17, 1945, was the first time he had heard from Rickey about any interest in African-American players. Sukeforth also noted that he had previously seen some Negro League games—he recalled watching Don Newcombe and Roy Campanella, among other players—but he wasn't sure if he had turned in any written reports on black players.

Rickey told Sukeforth that he was to take in the August 24th game of the Kansas City Monarchs in Comiskey Park, and that he should focus on the Monarch shortstop—Robinson. Rickey told him that he had good reports on Robinson, but that there was some doubt as to whether Robinson had a really good throwing arm. He specifically directed Sukeforth to ask Robinson to practice making throws from deep in the shortstop hole in practice.

At this point, Rickey's directions grew more clandestine. Sukeforth remembered Rickey directing him that "if I liked his arm to bring the fellow in, if I liked him and his schedule would permit." Rickey admitted that he wanted Robinson to sneak away from the Monarchs "without anybody knowing anything about it." He told Sukeforth to avoid publicity, but that if he was asked, he should give his own name.

A great scout must be a seer. He must not only see the tools and plays in front of him, but he must also project his team's needs, the player's development, and, particularly relevant in the case of Robinson, a series of extraneous factors not directly involving baseball, but involving a player's ability to bear up under the pressures and exertions endemic to all players. Needless to say, the pressures and outside factors bearing on Robinson would be extraordinary, and Sukeforth handled the "scouting" like a visionary.

Sukeforth tried unsuccessfully to find Robinson in a Chicago hotel before the game, but the Monarchs had traveled up by bus, so this did not work. Instead, he simply went to the ballpark, got a ticket, and watched to see who Robinson was. When he spotted him at the game, Sukeforth called him over and introduced himself. He explained his mission, and Robinson told him that he would have been glad to help him except that he had fallen on his shoulder and wouldn't be able to play for a week or so. Sukeforth asked Robinson to meet him at the Stevens Hotel after the game.

It was here that Sukeforth's scouting of Robinson began in earnest. After Sukeforth tipped the elevator operator to make sure Robinson had no (racial) trouble getting to his room, the two men met later in the evening. Sukeforth questioned Robinson on a variety of topics. Notably, he recalled asking him about his discharge from the army. Robinson, likely wary of the issue, told him only about his ankle injury—true enough, if only a piece of the truth. Robinson wanted to make a good impression and he succeeded. "The more we talked, the better I liked him," Sukeforth recalled. "There was something about that man that just gripped you. He was tough, he was intelligent, and he was proud."

He also was not naïve enough to dismiss Rickey's reason for wanting to see him in midseason. He had asked Sukeforth at the ballpark, and now he continued asking at the hotel. "Why is Mr. Rickey interested in my arm? Why does he want to see me?" Sukeforth told Robinson that he didn't know, but the topic came up again and again. Eventually, Robinson, tired of speculating, asked, "Mr. Sukeforth, what do you think?"

"Jack, I think this could be the real thing," Sukeforth replied.

Sukeforth told Robinson that he had to see a game in Toledo on Sunday, and that if Robinson met him there, he would accompany him on to Brooklyn. A handwritten note survives that initial scouting, and serves to memorialize the occasion. Sukeforth's report to Rickey reads, "Player fell on shoulder last Tuesday. Will be out of games few more days. I want to see Columbus-Toledo series Sunday–Monday. Will have player meet me in Toledo Mon night and accompany up to NY if satisfactory to you."

It was satisfactory.

Sukeforth and Robinson talked more on the train, and by the time they arrived in New York on Monday, the two men had gained the essential measure of each other. Robinson checked into the Teresa Hotel in Harlem on Monday night and on Tuesday morning, August 28, 1945, the famous Rickey/Robinson meeting was arranged and attended by Sukeforth.

Most of what we know about Sukeforth's experiences in that meeting comes from a conversation he had in January 1950 with Rickey. The occasion for the remembrance was a meeting called by Rickey to review the facts of the situation during the filming of the first Robinson biopic, *The Jackie Robinson Story*. Sukeforth's remarks are even more special because they are made on the precipice at which the Rickey/Robinson meeting would go from important insider information to legendary Hollywood moment.

Looking back in January 1950, Sukeforth recalled the meeting lasting "about three hours." In a moment of understatement, Sukeforth said to Rickey, "I did not have much to say after the introductions. You took over and asked him a few thousand questions."

He continued:

> You said that if you could get your hands on a great colored ball player, you would be tempted to put him in Montreal or even Brooklyn, providing he was the right temperament, had poise, and was the type of fellow who could take the insults and carry the flag for his race. You said, "I don't think you are that fellow. If somebody called you a black so-and-so, you would start a fight and that would set the cause back 100 years." And then followed a few more thousand questions and a lot of drama. You were at your best that day. I remember Robinson's answers, after a lot of thought. He finally said, "Mr. Rickey, I think I can play ball, but I will promise

you that I will do the second part of the job. I won't be involved in an incident," and he meant that he would do all right off the field, too.

In that August 1945 meeting, Rickey was impressed, but he was far from alone. Looking back, Sukeforth recalled the variety of questions, with Robinson asked about "his habits and deportment and associations and his background in California, particularly in competitive sports." He remembered, "I was impressed with the fellow and the way he handled himself. He would not go off half cocked. . . . You told Robinson you would have more than a good player. He seemed to understand."

Remembering the meeting in 1950, Rickey and Sukeforth discussed their memories for a few moments more. At one point, Rickey mentioned his own anger that the film would portray some incidents of racial difficulty within the Dodgers that he did not believe actually occurred. He asked Sukeforth if he had any comments on the film script, and Sukeforth admitted, "No, I don't think so, Mr. Rickey. I think they are going to write it up the way they want it, regardless."

The reality of Clyde Sukeforth would be banished beneath the image of actor Billy Wayne in *The Jackie Robinson Story*. Sukeforth, the story would go, was the unwitting architect of greatness, bringing two men together under unknown plans. He was some sort of New England Forrest Gump, happening to be in the right place when history occurred. But that's the movie—that's not the reality.

One aspect of Robinson's rise to major-league stardom that is consistently overlooked is just how much baseball he had to learn in a short span. Sure, he had played in college at UCLA—but he had also lettered in three other sports, and batted .097 in his last season of college baseball. He was also four years removed from those days when he had his less-than-full season apprenticeship in the Negro Leagues. From there, it was on to the highest level of minor-league baseball in 1946, and the big leagues the following year. The closest parallel to what Robinson accomplished in a purely baseball sense is probably the career of New York Mets farmhand Tim Tebow, a great athlete who had not played high-level baseball in years. The difference was that Robinson did not have the luxury of a learning curve like Tebow. He simply had to star from his first appearance on a Montreal or Brooklyn field.

Obviously, Robinson was a great natural athlete, but equally obvious, although often forgotten, is that he was extremely coachable. The man who imparted or supported a fair number of those lessons was Sukeforth. In Robinson's first spring training, back in 1946, Sukeforth urged him not to overdo it on throws from his shortstop position. Sensitive to slights about his lack of a throwing arm, Robinson ignored the warning and promptly came down with a very untimely sore arm.

Near the end of his life, Robinson remembered his struggles in spring training 1946. He recalled Rickey pushing him to play more aggressively, be more of a gambler. If Rickey took the bad-cop role, Sukeforth took on the good-cop persona. "Clyde showed his support and concern by massaging my morale and trying to get me to loosen up," remembered Robinson.

The support was probably fairly easy to show to such a quick pupil. After developing his sore arm, Robinson was moved, first to second base, and then to first base, where he barely had to throw at all. Rickey took an hour one morning to coach Robinson on the intricacies of the new position. "He is apt and learns things exceptionally fast," said Rickey. A fellow player, Al Campanis, later recalled that Robinson "had the greatest aptitude of any player I've ever seen," and that "in one half hour, he learned to make the double play pivot correctly [at second base]." Montreal infielders Lou Rochelli and Stan Breard were also both helpful to Robinson as he tried to learn new positions. Sukeforth noted coach George Sisler also helping Robinson learn some of the finer points of playing first base, but also later recalled, "[H]e played that first base like he was born there."

Robinson's short learning curve was hardly unique to his year in Montreal. In his year in Kansas City, one author noted, "The old-time baseball men pulled together in an effort to teach Robinson the trade as soon as possible."

The lessons continued into the winter of 1945–1946 as Robinson roomed with Gene Benson on his Venezuela barnstorming trip. Benson tutored Robinson on his technique for hitting curveballs, but also encouraged Robinson in the mental aspects of baseball. "I'd say to him, the big thing about playing baseball . . . is don't ever let yourself tighten up," remembered Benson. He also told Robinson sometimes, in reference to the big leagues, "Where you're going is easier than where you're coming from."

In some sense, Sukeforth maintained the continuity of the lessons from these baseball mentors. Even once Robinson made the Dodgers in 1947, when he experienced his initial big-league slump, an 0-for-20 dive to end April and drop his batting average to .225, it was Sukeforth who "kept encouraging him, expressing . . . confidence in his ability to help the team."

Sukeforth's confidence in Robinson sprang from his decades of baseball experience and from his own observation of Robinson's remarkable character and work ethic. In 1987, Sukeforth wrote a letter to Rachel Robinson in which he recalled standing by Jackie on the latter's first day of spring training 1946 in Sanford, Florida. Sukeforth stated that "the very atmosphere was charged" and remembered that as he and Robinson approached the field, Jackie said to him, "This is it!" That moment, wrote Sukeforth, "seemed like a challenging statement from a determined young man, and that it proved to be."

In a moment of poetic justice, Sukeforth not only attended Robinson's coronation as a major-league player a year later, but he played a major role in the game itself. Brooklyn manager Leo Durocher was set to manage Robinson, had directed his move to first base, and had famously broken up a group of rebelling anti-Robinson Dodger players in spring training, telling them, among other things to "shove your petition up your ass." (Interestingly, some sources maintain that Sukeforth was the source who had sussed out the existence of the petition and brought it to Rickey's and thus Durocher's attention.)

However, on April 9, 1947, six days before the season began, a series of accumulated incidents involving Durocher led to him being suspended from baseball for the season by Commissioner Chandler. Some have speculated that the late move to suspend Durocher loomed as a potential roadblock to Robinson's big-league path. Rickey acted quickly, asking Sukeforth to manage the team, which he declined. However, he did take over as interim manager until Rickey could locate a long-term skipper.

If the discipline of Durocher was intended to make Robinson's transition to Brooklyn difficult, that was not taking into account his feelings about Sukeforth. In 1948's *Jackie Robinson: My Own Story*, he noted, "I knew that he was definitely in my corner. . . . [A]ll through my efforts to make good, he had been my friend and advisor. I think he wanted me to succeed almost as much as my wife and mother did. . . . Many times during spring training, I used to say, 'I wish Sukey was the Brooklyn manager. I bet he'd ask Mr. Rickey to bring me up.'"

Robinson was promoted the day after Durocher's suspension was announced, and so Sukeforth found himself taking Robinson around the Brooklyn locker room and introducing him before his first exhibition game on the big-league roster. A few days later, Sukeforth penciled Robinson's name into a big-league lineup, which he did on Opening Day against the Boston Braves. The interim manager eschewed any motivational pep talks, later recalling, "I didn't tell Jack anything special. Jack had enough to think about."

In the two games that spanned Sukeforth's managerial career, he led the team during Robinson's first game, first at-bat, first run scored, and first base hit, a bunt single in the fifth inning of the team's second game with Boston. Brooklyn won both games, and with a lifetime big-league managing mark of 2-0, Sukeforth was relieved by Burt Shotton.

With Shotton in charge, Sukeforth could return to a coaching role, in which he served as a conduit between Rickey and Robinson. The former could not be in the dugout, much less the field, and so Sukeforth found himself combining an on-the-field presence with the big-picture perspective of Rickey. Early in the season, when Pirates pitcher Fritz Ostermueller beaned Robinson and the Dodger bench exploded in anger, it was Sukeforth who told the media, "The guys on the team are all for him. Mr. Jackie Robinson's going to do all right."

Sukeforth was capable of angry explosions himself. With manager Shotton stuck in the dugout due to his desire to not wear a uniform, it was Sukeforth who became the arguing presence of the Dodger management. No doubt Robinson, as a player who rarely missed an opportunity to question an umpire, appreciated Sukeforth's contributions in that area. On May 12th, after several questionable calls, Sukeforth lit into home plate umpire George Magerkurth so vociferously that Magerkurth cleared the Brooklyn dugout, leaving only Shotton, coach Jake Pitler, and players Hugh Casey and Cookie Lavagetto on the Dodger bench. Robinson was on the field at the time, so he was not part of Magerkurth's purge, but particularly in an era when Robinson was going out of his way to avoid any untoward incidents, he likely enjoyed Sukeforth's tirade.

Other times, Sukeforth helped Robinson keep the peace. On September 11th, with Brooklyn trying to hold on to the lead in the NL pennant race, when Cardinal catcher Joe Garagiola stepped on Robinson's foot at first base and then got into a heated altercation at home plate, it was Sukeforth who came out to restrain Robinson. When there was no other form of support to give Robinson, Sukeforth often played cards with the notoriously competitive player.

Robinson later recalled that on the one occasion he could remember when Shotton used racially offensive language in the locker room— dismissing an outsider as acting "nigger rich"—that he believed it was Sukeforth in whom he had confided. Sukeforth brought the principals together, which elicited an apology from Shotton, as he had not intended the term to be offensive and certainly was not referring to Robinson. Robinson kindly but firmly suggested that perhaps the term could be avoided altogether, and he did not recall any subsequent issues.

As Robinson's historic 1947 season unfolded, he knew that aside from his family and friends, he had support from the Brooklyn front office, from the African-American press, and from Sukeforth. It may not seem like much—a kind word here, a card game there, a sense of togetherness passed on. But it was. After that 1947 season, Robinson completed a publicity questionnaire for the National League. After all the standard biographical information, he was asked, "What manager, scout or players helped you most during your career?" He penciled in "Clyde Sukeforth," and when the follow-up question asked "How?" he wrote "Encouragement."

As part of the Branch Rickey brain trust, Sukeforth's days in Brooklyn were numbered after Rickey was supplanted by Walter O'Malley after the 1950 season. He was retained by new manager Charlie Dressen after the Burt Shotton era concluded with Rickey's departure.

The 1951 season began well for the Dodgers, who had won two pennants in the last four seasons, and had gone to the season's final day before losing in 1950. Brooklyn moved into first place on May 13th, and stretched their lead to 13 games ahead of the second-place Giants on August 11th. The Dodgers never fell out of first place but needed a superhuman effort from Robinson in the season's final game against the Dodgers to end the season in a tie for first place with the late-charging Giants. With the Dodgers knowing that they had to win over the Phillies in order to force a playoff for the pennant, Robinson made a brilliant bases-loaded grab of a Eddie Waitkus line drive to end the 12th inning. The catch jammed Robinson's elbow into his stomach so hard that he knocked the wind out of himself and, apparently, briefly knocked himself unconscious. With help from Reese, Robinson stayed in the game, and homered in the 14th inning for the deciding run in the Dodgers' 9-8 victory.

After the Dodgers and Giants split the first two games of the playoff, the winner-take-all third game was played in the Polo Grounds. The Dodgers held a 4-1 lead into the ninth inning, with Robinson contributing a first-inning RBI single, and Don Newcombe pitching masterfully. In the ninth, the Giants scored a run scored off Newcombe, who was visibly tiring, and with two Giants runners on base, Dressen called the Dodger bullpen.

Clyde Sukeforth was the bullpen coach and was presiding over a pair of pitchers who were warming in the bullpen, starters Ralph Branca and Carl Erskine. When Dressen called him, popular rumor had it that Erskine bounced a curveball in the dirt and Sukeforth reported this fact to Dressen. Erskine, in his memoir, recalled Sukeforth saying, "They're both OK, but Erskine is bouncing his overhand curve at times." Sukeforth denies the bouncing the curve story. In fact, he recalled catching Erskine, and that his curveball was not sharp. He remembered telling Dressen, "Branko's doing well."

In any case, the call was for Branca, and his second pitch was blasted into the left field bleachers by Bobby Thomson, ending the game and season. Robinson stood at his second-base position, watching Thomson circle the bases, making sure his foe touched every base before he left his position. That game was Sukeforth's final one in a Dodger uniform. Branca and Dressen remained, but Sukeforth was gone.

All was not lost for Sukeforth in 1951, however. A widower since 1938, he remarried on December 2nd, to Grethel Winchenbach, a fellow resident of Waldoboro, Maine. The 50-year-old Sukeforth spent nearly half a century of life with Grethel, until she passed away in 1999.

⌒

Parting ways with the Dodgers did not render Sukeforth a homebody. He followed Branch Rickey to Pittsburgh, where he scouted and coached for the Pirates. Demonstrating that his scouting eye remained sharp, Sukeforth was a champion of Roberto Clemente, then a forgotten minor leaguer in the Dodger system.

Watching Clemente warm up before the game, Sukeforth was wowed by his legendary throwing arm. During that evening's game, Clemente pinch hit, and Sukeforth saw him run out a routine ground ball so quickly that the humdrum play became close. Clemente may have been under the radar of most of baseball, but Sukeforth recalled, "I said to myself, there's a boy who can do two things as well as any man who ever lived."

As the Dodgers prepared for the minor-league draft, other scouts spoke against Clemente, but Sukeforth ended the conversation by noting, "[T]here's a question in my mind as to whether or not [Clemente's throwing arm] is better than Furillo's. It's right in the same class as Furillo's and it may even be a little bit better." Rickey was intrigued, followed up on the tip, and drafted Clemente. Once again, Clyde Sukeforth had been the seer, finding qualities in a talented young player that others hadn't observed.

Sukeforth stayed on with the Pirates first as a coach, and later as a scout and eventual minor-league manager. He turned down the opportunity to manage in the major leagues again in 1957, when the Pirates asked him to follow former Dodger Bobby Bragan as their big-league skipper. Meanwhile, unlike Rickey, who had been forced out, he was in the organization during Pittsburgh's thrilling 1960 World Series victory. In fact, in 1965, Sukeforth was coaxed back to managing for a single season, when he managed the Gastonia Pirates, the Western Carolinas League affiliate of the Pirates. He was chosen to manage in the league's All-Star Game, and his 70-54 mark led the Pirates, who included Al Oliver and Bob Robertson, to near the top of the league.

After his days in Pittsburgh, he scouted for the Braves, both in Milwaukee and in Atlanta. In early 1971, he had been around long enough as a scout to see the beginning of network scouting, as he worked for a group that combined efforts for the Braves, Yankees, Angels, and Cubs. Eventually, gradually, Sukeforth pulled away from baseball.

In the summer of 1972, Sukeforth saw an upcoming event honoring Robinson at Mama Leone's restaurant in New York, and decided to check in on his former prodigy. "I knew Jack wasn't feeling well," he later remembered, "I figured I'm not going to have many opportunities to see this fellow again." Indeed, Robinson by this time was nearly blind and otherwise suffering from the effects of diabetes and heart concerns.

Sukeforth attended the dinner, and when word of his appearance got around, the organizers asked him to say a few words. "I didn't expect to have anything to say," recalled Sukeforth. "I just wanted to see Jack." The comments he made do not survive, but Sukeforth recalled telling his audience, "I didn't think my part in Jack's career was that important. My relationship with Jack was just the same as it would have been with any ballplayer, black or white." At least one person present took exception to those comments.

A few days later, Sukeforth received a letter in the mail. On the letterhead of the Jackie Robinson Construction Corporation, Robinson's letter noted, "Please understand that I do not have any reservations in praise for the role that Clyde Sukeforth played in the growth and development of my beginnings in baseball. I have been very appreciative of the fact that whenever there were problems in the earlier days, I could always go to you, talk with you, and receive the warm and friendly advise [*sic*] that I always did."

Robinson continued, "While there has not been enough said of your significant contribution in the Rickey-Robinson experiment, I consider your role, next to Mr. Rickey's and my wife's—yes, bigger than any other persons with whom I came in contact. I have always considered you to be one of the true giants in this initial endeavor in baseball, for which I am truly appreciative."

Robinson expressed his desire to visit Sukeforth and pledged to get in touch with him when next he would be in Maine. He concluded, "May you never find it convenient to underplay the role you played to make the Rickey-Robinson experiment a success."

Three months later, Robinson passed away. Asked about the letter years later, Sukeforth stated, "That was kind of him."

When considering the relationship between Sukeforth and Robinson, there are perhaps few documentable events that would elevate the relationship to the level indicated by Robinson. However, given Robinson's own comments and actions, it appears certain that for every incident in which Sukeforth supported or accepted or befriended Robinson that is known, there are likely many more that were private moments inside hotels, locker rooms, trains, or airplanes.

Sukeforth's lengthy baseball career spanned the age of the generalist, when he broke in as a young man who could scout, coach, manage, and generally play a background role in the support and development of young players. It is little wonder that he and Rickey developed such a friendship, as the two ex-catchers both came up through baseball performing what in modern times would be four or five different jobs.

In some ways, the standardization of scouting into a quasi-official industry, well on the way by the time Sukeforth left baseball, has taken much of the mystery out of that role. Given the opportunity to view prospects in top competition, the focus has shifted in many areas to a more intangible, off-the-field assessment. As the range of baseball has expanded from a sport for white Americans to a truly international and interracial game, scouts have to comprehend and access a much wider variety of cultural norms.

To some extent, the leadership of Sukeforth and other great Dodger scouts has set a standard that the organization has followed by being bold in international scouting. First, the Dodgers were one of the major players in Mexico and Latin America, with stars from Fernando Valenzuela to Pedro Martínez. When Asian prospects were sought, again the Dodgers were at the front of the movement, with players like Hideo Nomo and Kenta Maeda. Part of the Dodger advantage was an attention to detail and connections in the international community, but part was a more streamlined process of mainlining talent into the Dodger culture.

Much of what made Sukeforth a significant figure to Robinson is now enveloped within the new arena of mental performance coaches. By 2018, 27 of the 30 major-league teams hired mental performance coaches, who employ a variety of techniques to help players cope with the pressure and difficulty of playing baseball. Admittedly, some of the new techniques and jargon, like imagery programs and visualization exercises, are a bit more new wave than anything that Sukeforth did for Robinson. But a large part of the process is talking about baseball, obtaining a positive mental attitude, and helping players cope with pressure, which was so persistent for Robinson that he was approaching a nervous breakdown during his 1946 season in Montreal.

Today, baseball constructs a massive support system to assess, sign, and improve players—and takes particular note of players who have cultural differences from many of their teammates. In the 1940s, the Dodgers had a general manager with a big idea, and Clyde Sukeforth. Managers changed, teammates came and went, but since their initial meeting in August 1945, Sukeforth was in Robinson's corner. It was well that Sukeforth was a jack-of-all-trades because the roles he fulfilled with Robinson, from his care and diligence in scouting Robinson's character as well as his baseball skills, to his support and advocacy for Robinson in difficult situations, required all of those skills. That skill set certainly aided Robinson, but ultimately, the triumph of Jackie Robinson also shows the multitasking excellence of Clyde Sukeforth. Sukeforth helped assess and establish Robinson as just the man for his times, in part because he himself was so far ahead of his own.

CHAPTER SIX

KINDLY OLD BURT SHOTTON: "I CANNOT POSSIBLY HURT YOU."

"We'll get you now, you prick!"

Stan Musial is remembered as one of the most gracious souls ever to be a legendary baseball player. Late in his career, though, an opposing manager drove him too far.

One too many times, the combative and combustible Leo Durocher ridiculed Musial and the Cardinals. Suddenly, Stan the Man shouted at him. Cardinal rookie catcher Tim McCarver recalled it as the only time that he ever heard Musial use any type of foul language. Leo Durocher could have that effect on people. And yet, this was the same Leo Durocher, managing savant but crown prince of questionable decision making, who years before was going to be entrusted with managing Jackie Robinson in his initial season in the major leagues.

But then fate and the inscrutable Happy Chandler intervened, suspending Durocher for the 1947 season five days before the regular season began and Robinson was set to break baseball's color barrier. In his office in Brooklyn, Branch Rickey—who sometimes enjoyed being dramatic—was near the point of collapse.

"I am falling out a window. I am on the ledge and going over! The sidewalk is twenty feet below! One name—one name can save me," Rickey told his circle of baseball advisors. Rickey had eight names on a sheet of paper as potential managers, and he sought his informal vetting committee's opinions.

Many of the names were usual suspects, most notably Joe McCarthy, the former Yankee manager who was retired because of ill health. But Rickey had already approached McCarthy and had been turned down.

Eventually, the group centered on one name, much to the surprise of everyone. The man who was chosen to save Rickey and the Dodgers

Jackie and Rachel Robinson share a moment together in the later years of their marriage. She wrote, "We had created a true partnership, a heady 'us against the world' kind of thing, and had been privileged to find a special mission early on."

Jackie Robinson and Branch Rickey found a common cause much deeper than winning baseball games. Robinson defined Rickey's legacy, and Rickey, after carefully charting a course, provided the necessary backing to make baseball's integration a reality.

Eternally a political creature, Happy Chandler was a self-made man and a frequent self-contradiction. As Commissioner of Baseball, he quietly helped pave the way for the integration of the sport, but his contributions are surrounded in mystery and myth.

Sportswriter Wendell Smith was a pivotal figure in both the integration of baseball and in the integrating of the press covering baseball. Friend, PR figure, and journalist rolled into one, Smith was a pivotal figure in Robinson's transition to the Major Leagues.

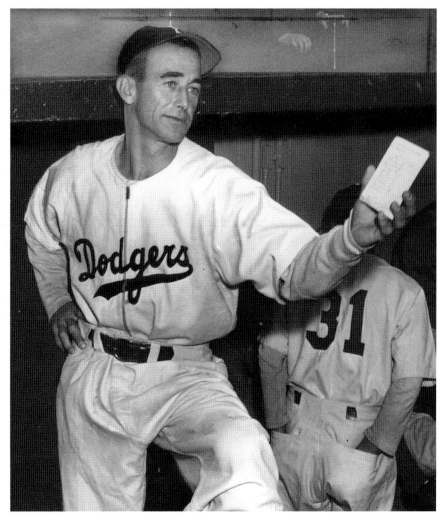

Clyde Sukeforth not only scouted Robinson, he coached him, encouraged him, and generally performed as a one-man support staff in aiding his transition into the Brooklyn system.

Dodger manager Burt Shotton, here dressed for the World Series, was a fascinating blend of the past and the future. His low-pressure, low-key demeanor helped Jackie Robinson become a star, and provided a signpost to the future of baseball managing.

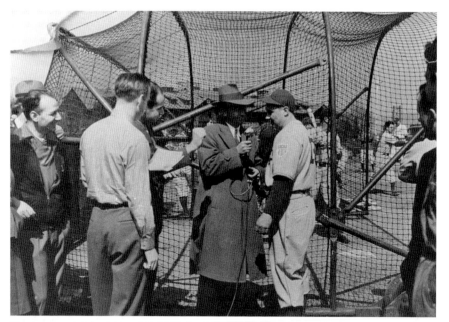

The immaculately dressed Red Barber broadcasting during World War II. Fellow broadcaster Bob Edwards recalled, "[H]e had looked deep into his soul and found something there he didn't like. Jackie Robinson helped him fix that."

Jackie Robinson and Pee Wee Reese golfed together, played cards together, and famously (some say mythologically) stood side by side in the forging of a brave new world. It was Robinson who wrote to his wife that Reese was a "fine team man," but each man spent years in Brooklyn living up to that label.

Dixie Walker has been cast as a villain for his initial opposition to Jackie Robinson, but Robinson's ability to change the lives of even those opposed to him stands as his greatest legacy. Walker, shown here sitting in front of (from left) Hugh Casey, Pee Wee Reese, Joe Hatten, and Eddie Stanky, told a reporter late in his life, "I've grown and Jackie knows it."

from doom was 62 years old, which would make him the oldest manager in the major leagues aside from the venerable and likely senile Connie Mack. His last full-time managing job had come in 1933, and that work had done little to recommend him. Rickey's managerial savior was an old man, out of baseball entirely, having not managed in nearly a decade and a half and sporting a lifetime record of 371-549 as a major-league manager.

Burton Edwin Shotton was in many ways the longest of long shots to lead the Brooklyn Dodgers into a new era of baseball. The game had passed him by long before, or so it looked to outsiders. In fact, Shotton ended up working out fine for Robinson and the Dodgers, in large part because he was the polar opposite of Leo Durocher. Durocher cajoled, wheedled, nagged, and projected an overpowering personality that held sway and dominion at all times over his team. He argued with umpires, he argued with the commissioner, he filled the notebooks of the press.

Burt Shotton was, in every sense, different. He sat in the dugout in slacks and a warm-up jacket. By major-league rule, as he was not in uniform, Shotton could not go onto the field to challenge umpires. He never had much to say to the media, earning him their indifference or even dismay, as when he was dubbed "Kindly Old Burt Shotton." As a manager, Shotton was careful about knowing his players, about trying to build up their confidence and comfort by projecting a solidity and a dependability that Durocher struggled to convey throughout his career.

Stan Musial would never have cause to swear at Burt Shotton. In fact, quietly, in 3½ seasons in Brooklyn, Shotton led the Dodgers to two pennants. He also impressed himself upon a generation of ballplayers as a template for what would later be dubbed a player's manager—a low-drama leader who trusted the men whose names he wrote on the lineup card to win games.

Shotton got along fine with the newest addition to his Dodger team, Jackie Robinson. He patiently stood by Robinson when he struggled, and the calmness and serenity he brought to the Dodger dugout and clubhouse had to be welcome at a time when everything else in Robinson's life could seem upside down. For his part, Robinson reciprocated in two major ways—he made Shotton a winner, which he had never previously experienced as a manager, and he helped the evolution of managers from overbearing attention seekers to quiet, business-first skippers who could adapt to the variety of players and cultures that soon filled dugouts and clubhouses. The Dodgers dipped into baseball's past to find Shotton, but Robinson helped him emerge as something of an unlikely template for the future of managing.

The evolution of baseball managers in many ways runs a parallel path to the evolution of baseball in general. The earliest managers weren't really managers—they tended to be player-managers who broadly functioned as team captains. But as baseball became more firmly entrenched in American culture, the manager ceased being just another player who had a few extra seasons under his belt and became a tactician, perhaps even a general.

The influence of John McGraw in the history of baseball would be hard to overstate, but suffice it to say that among many contributions, McGraw was the father of modern baseball managers. He had been a fine player in his younger days, and took over as a manger when he was still in his 20s. He won 2,784 games as a manager, and his innovations were numerous. Bill James has written that McGraw "did more to establish the profession of managing than anyone else in history," and credits McGraw and Connie Mack with establishing a baseball orthodoxy in many of the smallest details of the game, from the mechanics of infield play to base-running technique, to the use of relief pitchers, bench players, and coaches.

McGraw, while a respected baseball tactician and an excellent hand at developing young players, was not a particularly pleasant man. Rogers Hornsby, who himself was rather disagreeable, recalled, "He'd fine players for speaking to somebody on the other team. Or being caught with a cigarette. He'd walk up and down the dugout and yell, 'Wipe those damn smiles off your face.'"

The other model for young managers was the aforementioned Connie Mack. Mack managed from the 1890s until 1950. While his lifetime statistics are weighed down by the fact that he stayed in a major-league dugout until he was 87 years old, in his prime, Mack was as good of a manager as McGraw—and brought a much different attitude to the table.

Like McGraw, Mack was an excellent scout of baseball talent, in the era when the manager's job was not limited to mere on-the-field tactics but also included player evaluation and signing. But unlike McGraw, Mack was quiet and patient. He wore a suit during games, abstained from profanity, and preferred to sign educated young players. Bill James once wrote, "Mack's philosophy was, you get good people, you treat them well, and you'll win."

As baseball moved through the 1940s, firebrands like McGraw tended to prevail over peaceable gentlemen like Mack. Again, Mack's cause wasn't helped by the fact that he spent his late 70s and early to mid 80s growing more senile watching the Philadelphia Athletics land deeply at the bottom of the American League standings annually. Contrasting Mack and McGraw, James noted in 1994, "McGraw's approach was and is much more common among managers and coaches in all sports."

Leo Durocher, set to manage the Dodgers in 1947, was definitely a man from the lineage of McGraw. One author noted, "If Durocher spoke a sentence without curses, it was probably an accident, soon to be corrected." Oft-divorced, at the center of penny-ante clubhouse gambling, Durocher was not a man for whom peace and gentility were at a premium. Jonathan Eig wrote, "While Durocher thrived on animosity, not all his players did, and some Dodgers despised their skipper."

Still, the odd couple of Branch Rickey and Durocher persisted, mostly because, for all his personal peccadillos, Leo won games. In his first eight years in Brooklyn, he won a pennant and only once finished below third place in the National League. For the historically moribund Dodger franchise, a little bit of hell-raising was a price the team was willing to pay.

But how would Robinson react to Durocher? For his part, Durocher was unequivocal in his initial support of Robinson, whether it had been fed to him by Rickey or was just a part of his generally contrarian nature. When word of a potential petition against Robinson reached Durocher, he quickly called a meeting of the other Dodgers and lit into them. "I don't care if the guy is yellow or black, or if he has stripes like a fuckin' zebra. I'm the manager of this team, and I say he plays," Durocher allegedly told his charges, before offering to make sure anyone who disagreed was traded. So from the outside of things, Durocher was vocally pro-Robinson.

There was no shielding the fact that Durocher was not an easy person to get along with. Dodgers Howie Schultz recalled his former boss, saying, "I don't agree with all the things he did and said, especially his treatment of us on the ballfield, and I don't suppose anyone else did either, but I don't think anyone ran a ballgame, once that first pitch was thrown, any better than Leo did. Still he was impatient with the limitations that rookies and young ballplayers have."

Of course, how Durocher would have managed Robinson in 1947 became a moot point. After April 10th, when news of Durocher's suspension went public, the issue became how would the new Dodger manager, who eventually was Burt Shotton, manage Robinson? By all indications, it was quite a different kettle of fish playing for Shotton than for Durocher. And despite those who maintain that the suspension of Durocher was one last-ditch conspiracy attempt to keep Robinson out of the major leagues, things worked out just fine without Leo.

It took a long memory for anyone to remember Burt Shotton as a major-league manager. Of all the players on the 1947 Dodgers, only two, Dixie Walker and reserve Arky Vaughn, had been active in the major leagues when Shotton last held a managing job. The greatest influence on Shotton's managing acumen was unsurprisingly that of his own onetime manager and longtime boss, Branch Rickey. Nearly the same age, of the same general persuasion and mentality about the game, Shotton must have been a welcome sight to Rickey, as he was the closest thing possible to the Mahatma taking over the team himself.

Shotton was born in the small town of Brownhelm, Ohio, on October 18, 1884. Aside from its association with Shotton, Brownhelm's other claim to fame was as the first local American government to elect an African-American man to public office, when John Mercer Langston became town clerk in 1855.

Shotton was born into a middle-class family, the son of a quarry engineer. Growing up, he had odds jobs like working as a fireman at the same quarry, tending the boilers at a laundry and later driving the laundry wagon, and unloading iron ore in his area near Cleveland.

As a youngster, Shotton had significant vision problems, but he also had tremendous foot speed. Shotton gained a lifelong nickname when his speed reminded some of early race car driver Barney Oldfield, who had become the first racer to drive a car 100 miles per hour. Shotton was promptly christened "Barney" by some rooter, perhaps with the Oak Point team in Lorain, where as a young prospect he earned $3.50 per Sunday afternoon game that he played.

Shotton was first a pitcher, and then a catcher, until one day the manager of his first professional team in the Ohio-Pennsylvania League told him he would wear his legs out catching and should become an outfielder. After an undistinguished first professional season in 1908, in 1909, Shotton hit .344 for Steubenville of the Ohio-Pennsylvania League and was promptly purchased by the St. Louis Browns, for whom he played 17 games that year.

During his meteoric rise that year, Shotton met Mary Daly, who he married after the season. They were married for 52 years. After another year's seasoning back in the minors, the Browns brought Shotton back to stay in 1911. Shotton became the Browns' everyday center fielder, and while he hit just .255, he was an excellent defensive outfielder and used his speed to steal 26 bases.

In the following season, 1912, Shotton developed into a complete player. He hit .290, but also was more than willing to take a walk, drawing 86 passes. He stole 35 bases and finished 12th in the American

League's Chalmers Award (MVP) voting. But it was the following year when his career truly took off.

The Browns hired a new manager in 1913, and Branch Rickey, only two years older than Shotton, also from rural Ohio, and also a respectable sort of man, instantly became a fan of Shotton. Years later, Shotton remembered, "Rickey was the first manager I ever knew who even pretended that ballplayers have brains." He continued, "[H]e tried to make us think things out for ourselves, instead of ordering us around like a bunch of dumb cattle." This impacted young Burt Shotton in profound ways.

Shotton starred every year in St. Louis until 1917. His batting average hung near .300 for most of the time, and he twice led the league in walks. He stole 40 or more bases in every season from 1913 to 1916. Like Rickey, Shotton enjoyed baseball based around adventure—for his many stolen bases, he also was among the runners most frequently caught stealing in his prime years.

Rickey told a writer after the 1916 season, "I tell you Bert is a much underrated player. Take into consideration his amazing speed, the number of times he gets free transportation to first, his general batting, and ground covering ability, and he is one of the half dozen best players in the game."

This wasn't an opinion held only by Rickey—in 1915, major-league players were asked to select an All-Star team, and the chosen outfield was Ty Cobb, Tris Speaker, and Burt Shotton.

But Rickey trusted Shotton so much that not only did he rate him highly as a player, but when his weekly Sabbath day came, he tabbed Shotton to manage the Browns in his absence. When Shotton's productivity began to dip, Rickey traded for him with his new team, the Cardinals, in 1919. Shotton's career ebbed out in St. Louis, as hits at-bat dropped from 270 to 180 to 48 to 30 and down to a single plate appearance in 1923.

When Shotton was finished as a player, he stayed on as a coach under Rickey from 1923 to 1925. When Rickey went from the dugout to the business office, he sent Shotton to Syracuse to manage, as part of his innovative farm system. Shotton took to the job immediately.

While his initial team struggled, finishing with a 70-91 mark, Shotton was a quick hit. One biographer noted, "The younger players responded to his system, largely because of the way he communicated it, firmly yet with fatherly patience. He would never embarrass a player publicly, but once alone in the clubhouse, he would not hesitate to scold one of his 'boys.'. . . He viewed his role not just as managing a team but molding individual players."

In his second season, Shotton's squad won 102 games, and the secret of his quiet excellence in managing was out. As a reward for his minor-league success, Shotton found himself named the manager of the Philadelphia Phillies. The Phillies were the most unredeemable franchise in professional sports. When Shotton was hired in 1928, the Phils were in the midst of a streak from 1918 to 1948 of finishing 4th or worse in the eight-team National League every season. In fact, their best performance during those three decades was a 78-76 fourth-place season under Shotton in 1932. It was their only winning season during that hopeless drought.

As a manager, Shotton tried to be patient, but the lack of talent from the Phillies doomed him as it had many before him. He was cut loose after the 1933 season, and in mid-1935 he resurfaced in the Cardinal organization with Branch Rickey. He led the Columbus Red Birds to American Association titles in 1937 and 1941, and he was named minor-league Manager of the Year by *The Sporting News* for the latter triumph.

Shotton then coached the Cleveland Indians under manager Lou Boudreau from 1942 to 1945. Boudreau was a 24-year-old player-manager when the veteran Shotton joined his staff. Boudreau appreciated his elder statesman, supposedly telling Shotton, "If I had a father, I know he'd want me to grow up to be just like you."

But sentiments aside, Shotton was in his 60s after the 1945 season, and was allowed to retire to Florida. One newspaper article covering this news recounted, "Shotton sealed his fate with the Indians one day last summer when, while in the third base coaching box he caught a foul fly, thus rendering automatically out the man who hit the ball." The writer noted that Shotton had also somehow missed the White Sox pulling the hidden-ball trick on Boudreau while Shotton was standing mere feet away and coaching third base. He had not exactly covered himself in glory as a third-base coach.

Accordingly, when Shotton left the Indians, he and Mary looked forward to spoiling their grandchildren, and Burt enjoyed fishing and puttering around in retirement. He would occasionally scout a bit for his friend, Branch Rickey. But he had experienced life as a big-league manager, and it hadn't been kind. His chance had passed, or so he—and most of baseball—assumed.

━━

When a telegraph arrived from Branch Rickey at Shotton's home in Florida, he stuck it in his pocket, where it sat until he mentioned it to his wife, who chastised his carelessness and told him to open it. The message was brief but cryptic: "BE IN BROOKLYN TOMORROW MORNING. SEE NOBODY. SAY NOTHING. RICKEY."

Shotton headed north the next morning, and Rickey met him at LaGuardia Airport. Shotton supposed Rickey wanted to talk about some players he had scouted, but instead, Rickey asked him to take the Dodger job, for the year only. Shotton accepted, but he later told writers he had not signed a contract as he had never had one with Rickey and did not need one.

So sudden and unexpected was Shotton's hiring that when Rickey dispatched him to the Polo Grounds, where the Dodgers would soon play their third game of the season, Shotton got lost in his driving and was late to the ballpark. He would not dress in a baseball uniform ("I took it off for the last time years ago," he told the media). He would generally wear a cap and a button-up Dodger jacket on top of his clothes, which often featured wildly colored shirts that earned him some ribbing from his Dodger veterans.

On that first day, April 18th, Shotton was rushed into the clubhouse by Clyde Sukeforth, who hastily introduced him to his new team.

The laconic Shotton wanted to make sure his players understood that he himself recognized the overwhelming suddenness of his task. As the team gathered around, Shotton told them, "You fellas can win the pennant in spite of me. Don't be afraid of me as a manager. I cannot possibly hurt you."

Part and parcel of the players who had to decide if Shotton could hurt them was Jackie Robinson. He was 1 for 6 in two games as a Dodger, and before the month was out, he would have an 0-for-20 slump. The Dodgers had other options at first base, including power hitter Howie Schultz. One author remarked, "Every day, when Burt Shotton filled out his lineup card, Robinson wondered if he would see Schultz's name instead of his own." Rumors floated that the Dodgers were trying to trade for future Hall of Famer Johnny Mize. But Shotton stayed the course.

Shotton later remarked, "As a manager, you need to know who to praise, who to kick in the seat of the pants and who to leave alone." He left Robinson alone, doubtlessly realizing, as Clyde Sukeforth had, that nothing he could say or do would make Robinson's load lighter to bear—nothing, except continuing to write his name in the lineup every day, which Shotton unerringly did.

Batting second and playing first base, Robinson found himself a fixture in the Dodger lineup. And given his manager's confidence and free rein to play aggressive, enterprising baseball, Robinson went from hitting .225 at the end of April to .266 at the end of May to .315 at the end of June (courtesy of a month when he hit .377 and stole eight bases).

Broadcaster Red Barber later wrote, "Shotton knew in short order he had a star in Jackie Robinson. . . . Rickey urged Shotton to encourage Robinson to run wild; Shotton needed no such urging. Robinson on base was always on his own." The veteran manager trusted the inexperienced rookie to strike whenever he wished, which would have been remarkable under any circumstances.

What role did Shotton play, other than trusting his rookie? He set an even emotional keel around the ballclub. A biographer noted of Shotton, "Unlike other managers who preceded him throughout his career, men like Ray Blades and Leo Durocher, he was never given to extreme highs or lows. He kept a balanced perspective, which unfortunately was at times misinterpreted by reporters and fans as aloofness."

The *Saturday Evening Post* opined in 1949, "Jackie's admirers . . . are apt to forget that his rise to big-league stardom has come almost entirely under the managership of wise old Burt Shotton. This may be a coincidence, but seasoned students of the game do not think so. In their opinion, Shotton did a better job than Durocher or almost anyone else could have done in bringing Robinson through the dangerous period when he was the only Negro player in the major leagues."

For his part, Shotton was quick to express his admiration of Robinson, whom he called "a perfect gentleman and one beauty of a ballplayer." Asked at one point if he would trade Robinson, Shotton replied that he would—if he could receive two pitchers in return who were each certified to win 30 games.

The Dodgers and Shotton were the surprise of the National League, led by Robinson's steady and brilliant play. When the team clinched the NL pennant on September 22nd, Shotton called it "one of the happiest moments of my life." He was quick to redirect any credit, noting, "I'm happy for the boys. They deserve a lot of credit for the way they hustled and fought against the odds all year."

After Shotton and the Dodgers lost the 1947 World Series to the Yankees, the reinstated Durocher retook the Dodger managing job and Shotton headed back to Florida. Shotton was officially employed as supervisor of the Dodgers' 26 minor-league managers, but his big-league days seemed to be behind him. It had been a good run, but now it was over, and Jackie Robinson could test his skills under one of baseball's great tacticians, if unfortunately also one of the game's legendary redasses. If Shotton's rise to the Dodger job had been surprising, his return would be even more so.

﹈

Those who had waited for the union of the ultracompetitive Robinson and the possibly even-more-competitive Durocher simply had their opportunity delayed for a season. But what a difference a year made, both in Robinson's play and in Durocher's reaction to him. In the offseason after 1947, Robinson had undergone a southern speaking tour. While the tour was a success, the Jim Crow mores of the time meant that Jackie was generally fed amply in private homes, with the sort of rich, luxurious food that was the pride of many a southern kitchen. Accordingly, his weight jumped to around 230 pounds. While Robinson had lost some of the excess weight by the time he reported to spring training, Durocher was not impressed.

Not for nothing was the veteran manager known as "The Lip." Seeing Robinson, he shouted at him, "What in the world happened to you? You look like an old woman. Look at all that fat around your midsection. Why you can't even bend over!" Observers noted Durocher walking around, muttering to himself, "He was thin for Shotton, but he's fat for me."

Durocher was scarcely more guarded in his comments to the media. At one point, he told reporters, "Robinson will shag flies till his tongue hangs out. [Coach] Jake Pitler will see to it that Jackie chases every fungo up a palm tree for the remainder of the Dodgers' stay." The media observed Robinson and Pete Reiser being put through their paces with extra workouts, even during the season.

Robinson would later deny any ill will toward Durocher, even when the skipper temporarily gave the second-base job—which the Dodgers had opened by dealing Eddie Stanky to Boston—to Gene Mauch. Shortly after his retirement, Robinson opened up in a private interview with Carl Rowan, saying, "[I]f you had a winning team, nobody is better than Durocher . . . but when he is losing, he loses everything, in my opinion; he gets upset, [and] makes the players angry."

This was what happened to the Dodgers in 1948. The team that had won the pennant the year before suddenly faltered. On July 11th, heading into the All-Star break, Durocher had led the Dodgers to just a 35-37 record, good for fifth in the eight-team National League and a sturdy 8½ games behind the league-leading Boston Braves. Robinson had slowly pulled himself into form and was hitting .295 at the time, although he had stolen only three bases.

Similarly, the New York Giants were having managerial issues. Skipper Mel Ott was 37-38 at the break, and owner Horace Stoneham wanted to make a change. He called Branch Rickey, asking whether Shotton was available to take the Giants job. Rickey, fed up with the difficulties he had experienced with Durocher, told Stoneham that either Shotton or Durocher was available. When Stoneham succumbed to what was the more glamorous pick (Durocher), Rickey promptly reinstalled Shotton as the Dodger manager.

It was probably for the best. While both men were active in baseball, Robinson and Durocher were frequently at each other's throats. Durocher would jockey Robinson and Robinson would retaliate by teasing Durocher about allegedly wearing Laraine Day's perfume. Day herself got involved when she touted Giant Alvin Dark as a superior second baseman to Robinson. Clearly, Day's baseball wisdom was about as sound as her husband's tact. Only once both men retired could Robinson and Durocher acknowledge each other's competitive excellence—when they were active, they couldn't stand each other.

Meanwhile, Shotton's lighter touch helped not only with Robinson but also with other young Brooklyn players. Ralph Branca had won 21 games under Shotton in '47, but had also struggled in early '48, yet pitched better under Shotton's tutelage. Other young players like Billy Cox and Duke Snider fared better with Shotton's patience than with Durocher's win-at-all-costs bluntness.

Shotton led Brooklyn to a 48-33 second-half mark. Robinson hit .297 in the season's second half but doubled his home run total from the first half and swiped 19 bases after the All-Star break. The Dodgers made a run at the pennant, climbing into a first-place tie on September 1st before eventually fading to third place.

The strong finish to 1948 set the table for a remarkable 1949 season for Robinson, Shotton, and the Dodger franchise. It was the year that may or may not have seen the removal of Robinson's pledge of quiet acceptance, but it certainly was the year of his finest all-around baseball.

Robinson led the National League in 1949 with a .342 batting average, and also with 37 stolen bases. He slugged out 38 doubles,

12 triples, and 16 home runs, which yielded a return of 124 RBIs, as well as 122 runs scored. Meanwhile, several of Shotton's other young prospects had break-through seasons. Gil Hodges had 23 home runs and 115 RBIs, up from 11 homers and 70 RBIs the previous year. Duke Snider's first everyday action yielded a .292 batting average and 23 home runs. Rookie pitcher Don Newcombe won 17 games for the Dodgers and became one of the first African-American pitchers in the big leagues.

Newcombe's testimony to Shotton's quiet ease with young players is insightful. Called up after two years in the minors, Newcombe promptly allowed four hits and three earned runs in one-third of an inning to the Cardinals. He remembered sitting in the clubhouse afterward, sure he would be sent back to the Montreal Royals, when Shotton approached him. Shotton asked how he felt, and the rookie answered, "I feel fine, Mr. Shotton." Shotton told him, "You threw pretty good tonight. You gave up some base hits, but you looked pretty good." The nervous Newcombe asked, "I guess I'm going back to Montreal, right?"

Shotton replied, "The hell you are. You're starting . . . against Cincinnati on Sunday. That's what I'm down here to tell you. How do you feel about that?"

Newcombe did start on the following Sunday, and he threw a five-hit shutout against the Reds. He went on to make the All-Star team and be chosen Rookie of the Year.

Kindly Old Burt Shotton led the 1949 Dodgers into the season's final day, where they needed a win over the Philadelphia Phillies to clinch the NL pennant. Newcombe started but ran out of gas and departed in favor of a fairly anonymous rookie pitcher, Jack Banta. Banta took over with a 7-6 lead in the sixth inning. The Phillies scored the tying run, but Banta shut down Philadelphia for four more innings, and when Snider knocked in a run in the tenth inning, the Dodgers had the margin that they extended to a 9-7 win, and Burt Shotton's second pennant in three big-league seasons.

Once again, the Dodgers fell to the Yankees in the World Series, but two pennants and a midseason resurrection in three years seemed to put

Shotton on safe footing. But Shotton's run with the Dodgers was easy come, easy go, and after one more season, he would be gone.

⟋

The Dodgers' 1950 season illustrates the razor-thin margin that a team with little pitching depth has over the course of a 154-game schedule. Robinson was again magnificent—hitting .328, scoring 99 runs, and knocking in 81. While his stolen base total dropped to 12, he did manage 80 walks against just 24 strikeouts. He was one of the best players in the game, and when supported by the now fully developed young talent of Gil Hodges (32 home runs, 113 RBIs) and Duke Snider (31 home runs, 107 RBIs), he helped establish one of the most fearsome hitting attacks in the National League. The Dodgers led the league in batting average, runs, home runs, and stolen bases.

But the pitching was inconsistent. Don Newcombe and Preacher Roe each won 19 games, but young pitchers like Carl Erskine (7-6, 4.72 ERA) and Ralph Branca (7-9, 4.69 ERA) could not put together enough quality innings to support the two aces. The Dodgers were fifth in the eight-team NL in ERA and last in home runs allowed.

The Dodgers bounced around throughout the season. The All-Star break found them in fourth place, and on September 1st, while they had climbed to second, they trailed the Phillies by seven games. On Monday, September 18th, Brooklyn's 76-61 mark left them nine games behind Philadelphia. But the Dodgers rallied to go 13-3 in their next 16 games and forced the season down to a single game against Philadelphia to possibly tie and force a playoff for the pennant.

Newcombe excelled for nine innings, and after Dodger Cal Abrams was thrown out at the plate in the bottom of the ninth inning, a 1-1 tie moved the game into extra innings. In the top of the tenth, though, a three-run homer by Philadelphia's Dick Sisler proved to be the difference, as the 4-1 loss left the Dodgers shy of the pennant.

Shotton's 89-65 season wasn't the sort of work that would normally get a manager fired, particularly coming on the heels of winning the pennant the season before. But the 1950 offseason found Branch Rickey on the outs, and successor Walter O'Malley had less than no interest in retaining a Rickey disciple as his manager. Former Dodger coach Charlie Dressen was tapped for the job, after Shotton, knowing the axe was coming, simply refused to meet with O'Malley.

This time, Shotton truly was finished. While rumors of him reuniting in Pittsburgh with Rickey flew, he was quite happy to return to Florida as a baseball lifer now into his mid-60s. Shotton's 326-215 mark with the Dodgers, had it constituted his entire career, would place him 4th all-time in winning percentage among MLB managers who skippered 500 or more games.

Jackie Robinson's remaining big-league career was ruled by Charlie Dressen and, after the 1953 season, by Walt Alston. Robinson enjoyed playing for Dressen, who was more combative than Shotton, although he is recalled by many for his healthy ego. For a veteran player, as Robinson then was, a manager who was a bit full of himself wasn't an issue.

The same could not be said of Alston. Robinson told Carl Rowan in 1958, "Alston has known it from the first year that I had no respect for him as a manager. Alston can't think fast enough." A play in 1954 at Wrigley Field likely cemented the poor dynamic between Robinson and Alston. When Duke Snider blasted a ball that carried into the bleachers but bounced back to the field, Robinson was incensed that the hit was ruled a double. He charged from the dugout and lambasted the umpire who made the call—only to find that no one was behind him. Robinson admitted, "Out there alone, with the fans riding me more every second, I felt foolish. I wanted to find a hole and crawl into it." Robinson accused Alston of "standing out there at third base like a wooden Indian," and the chilly relations between the two grew positively arctic.

Interestingly, one of the possibilities for the replacement of Dressen after the 1953 season that had been discussed was making Pee Wee

Reese a player-manager. Robinson publicly supported that idea, and it doubtlessly would have been a better fit for him.

Robinson's assessment of Shotton as a manager was positive, but never exceptionally glowing. He told Carl Rowan in 1958, "Shotton was a good sound baseball man: he was quick. Shotton's only trouble was that he never came out of the dugout . . . I liked the manager that would fight your battles."

He ranked Shotton third of his four Dodger managers, but the only criticism, aside from Shotton's inability to ramble onto the field to defend a point, was an incident when Shotton told the Dodgers in the locker room one day that the players "didn't want to get like certain ball players that had become nigger rich and stopped hustling." Robinson discussed the matter with Clyde Sukeforth, and Shotton later came to Robinson, saying that he hoped Robinson wasn't offended, and that the offensive phrase "was just an expression and he didn't mean it that way." Robinson countered that "there are many expressions that should not be used no matter what." Shotton apologized.

That incident aside, Robinson noted in 1949, "I love to play for Shotton." In another interview, he commented, "When Shotton wants to bawl out a player he takes him aside and does it in private. That gives you a sort of lift."

Other Dodgers singled out Shotton for his treatment of players. Pee Wee Reese, an acknowledged Durocher backer, once stated, "I think Shotton has a great way with younger ballplayers, maybe does better with some of them than Leo did."

Carl Furillo called him "a prince," and Carl Erskine added that he was "an outstanding man" and "a class individual." Don Newcombe, likely mindful of Shotton's patience after his failed first pitching appearance, remembered him as "a damn nice man."

If others were not as kind in their memories, one thing is clear in reading the comments of the Boys of Summer in regard to their skippers—no two players ever saw things the same way. One would criticize Durocher and credit Dressen. The next would speak against Dressen and back Durocher. Or credit Walter Alston with the team's success. Baseball is fickle, and perhaps the ultimate regard for Shotton lies in the fact that the area he is best credited for—understanding and supporting his players—has become a bigger and bigger part of the modern manager's job. Time's judgment is final.

Once Robinson retired from baseball following the 1956 season, many in the game wondered if he might become a manager. Ultimately, Robinson mostly stayed away from baseball after his retirement. He only very occasionally attended a game, as the sport didn't keep his attention the way it had when he played it.

In 1957, Robinson considered the issue in a magazine article titled "Why Can't I Manage in the Majors?" Robinson concluded, "My managers know that I gave them everything I had as a player. I believe my players would give me everything they have if I were a manager. Maybe I wouldn't be a good manager, but the reason would come from what was inside me, not outside me and inside my players."

The call to manage never came, although rumors abounded early in Robinson's retirement of minor-league jobs. The cause was never far from Robinson's mind, and in his last public appearance at the 1972 World Series, he told the assembled crowd, "I am extremely proud and pleased to be here this afternoon, but must admit I'm gonna be tremendously more pleased and more proud when I look at that third base coaching line one day and see a black face managing in baseball."

Robinson passed away within a month, and so he never got the chance to see a black face managing in the major leagues. But as the face of baseball was changing, and the role of managers was changing, other fans soon would see darker faces in the dugout. They'd also see a lot of managers who approached the game more like Burt Shotton than like Leo Durocher.

After his 1950 canning, Shotton did indeed elect to stay home in Florida and pass his remaining days with his family. Rickey hired him as a consultant for the ill-fated Continental Baseball League, and at one point, he had him supervise the managers of the Class D Western Carolina League.

He was at home on July 29, 1962, when he suffered a fatal heart attack. Shotton was not particularly remembered—an infamous column on the occasion of his death by UPI writer Oscar Fraley claimed that he was "unpopular with his players" and "a man with a scorching tongue and a crusty exterior." Perhaps Fraley showed his colors a bit by holding it against Shotton that he "left the scene . . . bitterly, holding it unfair that he hadn't been retained when Walter O'Malley took over." As if it were the most natural thing in the world to fire a manager who had won two pennants in three full years as a manager, and missed a third on the final day of the season.

Fraley also rained on Shotton that he "was quick to accept credit and slow to accept fault." Nothing could be more demonstrably untrue, time and again. One biographer noted of Shotton, "His managerial theory was 'good players make a good manager, not vice versa.'"

A much more accurate epitaph could have come from Branch Rickey, who was asked about Shotton's strength as a manager. He stated, "Wisdom in handling men. . . . You never have discipline when it's only super-imposed and Shotton knows that. He tries to get discipline that is self-imposed. . . . A team that's well-disciplined doesn't have to be watched at all." For Shotton's many detractors, the future of baseball would place a premium on managers who were better at handling players, and perhaps less inclined to kick dirt on an umpire or chastise their starting second baseman in the newspapers.

Changes in the culture of baseball likely mandated changes in managing. As African-American and Latino players flooded the game, a manager had to be someone who was more comfortable building a consensus than expecting others to pick up his peculiar preferences of communication and accountability. Many major African-American and Latino players feuded with managers, often due to a minimal understanding.

In July 1964, Giants manager Alvin Dark, who had occupied the Boston and then New York dugouts and had gone against Jackie Robinson in many of those memorable pennant races of the late '40s and early '50s, showed such a lack of understanding. Dark told an interviewer that his team was having trouble "because we have so many Negro and Spanish-speaking players on the team. They are just not able to perform up to the white player when it comes to mental alertness. You can't make most Negro and Spanish players have the pride in their team that you get from the white players."

Let the record reflect that the Negro and Spanish-speaking players of whom Dark was complaining included Willie Mays, Willie McCovey, Orlando Cepeda, and Juan Marichal. Of the five Giants who posted WAR of better than 3.0 for the 1964 season, four were black or Spanish-speaking. Dark moved on after that season, but had no problem getting additional managing jobs with the Kansas City A's, Cleveland Indians, Oakland A's (where he won a World Series with help from Reggie Jackson, Bert Campaneris, and Vida Blue, among other black and Spanish-speaking players), and the San Diego Padres.

Five years later, in *Ball Four*, Jim Bouton chronicled a teammate who said of African-American outfielder Tommy Davis, "You know, for a colored player, he's not a bad hustler. Hell, he wants to play ball." Davis's .294 career batting average and 2,121 hits might also have attested to the fact that he wanted to play ball.

Stereotypes die slowly. One major step came in 1971, when Pittsburgh manager Danny Murtagh fielded a lineup of nine dark-skinned players in a game. Murtagh was a veteran manager who had initially clashed with Roberto Clemente in Pittsburgh. Asked after the game if he was aware of the significance of his lineup, he quipped, "I knew we had nine Pirates."

In 1975, Cleveland hired Frank Robinson to become a player-manager, and he broke the major-league managing color line. While baseball was slow to hire additional African-American or Latino managers, in time progress was made. In 1992, Cito Gaston of the Toronto

Blue Jays, who had come up as a player under the tutelage of veteran Hank Aaron, who often invoked Jackie Robinson as a teaching example, became the first African-American manager to win a World Series. Of the 64 managers who have won 1,000 major-league games, only three are men of color—Dusty Baker, Frank Robinson, and Felipe Alou.

However, progress has come in other forms. The desire to communicate authentically and directly with players became important enough that many managers mastered at least pidgin variations of Spanish. In the 1981 World Series, when Dodger skipper Tommy Lasorda came to the mound to encourage Mexican rookie Fernando Valenzuela, he did so in Spanish. When Valenzuela finished a 149-pitch complete game, Lasorda was one of the first to congratulate him, wrapping one big hand around Valenzuela and the other around Italian-American catcher Mike Scioscia, who would one day become an excellent manager in his own right. If the times change faster than the managerial roster, then maybe the managers have adapted.

Back in 1949, Burt Shotton told the *Saturday Evening Post*, "The only thing a manager can really do is know his men. There's no use telling a man to do something he can't do. And there's no use bawling a man out because he tries to do something and can't. . . . What I want to know about my boys is this: Are they really trying? And are they really keeping themselves in shape? If they are, they'll be all right."

Was Shotton a prototype of what was to come? Maybe so.

Flash-forward 67 years to 2016. A connection may seem apparent. Cubs pitcher Jon Lester said of his manager, Joe Maddon, who was about to lead the Cubs to break their 108-year World Series drought, "Joe's done a good job of communicating. I think that's what makes him a good manager. He communicates. He pulls guys aside. He talks to them as a man. I think that's a big thing."

Teammate Ben Zobrist offered, "He very rarely tries to light a fire under us because he believes in the professionalism of the player, and it's your job to be prepared yourself. And he wants to put you in a position to do what you know already how to do."

Sounds awfully familiar.

How did Jackie Robinson change the life of Burt Shotton? Well, for one thing, he made him a winner. The manager with a career .403 winning percentage and a history of teams finishing eighth, fifth, eighth, sixth, fourth, and seventh managed the Dodgers at a .603 clip, including pennants in 1947 and 1949. Shotton found himself managing in the World Series and in the All-Star Game.

Robinson also gave Shotton the first crack at a legacy of running a multiracial clubhouse. Sure, baseball had occasional foreign-born players, but it took 1947 for modern baseball to assimilate any type of melting-pot legacy. Robinson was a volatile player under difficult circumstances. He visibly chafed at working with one Hall of Fame manager, but Shotton's trusting, egoless style of managing fit him well in a tumultuous era of his career.

And because of Shotton's solid work with Robinson, and later with Campanella and Newcombe, Shotton became something approximating a prototype for the modern manager. He trusted the training and experience the Dodgers farm system had provided, and saw himself less as a teacher who had to drill players into becoming players than as what he was—an elderly man who inherited a group of talented, but often inexperienced, players who were working through their own insecurities and finding their own identities in the game of baseball. When he criticized, he did it privately and constructively. An atmosphere of respect pervaded his Dodger teams.

For the many aspects of Robinson's integration of baseball that were planned and replanned, and carefully weighed, the selection of Shotton five days before the color barrier was broken seems to be serendipitous. After all, Branch Rickey told his advisors the day that Shotton was chosen that he was falling out a window, and only the right manager could stop him. Shotton wasn't the likely choice, and he wasn't the glamorous choice, but for Jackie Robinson, he was the right choice. As Robinson took the game places it had never been, so too he took Shotton into the top of the standings, and into a small peek at baseball's future.

CHAPTER SEVEN

MEN AND BROTHERS:
RED BARBER AND JACKIE ROBINSON

Walter Lanier "Red" Barber was at a loss for words. Barber, professional manipulator of the English language, distinguished major-league broadcaster for the Cincinnati Reds from 1934 to 1938 and then the voice of the Brooklyn Dodgers beginning in 1939 until that date in March 1945 when he went to lunch with Branch Rickey, was never at a loss for words. But now he was.

Barber had planned to become a college professor, not commentate on baseball games. But his peculiar turns of phrase had already become the stuff of legend in Brooklyn. His command of the nuances of the English language was such that one of his favorite catchphrases, that a batter in a favorable count was "sitting in the cat-bird seat," had caught the ear of humorist and writer James Thurber, who thus titled a 1942 *New Yorker*–published short story, "The Catbird Seat." Lest anyone miss the source, one of Thurber's characters explains an office worker's use of Barber's colorful vocabulary. "She must be a Dodger fan," a character says to another. "Red Barber announces the Dodger games over the radio and he uses those expressions—picked 'em up down South."

But Barber, the adopted voice of Brooklyn, had picked up some other things down South, including his worldview. And Branch Rickey was threatening the foundation of Barber's very ethical code.

"I'm going to tell you something," Barber recalled the garrulous Rickey telling him quietly at a back table in Joe's Restaurant, as Rickey smeared butter on a roll. "I'm going to tell you something that even my board of directors doesn't know. No one knows outside of the family."

Rickey told Barber that day about another day many years before, when Charlie Thomas, "a splendid young man," had been refused registration at the Oliver Hotel in South Bend, Indiana. He told Barber of the angst of young Thomas, of his tears, and his brokenhearted cry that it was all because of his skin, and that if he could only tear it off, he would be like everyone else.

Rickey continued, assaulting his dinner roll throughout the conversation with his knife. "I have never been able to shake the picture of that fine young man tearing at his hands. . . . As the years have come and gone, this has hurt me inside. And I have made up my mind that before I pass on I am going to do something about it."

Unburdening himself, Rickey got immediately to the point.

"What I am telling you is this: there is a Negro ballplayer coming to the Dodgers, not the Brown Dodgers [Negro League team]. I don't know who he is, and I don't know where he is, and I don't know when he's coming. But he is coming. And he is coming soon, just as soon as we can find him."

"I didn't say a word," Barber would later write. "I couldn't."

Reflecting on that historic meeting, questioning why Rickey decided to tell this information to him, Barber observed, "I don't think [Rickey] needed me as his confessor. And certainly, when he spoke to me about it, I gave him back no support. I gave him back 100 per cent silence, because he had shaken me. He had shaken me to my heels."

Barber concluded, "And I think that is why he told me, because he knew that it would shake me."

The meeting ended, with no support or opposition offered by Barber. He returned home and told his wife, Lylah, about the astonishing meeting.

"I'm going to quit," he told her. "I don't think I want—I don't know whether I can—"

Lylah Barber was a southern lady of the same relative age and customs as her husband. She also was a southern lady who had grown used to living in the greater New York City area, to fine dining, good company, superb shopping, and the other refinements that went with the city.

She was in no hurry to leave. She also understood her husband, and the better angels of his nature, perhaps better than he.

"Well, it's your job and you're the one who's going to have to make the decision," she told him. "But it's not immediate. You don't have to do anything about it right now. Why don't we have a martini? And then let's have dinner."

That reconsideration would change the way that Jackie Robinson was welcomed to Brooklyn, and the way that the millions of fans who rooted via the magical waves of radio rather than from the bleachers at Ebbets Field would know the man who became a hero and an inspiration for so many. But perhaps even more, it would change Red Barber.

Walter Lanier Barber was born in Columbus, Mississippi, on February 17, 1908. He was the son of a railroad engineer and an English teacher. "My mother gave me an ear for language," he later wrote. Selena Barber had graduated from the Mississippi State College for Women at age 16 and wrote a grammar textbook that was used by the public schools of Mississippi. Barber recalled that his father "did not have the education my mother had, but he was a wonderful storyteller, a natural raconteur."

At around age 10, Barber and his family moved to Florida, after the railroads of Mississippi were decimated by a boll weevil infestation of the cotton crop. Florida became Barber's home, although the family moved around the cities of the Sunshine State depending on William Barber's ability to find railroad work in one locale or another.

Young Red Barber grew up to love sports. Despite standing only 5'8" and weighing 165 pounds, Barber was a talented halfback in high school football. But meanwhile, he also fell in love with entertainment. He would watch the traveling minstrel shows that made their way through rural Florida, and he believed that he might follow that career line. Barber later recalled participating in amateur shows as a blackface comedian (he noted that this "was an accepted art form in those days"). "I liked to try the little eccentric dances," he remembered. "I loved to tell jokes and sing songs. It became a passion with me." In fact, Barber was prepared to travel to Cincinnati to join a minstrel show when a telegraph arrived telling him the show had disbanded. "Vaudeville was dying . . . but the minstrel shows were beating vaudeville to the grave," Barber wrote. His dreams of entertaining dashed by a change in popular taste, Barber would soon be on the cutting edge of entertainment.

While Barber's family was solidly middle class, that left little discretionary income for education beyond high school. After high school, Barber got a job roofing a house. He remembered, "Central Florida is, in a word, hot in the middle of summer, and when your job is to stand over a boiling pitch pot and take two buckets of melted, steaming pitch up a ladder onto a hot roof under a broiling sun and then help a man spread that pitch over the roof, you are more than just a bit warm." Given the circumstances, Barber became introspective quickly. He acknowledged that while he wasn't sure what he wanted to do with his life, it wasn't roofing houses in the Florida sun.

Barber decided to try attending the University of Florida. While he knew that he could attend without tuition, he also knew he would have to work odd jobs to pay for his housing, meals, and fees. "I told myself, going to college may not be the right thing," Barber wrote, "but . . . [i]t's got to be better than this."

Barber struggled to get by at Florida. He went out for the freshman football team but was injured in a scrimmage, and he found the coaches unwilling to help him find work to stay in school. In fact, Barber was ready to leave Gainesville late in his freshman year when an observant professor saw him headed away, stopped him, and helped him find a place to both eat and stay. Barber's economic crisis passed, and he became ensconced in Gainesville.

Another lucky break came a few years later, when a fellow student, Ralph Fulghum, happened upon Barber in the University Club, and complained that he had to read three papers on the campus radio station's farm program. Seeing the potential for help, he solicited Barber to read the middle of the three papers. Barber, deep in writing a paper on King James I, pleaded his ignorance of both radio and farm programming and his extreme busyness. But when Fulghum offered him dinner in exchange for reading the paper, he forgot the other issues.

And so Red Barber's first radio appearance was reading a paper on WRUF, "On Certain Aspects of Bovine Obstetrics." On Barber's way out, he was accosted by the director of the campus radio station, who had heard his smooth but expressive voice and asked him to work as a part-time student announcer. Given the number of jobs Barber kept to manage his student expenses, he was not interested in adding to the load and declined. But the director, Major Powell, stayed after Barber, and eventually asked him how much Powell would have to pay to obtain his services.

Barber did some quick calculating, added up all his expenses, and added an additional fairly steep fee for pocket money. "I can put a spoke in his wheel right quick," he recalled thinking, "I'll ask him for all the money in the world." He asked for $50 a week, and Major Powell quickly assented. Barber quit his other odd jobs and became a radio man.

He failed miserably in his first sports broadcast, a Florida football game. But thereafter, he studiously attended practice, questioned an assistant coach, and returned to the job much more prepared and performed a relatively proficient second broadcast. Soon, Barber became a radio junkie. During his junior year, he was offered a full-time announcer's job, at $150 per month, but was told he would have to quit school to take the position.

"I had fallen completely in love with radio," wrote Barber. "When a person is doing good work, he knows it." Barber was doing good work, and he quit school and took the job. He was the chief announcer at WRUF for three years.

There was likely another factor in Barber's decision to turn full-time professional in the radio world. By this time, he had met and courted Lylah Scarbrough, a nurse who had treated him in the infirmary after a car accident. Barber wrote, "The day I got out of the infirmary I asked her for a date, and she accepted. On our second date we agreed that we'd marry each other. We didn't set a date. We merely agreed that some day we were going to get married, and we kept steady company after that."

The two did marry in March 1931, soon after Barber made his full-time radio jump. In 1934, when Barber found himself ready to leave

WRUF, he was looking for a national job just as baseball radio broadcasting entered its golden age. Unlike his failed attempt at being in a minstrel show, on this matter, his timing was perfect.

⁓

As radio moved into its golden era, it had something of an on-again, off-again relationship with baseball. First, broadcasting baseball meant either providing coverage by reenactment, which was common for several decades, or handling the technical difficulties in broadcasting remotely from the relevant stadium. Team owners were reluctant to promote broadcasts because the theory of the day was that if fans could listen to games for free on the radio, why would they spend hard-earned money to come to the ballpark at all?

The first radio broadcast of baseball was a Pirates-Phillies game on Pittsburgh's KDKA on August 5, 1921. The first World Series broadcasts that fall, covered by the same station as well as WJZ of Newark, New Jersey, featured a broadcaster—or more accurately, a sportswriter, either Grantland Rice or Tommy Cowan—broadcasting the games via reports from a telegraph machine.

In 1923, baseball found its first radio star. Sportswriter W. O. McGeehan and radio personality Graham McNamee were broadcasting the World Series together for Westinghouse, with McGeehan serving as ostensibly the featured broadcaster. But during the third game of the Series, he turned the microphone over to McNamee. A baseball neophyte, McNamee learned the game on the job, but he knew how to carry an exciting broadcast. Author Bill Bryson writes of McNamee's technique, "McNamee described the crowds, the weather, the air of excitement that was rippling through the park. He picked out celebrities. He made the listeners feel present and welcome, like old friends. People loved his broadcasts even if he didn't always entirely grasp what was happening on the field."

The success of McNamee aside, baseball owners did not hurry to embrace radio broadcasts. Many owners were wary of the adverse effects of broadcasts on ticket sales, and accordingly limited broadcasts. More confoundingly, New York's three teams, under a triparty agreement, not only did not allow any broadcasts but also would not allow broadcast re-creations of any of their games. Accordingly, in 1938, when Reds pitcher Johnny Vander Meer pitched his second consecutive no-hitter in a game at Brooklyn, there was no radio coverage of that game at all, and Reds fans didn't know of Vander Meer's feat until they read the next morning's newspapers.

One of the quickest exceptions to the negative attitude toward baseball broadcasts came in Cincinnati. The first Reds broadcasts were prepared on a limited schedule in 1929, but the Reds grew much more interested in broadcasts when the team was purchased by Powel Crosley Jr. before the 1934 season. Crosley owned Cincinnati radio station WLW, which dubbed itself "The Nation's Station." Some noted that during World War II, WLW broadcasts could be heard as far away as Europe or South America.

The potential loss of money from ticket sales to Crosley was offset by the possibility of a gain of income to WLW from covering baseball. That said, despite his positive attitude toward radio, Crosley did not invest too deeply in baseball—it wasn't WLW that would broadcast Reds games; it was smaller sister station WSAI, which Crosley also owned.

Competition reigned in Cincinnati, as WSAI's broadcast often went head-to-head with a WFBE broadcast of Reds games. The original WFBE Reds announcer was a 300-pound man named Harry Hartman, who is remembered for an exuberant style that featured him shouting things like "BLAMMO!" or "BELTO!" in response to particularly impressive feats of hitting.

With Hartman firmly entrenched on WFBE, Powel Crosley left the matter of his opposition to Reds head honcho Larry MacPhail. Crosley decided to go in a very different direction than the combustible, excitable Hartman, a man who would take his shirt off during his broadcast on a particularly warm day. Oft-noted as a man with a good eye for baseball talent, MacPhail might also be noted as a man with a good ear for baseball talent, because he "discovered" Red Barber.

Barber's path to Cincinnati was anything but smooth. In the summer and fall of 1933, when he had grown tired of life in Gainesville and with a burgeoning family to support, Barber took his vacation time from WRUF in Gainesville and traveled across the country. He rode a bus into a city—Atlanta, Charlotte, Louisville, Cincinnati, or Chicago—went into the biggest local radio stations, and asked for an audition. As one would imagine, jobs were scarce in 1933. Finally, at WLW, Barber found a waiting job—or actually two, he was told. Barber asked to go back to Florida and give notice.

Back in Florida, Barber got a telegram from WLW—"Regret due to change in conditions, job no longer open." He wrote, "I rolled over on the bed and cried."

The following spring, Barber was surprised on March 4th to receive another telegram from WLW. It read, "Will you do Cincinnati Reds games? Twenty five dollars a week." Barber wired back his acceptance immediately. It was a pay cut, and it called for him to go work for the same station he had doubtlessly cursed consistently for the past half-year. But Barber saw beyond the lower salary and the slight for the chance at stardom, and he took the leap.

Reporting to Reds training camp in Florida, Barber felt immediately at home. "It was a new world for me," he recalled. "I knew how Columbus had felt. This was the big league, and I was in it."

The first major-league game Barber ever saw was one he broadcast, the Cubs at the Reds on Opening Day, 1934. He termed it "the most joyous day of my life, next to my wedding day." If Barber's dreams of the big time had come true, there was precious little big time and much day-to-day work involved. He later recalled broadcasting no more than 18 games in the 1934 season, calling baseball broadcasting "quite casual" in that age. MacPhail scheduled 14 or 15 broadcasts, and if a particular game was sold out, he might add another game to the radio schedule. Barber was "fairly certain that WSAI did not pay . . . one nickel for radio rights, even in a bookkeeping sense." So aside from his occasional baseball broadcasts, Barber was a regular studio announcer for WSAI. The day-to-day grind of broadcasting was far from glamorous, but Barber was always learning and improving his technique.

His next big break came in 1935. The Mutual Network sought to broadcast the World Series, but Commissioner Landis had to approve any such broadcasts. Mutual had only three stations, and they volunteered to add WLW to their network. WLW indicated that it was amenable only if one of its announcers was included in the broadcast. Landis approved the decision, and the result was that Barber, who had previously been only at WSAI, joined the broadcast along with Bob Elson and Quinn Ryan. Barber split the broadcasting responsibility with Elson, leaving Ryan to do the pregame and postgame coverage, and the 27-year-old broadcaster, who had seen his first big-league game the year before, brought the Series into millions of households.

The following year, WLW threw in with the NBC Network, which resulted in Barber broadcasting the Series under the watchful eye of Graham McNamee. Barber admitted, "I kept thinking about those days when I first listened to radio and dreamed of being up there with McNamee. And now the dream had come true. . . . It was an extraordinary sensation." Barber related that after a few innings, during a pause, he felt a squeeze on his left arm and McNamee told him, "Kid, you've got it." The torch had been passed.

Barber stayed in Cincinnati until after the 1938 season. When Larry MacPhail, who had left the Reds after the 1936 season, moved in to fill the open Brooklyn Dodgers job, he had designs on breaking up New York's nonbroadcast monopoly, and he knew just the announcer whom he wished to utilize. The nonbroadcast contract had just been renewed, in a five-year deal inked in 1938. MacPhail told the Yankees and Giants that *he* hadn't signed anything, and he didn't intend to follow it. Angered, Giants secretary Eddie Brannick told him, "If you dare broadcast . . . we'll get a 50,000-watt radio station, and we'll get the best baseball broadcaster in the world, and we'll blast you into the river."

As author Peter Golenbock noted, "MacPhail did to the Giants what Brannick had threatened to do to him." He inked a deal with General

Mills for sponsorship, with 50,000-watt station WOR for broadcasting, and hired Barber. The Dodgers decided to broadcast all games from Ebbets Field and to broadcast re-creations of the team's road games. Incidentally, the lack of attendance forecast by the other New York moguls didn't materialize. Dodger attendance improved by nearly half in Barber's first year behind the microphone. Given the national platform to broadcast, now with several years of experience under his belt, Barber's glory years began in earnest. It was his time in Brooklyn that led to Barber being acclaimed as "the most influential sportscaster in American history."

The discussions of Red Barber may fixate on his accent or his colloquialisms or his preparation, but they generally end up coming back to his absolutely unsurpassed professional technique. One author writes that Barber "was by far the most detail-oriented play-by-play voice of his day. He prepared endlessly and obsessed over accuracy. He had his own syntax and cadence. He believed it inappropriate for him to root for the Dodgers, because he saw himself as a reporter, not as a fan or as some kind of hanger-on. Barber could weave a narrative with the best storytellers, but his voice was always authoritative, a constant reminder that you were listening to him."

In a December 1939 column in *The Sporting News*, Barber is purported to have qualified 14 pieces of advice for potential broadcasters. As one of those rules cited is "Read *The Sporting News* through every week," the list might be taken with something of a grain of salt. But one key does ring true. Rule 13 of Barber's maxims is, "Get the background of your city, of your ball club, of your players. Learn all you can about your listening public, about the city and its suburbs, and humanize your announcing." If that rule rings truer than a few of the others, it's because Barber demonstrably did that very thing on his arrival in Brooklyn.

"When I took the job I knew nothing about Brooklyn," Barber recalled. "Eventually, I made it a point to find out everything I could about it. Whenever we had an off day, Lylah and I would take the baby and jump in the car and drive aimlessly through Brooklyn. We didn't take a map. We just drove, in and out and all around, and I learned about Brooklyn." He continued, "When I went to Ebbets Field each day to broadcast, I'd ride the subway and then I'd walk from my subway stop to the ball park. . . . I think I really got the feeling of Brooklyn by walking along and talking to the people who stood in front of the stores."

Brooklyn was as fascinating to Barber as he would later become to Brooklynites. He wrote, "Brooklyn was suffering from a borough-wide inferiority complex. That complex was compounded by the fact that so many people there felt they were foreigners. They talk about America being the melting pot. Brooklyn was, and it still is. There were more different racial and national strains in Brooklyn than anywhere else, and a lot of those people didn't speak English too impeccably, if they could speak it at all. . . . Some people who emigrated . . . went over to Brooklyn to join friends or relatives, settled in a certain neighborhood, and never left that neighborhood for the rest of their lives. . . . But these people who thought in terms of their own group and then their own neighborhood began to think in terms of Brooklyn. This was their town."

Many of the touchstones of Barber's style would seem unlikely to attract a rabid following of Brooklyn Dodger fans. Far from hiding his southern roots, Barber played to them with his love of rural colloquialisms. Despite broadcasting to a base of rabid fans, Barber did not pander to his audience but reported objectively on what he saw. He was literate, intelligent, and quietly comfortable behind a microphone. And Dodgers fans fell in love.

Television personality Larry King noted, "Red Barber was an indelible part of my life. He was the best sports announcer I ever heard. . . . I never heard anyone do a baseball game like him." King continued, "Red was a poet in the broadcast booth. He could make a 10 to 1 game interesting with his little insights, little truisms about baseball players."

Author Thomas Oliphant explained in his memoir, "In our household, Red Barber was God and the first voice that brought Dodger baseball to my ears."

No less an authority than the *New York Times* paid tribute to Barber's "scrupulous grammar, superb syntax, and meticulous preparation."

The regard worked both ways. Barber admitted, "In time, despite my southern accent . . . I felt that I was as much a part of Brooklyn as the fellow who had been born there. I didn't broadcast with a Brooklyn accent, but I did broadcast with a Brooklyn heart."

Barber's Brooklyn heart was especially on display when he became involved in extensive local blood drives during World War II. Doing so forced Barber to break a long-standing radio taboo against the mention of blood, but he asked Larry MacPhail, and given the exigencies of the situation, it was cleared.

Barber remembered, "From that [first] day on to the end of the war, there was never a broadcast of a Brooklyn Dodger game that did not include a blood-donor appeal." Given the massive success of that advertising campaign, Barber eventually cited it as "one thing from that career that I am truly proud of."

However, while Barber evinced concern for his fellow Americans and did believe that he had grown to broadcast with a Brooklyn heart, traces of his southern roots remained with him.

Lylah Barber remembered an incident back in Cincinnati, in which she and Red had traveled to see the Cincinnati Symphony. She recalled, "When we arrived we discovered that we would be sitting next to a black couple. Hastily, but quietly with our carefully taught Southern prejudice intact, we moved to still higher seats in the last row of the gallery, which was unoccupied." Lylah admitted, "I didn't hear much of the music. I was too busy examining myself and my own emotions. I watched the black couple down below . . . obviously enjoying the music. By the end of the concert I reluctantly accepted the knowledge that my reaction had only hurt me."

Barber later looked back on his youth and acknowledged, "I was raised by wonderful, tolerant people who taught me never to speak unkindly to anyone or to take advantage of anyone. The Negroes who came and went through our lives were always treated with the utmost respect and a great deal of warmth and a great deal of affection. But there was a line drawn, and that line was always there."

Branch Rickey's meeting in Joe's Restaurant threatened that line, and forced Barber to consider the demarcation of his own spiritual existence in a changing world.

~~

As Barber's decision was a spiritual one—there being no actual Jackie Robinson figure to consider but a mere principle of racial integration instead—his spiritual life bears consideration. In one of his many books, Barber pinpointed a key moment in his spiritual development as New Year's Eve, 1931. He had married Lylah earlier that year, but on New Year's Eve, he was shocked by news of his mother's death at age 55. Riding to comfort his father on that night, Barber grew angrier and angrier, as he considered that his mother had become an invalid in her early 50s and was then deceased at 55. "My anger grew and hardened," he wrote. "I did not go to church again for over ten years. I wanted nothing from God or from his ministers."

Barber indeed remained abjectly uninterested in spiritual matters, his issues with faith doubtlessly deepening as his wife, Lylah, had two miscarriages. But in 1937, their daughter Sarah was born. When she was five years old, Lylah, who was an Episcopalian, took her to Sunday school. Red recognized that his daughter was an intelligent enough child that she would soon ask why her father didn't go to church. He considered the matter, and finding no good answer, he announced one Sunday in late 1942 that he would go to church with his wife and daughter.

"I was an instant convert," Barber wrote of his spiritual renewal. "I hadn't known I was so dry, so thirsty, so lonely. I wasn't angry at God anymore; and most important, I found that God had not been angry with me. All I ever got from God when I returned to his house of worship was a complete welcome without once being asked, 'Where have you been?'"

The following spring Red was confirmed into the Episcopal church. Perhaps his reservoir of religious faith was what inspired Lylah, who said that after her husband's March 1945 meeting with Rickey, "I knew Red would get his thinking straightened out."

Barber sat down after his meeting with Rickey and did some serious soul-searching. He acknowledged that he enjoyed his work with the Dodgers, but by the same token, he recalled his father telling him, "Son, don't let anybody ever tell you that the job you have is the only job you can have. And don't ever let a man make you afraid of your job." So it wasn't an attachment to his job that he found sticking him in the conscience.

Barber then began to question himself as to why the possibility of working with a black player, broadcasting the games of a black player, even traveling with a black player, bothered him. "I had been carefully taught," he reflected. "I had been taught by everybody I had been around. I had been carefully taught by Negroes and whites alike. I was a product of a civilization; that line that was always there was indelible."

But digging deeper, Barber asked himself, "How much control did I have over the parents I was born to?" The answer was none, and he might just as easily have been born to different parents, in a different time, in a different place, and perhaps even with a different color of skin. He then acknowledged, "I figured out that I didn't have anything to be so proud of after all, this accident of the color of my skin."

But the soul-searching took on a greater impact when Barber happened to be approached by the rector of his church, St. James the Less in Scarsdale. He was asked to do a radio show, and his topic, taken from a sentence written by Saint Paul, was "Men and Brothers." Barber later admitted, "You look back and you say to yourself, how marvelous it is the way things synchronize in your life, how they fit and mesh together, the timing. . . . [W]hile I was trying to work out this thing of who I am, and this accident of birth, and losing a lot of false pride. . . . the rector asked me to talk about men and brothers, with the idea being that whether you were a Jew or a Christian, you were brothers."

The topic was chosen in response to some ugly anti-Semitic episodes in Barber's Scarsdale neighborhood, but it resonated deeper for the man tapped to give the talk.

"I suddenly found," recalled Barber, "that I wasn't nearly so interested in the relationship between Christians and Jews, Jews and Christians, as I was about the relationship between one white southern broadcaster and one unknown Negro ballplayer who was coming."

The matter now being properly framed in Barber's mind, his next question was one of action. Now that he was inclined to sympathize with the plight of the man who would eventually be Jackie Robinson, he had to figure out what exactly his role would be.

Ironically, the final factor in Barber's acceptance of Robinson was a voice from the dead, a voice of one of the men who had played a major role in keeping blacks out of baseball. While pondering his role, Barber flashed upon a memory of the late Kenesaw Mountain Landis. After the 1934 World Series, when broadcaster Ted Husing had been very critical of the umpires, Landis met with all of the broadcasters who would work the 1935 Series, including Barber. His mandate to all of them, the words that echoed back to Barber a decade later, had been, "You are not to manage, you are not to play, you are not to umpire, you are to report. Report everything you can see, but leave your opinions in your hotel room. Report."

"I heard that word, 'Report,' and peace came," Barber related. "I knew who I was and what I was to do and how I was to do it."

In other version of his story, Barber did not credit Landis, but veteran National League umpire Bill Klem, who famously said, "All there is to umpiring is umpiring the ball." The import of the message, regardless of who the inspiration was, remained identical. Barber was not the director of the grand experiment, he was not a manager or a coach who had to instruct Robinson, and he wasn't—even in this crucial assignment—a fan who would root ceaselessly for the home team. He was a reporter, and he would report. Prejudice being conquered, the onus was on baseball, which was all that Rickey, Robinson, or anyone else could have ever hoped.

And so, when Jackie Robinson signed in October 1945, tore through the International League in 1946, and broke spring training with the Dodgers in 1947, one man who was completely prepared was Red Barber. Fellow broadcaster Bob Edwards wrote, "Barber was another important sender of signals that year. . . . The fans were waiting to hear what Red would say. Red said nothing extraordinary—it was what Red didn't say that made an impression. He never said the word 'black' or 'brown' or 'Negro' or 'colored.' He just said 'Robinson' in the same way he would say 'Stanky,' 'Reiser' or 'Casey.' Robinson was just another infielder. Well, maybe not *just* another infielder."

Among many things he later wrote in praise of Robinson, Barber noted, "Robinson on base—on any base, first, second, third—was the most exciting player I've ever seen. When Robinson was on base every eye in the ball park was on him." That kind of excellence couldn't be objectively withheld from Barber's broadcasts, and his admiration for Robinson the player shone through even his seasoned objectivity.

Even a stick in the relative mud like *The Sporting News* considered Barber and Mel Allen's broadcast of the 1947 Series and offered, "Barber and Allen, noticeably fair and objective, did justice to Robinson as the first Negro to play in a World's Series, but stayed away from mawkishness."

No mawkishness was needed as the success of the Dodgers in 1947—winning their first pennant in six seasons—and the ensuing economic payoff to Robinson's Dodger teammates were significant building blocks to his acceptance.

"It was more than that for Red," Edwards continued, "because he had looked deep into his soul and found something there he didn't like. Jackie Robinson helped him fix that. Red told me that Robinson had done far more for him than he had ever done for Robinson."

Both Edwards and Lylah Barber told a story that demonstrated Red Barber's acceptance of Robinson. Shortly after Robinson's debut, a pair of Florida friends were visiting the Barbers. Red offered the couple passes as his guests at Ebbets Field, at which the husband said, "I'll never set foot in Ebbets Field as long as that nigger is playing there."

Barber wasn't confrontational. He didn't rant or rail, but calmly told his former friend, "We won't miss you."

Neither Barber, nor the Dodgers, nor baseball missed those who were left behind in the waves of integration. The confluence of a decidedly southern announcer and the denizens of Brooklyn took on even deeper overtones as Barber was the voice of the first team that began to truly resemble America's team.

The Dodgers' diversity became increasingly apparent when television joined radio as a burgeoning media outlet for baseball. In 1948, the Dodgers decided to provide radio coverage not only for home games but also for all road games on the radio. Barber worked the fifth and sixth innings of Dodger games on television, and then called the rest of the games on the radio. Barber worked the television broadcasts of the 1948 World Series.

Adding the visual media both to Robinson's spectacular brand of baseball and to the Dodgers' melting pot of baseball talent made the representative nature of the squad stand out even more sharply. Take, for instance, the 1953 World Series between the Dodgers and the Yankees. The Yankees were still two years away from integrating, and they were the team of Mickey Mantle and Whitey Ford. The Dodgers, on the other hand, started Robinson, Jim Gilliam, and Roy Campanella in their normal lineup, and even with Don Newcombe in the military, reliever Joe Page added some color to the pitching staff.

One person who wasn't at that 1953 World Series was Red Barber, as he was about to be exiled from the Dodger family.

⌒

Barber always aligned himself closely with Branch Rickey, which meant that after Rickey left the team following the 1950 season, he found himself on somewhat thin ice with Walter O'Malley. Barber had a year left on his contract when Rickey left town, but he met with O'Malley soon thereafter, telling him that he would not hold the Dodgers to the contract if O'Malley didn't wish him to remain as broadcaster.

O'Malley assured Barber that he was welcome. Barber didn't attempt to keep secrets.

"I was a close friend of Rickey's, I still am, and I intend to remain one," he told O'Malley. "I'd be happy to keep this job, and I'll do everything I can for you. I won't be talking about Rickey all the time. But if I stay here I do want you to let me keep my friendship with him."

O'Malley again assured Barber that this would not be a problem. But it always was a problem.

"I should have quit right then," Barber wrote years later.

Barber shared the story of O'Malley asking him about a manager, and Barber backed Shotton as "the best manager I know of right now." This didn't suit O'Malley, as Shotton was a Rickey disciple. Barber also mentioned Eddie Dyer from the Cardinals and former Dodger Dixie Walker. At that point, O'Malley told Barber he was hiring Charlie Dressen. This typified the cat-and-mouse games that O'Malley liked to play with Barber.

O'Malley and Barber never argued, but Barber admitted that the gulf between them "was just a combination of small things that kept growing and growing." The matter came to a head when Barber, tired of Gillette's penny-pinching ways in its World Series coverage, decided that he would turn down the 1953 Fall Classic unless he was paid a more reasonable fee for his work. Gillette had paid Barber $1,400 for broadcasting the seven-game 1952 Series.

When Gillette offered Barber the same fee for 1953, he turned them down flat. A stewing O'Malley recommended one of Barber's assistant broadcasters, a young Fordham alum named Vin Scully, to fill the post. Barber and the Dodgers were through.

And so, the exodus of the Dodgers continued. Rickey and Shotton were gone after 1950, Barber was gone after 1953, Robinson went after 1956, and the team left Brooklyn entirely after 1957. Barber took a job for the New York Yankees, working alongside his former rival Mel Allen in television and radio broadcasting. Barber got along with Allen, but he was now a supporting player in another man's broadcasting booth. He handled pregame and postgame shows, broadcast a few innings, and only traveled with the team occasionally.

One issue was Barber's own lukewarm feeling toward television. After dominating the radio coverage of baseball, he found the visual medium to be a very different challenge. He once explained, "On TV it's the director's show, and the broadcaster is an instrument of his, like a camera. On radio, it's my show, where my knowledge and experience and taste and judgment decide what goes and what doesn't. On radio, you're an artist. On TV, you're a servant."

Another annoyance for Barber was the imposition of former-players-turned-commentators. Much of his ire was reserved for former catcher Joe Garagiola, who may be best remembered in the context of Jackie Robinson for spiking Robinson and then arguing with him in 1947. Garagiola once stepped on Robinson's feet, but he frequently stepped on Barber's words in the broadcasting booth, a sin that the venerable Barber found difficult to forgive.

After the 1966 season, the Yankees, mired in a decline to mediocrity, decided not to renew Barber's contract. At 58 years old, he retired from full-time announcing and returned to Florida. While Barber had spent 32 seasons as a baseball broadcaster, he would prove that he had far more to offer.

~

Barber had always been a superb writer, and given the time, he produced four books in four years, running the gamut from a memoir of his own life to a spiritual book that included his memories of many nonbaseball moments of spiritual import in his own life and then a handful of lay sermons he had delivered around the world. Given a few years of respite, in 1982 he authored *1947: When All Hell Broke Loose in Baseball*, a fascinating account of the power play between Larry MacPhail and Branch Rickey and a recollection of the unforgettable 1947 season that culminated in a Dodgers/Yankees World Series. The cover of that book noted 1947 as "the year Jackie Robinson broke the color barrier," and the cover photo is Robinson stealing home.

In 1978, the Baseball Hall of Fame made Barber along with Mel Allen the first two recipients ever of the Ford C. Frick Award, presented annually to a broadcaster for "major contributions to baseball." This is the broadcasting version of enshrinement in the Hall of Fame, and Barber was further honored by being named to the Veterans' Committee, which considered the Hall of Fame credentials of players outside the realm of the BBWAA vote of recently retired players. Despite the honors, Barber's broadcasting career was far from finished.

In the late 1970s, a young female radio producer from National Public Radio asked her father about Red Barber. Barber's name kept popping up in conjunction with Jackie Robinson, and the producer, Ketzel Levine, was working on a Robinson story for Black History Month. Her father told her that Barber, in overcoming his own southern prejudice and treating Robinson as if his color truly was irrelevant "sent a signal to the fans in Brooklyn and elsewhere in baseball: black ballplayers were to be accepted. Integration was here to stay."

Levine interviewed Barber on a couple of occasions, and then offered him a job to do a weekly commentary for NPR's *Morning Edition*. Soon, Barber had a standing weekly four-minute spot at 7:35 a.m. Friday mornings with NPR host Bob Edwards. For those who heard him in the 1930s and 1940s, the Barber who broadcasted Dodger games was a revelation in sportscasting. But for those who heard him in the 1980s and early 1990s on NPR, the Red Barber who spoke for four minutes on Friday mornings to "Colonel Bob," as he dubbed Edwards, was even more fascinating.

Barber refused to do anything but live, ad-libbed conversation. Edwards might intend to ask him about a sports issue but end up discussing the plants growing in Barber's garden for four minutes. Barber might discuss literature, music, or perhaps even Jackie Robinson. But whatever he talked about, he charmed his audience.

Edwards later reflected, "[F]or many listeners, Red was a reminder of a father, a grandfather, or a favorite uncle they had—or wished they had."

Another generation got to know Barber through Ken Burns's award-winning *Baseball* documentary. Barber held forth on many topics that were included in the nine-volume series, but he was always at his most poignant when discussing the player who had changed his life forever.

Unfortunately, by the time *Baseball* was released—its initial incarnation coming on public television, thus neatly bookending Barber's radio career that had begun on a public broadcasting station and ended with his NPR work—Barber had passed away. He begged off an NPR show the day before broadcast on October 8, 1992. The next day, he underwent surgery for an intestinal blockage and went into a coma from which he did not recover. Barber died on October 22, 1992.

The influence of Jackie Robinson on Red Barber didn't end in 1945 when Barber worked out his feelings on the as-yet-unknown player who became Robinson, or in 1947, when Robinson revealed himself to be the most exciting baserunner Barber ever saw. Barber wrote in 1969:

> Rickey and Jackie Robinson had made me think. Selma, Alabama had made me think. So had Birmingham. So had Philadelphia, Mississippi. So had the battle over segregated schools. So had racial riots in city after city. Black Power and Black Muslims and George Wallace of Alabama and Governor Ross Barnett of Mississippi and the riots at the University of Mississippi over one Negro man going to school there made me think.

Robinson's greatest influence on Barber wasn't at an end point with the game of baseball. The game of baseball was a beginning. Barber realized that if his knee-jerk reaction to calling baseball games alongside a black player had been so wrong, his first thought on other matters of racial equality might also require further examination.

In the chapter of his book that accompanied Barber's reflective comments, an African-American football coach told Barber, "A converted white man—by that I mean a white man who has made up his mind to be fair—is the best friend a black man can have."

Red Barber came away from his March 1945 conversation with Branch Rickey as a converted white man. Jackie Robinson was the reality to the soul cleansing that Barber had already instituted. Determined to treat Robinson as just another player, Barber soon had to amend that description to just another *exceptional* player. That fairness reverberated from his broadcasts, across a borough with an inferiority complex, where its residents—Jewish, Hispanic, black, and white—heard a brave new world in Barber's broadcasts. Barber may have intended only to report, only to broadcast the game in front of him, but his own story was a constant counterpoint to the story of the game.

"[I]f there is any thanks involved, any appreciation," Barber wrote in his memoir, "I thank Jackie Robinson. He did far more for me than I did for him."

CHAPTER EIGHT

PEE WEE REESE: "STANDING BY ME."

In late April 1902, an African-American man named Ernest Dewley got into some trouble in a saloon in the one-horse town of Guston, Kentucky. The saloonkeeper, Frank Pickerel, ejected Dewley from his premises. He had the misfortune to happen upon Dewley at the train station later that day, and Dewley, no doubt still angry at being kicked out of the saloon, took out a pistol and opened fire on Pickerel. He didn't hit Pickerel, but he did hit a bystander named Harry Dowell. Dowell was wounded but not killed in the shooting.

Police took Dewley into custody and placed him in the county jail in Brandenburg, the capital of Meade County, slightly southwest of Louisville. It didn't matter. That night, a lynch mob came to the jail and demanded the keys. The jailer didn't give up the keys, so the mob battered down the doors, took Dewley a mile and a half down the road, and hanged him to death, shooting his corpse many times as a final insult.

Carl Reese was a teenager in Meade County, and the Dewley lynching was national news for a brief period. Years later, in the late 1920s, Carl was a middle-aged father and a railroad detective for the L&N Railroad. He took his son to Brandenburg and showed him a tree. One version of the story holds that Carl told Harold, "When a nigger gets uppity, this is where we string him up. We hang him high. That's why we call this the Hanging Tree."

Other accounts suggest that Carl showed this tree to Harold in a very different spirit. In any case, when Harold grew into adulthood and showed his son Mark the same tree, Mark's memory was that "there was definitely an emotion in his voice, an emotion that said to me . . . that it was a terrible thing that human beings did to another human being, and only because of the color of their skin." Mark told an interviewer, "I imagine that when his dad told him the story, there was a similar emotion."

In whichever spirit the conversation was held, part of what made Harold a wiser young man than most of his time was that he heard the story and processed it into an unacceptable act of hate. White men might have the power to treat a black man this way, but it shouldn't be done. Young Harold refused to be defined by the past of his land or his people.

It is an odd thing that the brutal lynching of Ernest Dewley started a chain of events that ended in one of the most enduring images of a pair of black and white men as friends and teammates. Today, the Hanging Tree in Brandenburg, Kentucky, is mostly forgotten. Today, in Brooklyn, New York, there is a statue of a white man putting his arm around a black man—his friend, his teammate. The path away from hate runs to redemption. It can be a winding path, but it is a glorious path. Particularly when shared by teammates.

~

Harold Henry Reese was born on July 23, 1918, and grew up on a farm between the small towns of Ekron and Brandenburg, Kentucky. When he was seven years old, his family moved to Louisville. Growing up in a much more urban environment made little difference in terms of any meaningful contact with African Americans. Reese told an interviewer late in his life, "The part [of town] that I grew up in, there were no blacks allowed in there. Blacks got in back of the buses, they had a special fountain to drink from. I don't guess I ever shook the hand of a black person really. . . . We never came into contact with them."

Reese did recall an incident when he was around 13 or 14, when his older brother shouted a racial slur at a group of about six African-American boys, telling them to "get off the street." When the group ran after the Reese boys, they had to take to their heels and run away home. "I thought it was stupid," Reese later said of his brother's taunt.

If there was little to mark Reese as a racial pioneer, there wasn't much more to mark him as a famous athlete. By the age at which his future double-play partner Jackie Robinson was shining in multiple sports, Reese had only one area of particular expertise—marbles. In early 1933, he tied as runner-up in the *Louisville Times* 1933 marbles tournament. The winner went to a regional tournament in Chicago, and in Reese's case, the runner-up got a lifelong nickname—"Pee Wee," a term applied to smaller marbles.

Reese was a physically slight young man—he would eventually fill out to a listed height of 5'10", but at least one source indicates that he didn't surpass a weight of 100 pounds until his senior year in high school. In any case, he barely got into any games during his high school career at Louisville's Dupont Manual High. After high school, Reese took on a series of jobs. His work as a telephone cable splicer improved his physique. "Climbing up and down those poles really built me up," he said.

Whatever the cause, Reese began to draw attention with his play in a local church league, as a star for the New Covenant Presbyterian Church team, which he led to the 1937 Louisville city championship. His play caught the notice of the city's minor-league franchise, the Louisville Colonels, who signed Reese for the 1938 season. Reese worked his way into the Colonel lineup "by accident," as he later told *The Sporting News*. He hit .277, stole 23 bases, and impressed the Louisville team enough that he picked up another nickname—The Little Colonel.

He also impressed the Boston Red Sox. Louisville, despite having what one article termed "a working agreement" with the Dodgers, was technically an independent franchise. In September 1938, the Boston Red Sox purchased the team for $195,000. Boston general manager Eddie Collins noted in the paper that one of the team's biggest assets was Reese, "for whom several major league clubs already have offered $40,000."

Reese's destiny seemed to lie with the Red Sox, but things quickly turned in a different direction. The Red Sox were run by player-manager Joe Cronin, who was a Hall of Fame shortstop himself. Cronin was in no hurry to cede his spot on the diamond to Reese.

Accordingly, on July 18, 1939, Reese was sold to the Dodgers for $35,000 and four players. Dodger president Larry MacPhail estimated the total value of the trade at $75,000, which would have been the most

Brooklyn had paid for any player to date. MacPhail cited Reese's age and inexperience as making the deal "quite a gamble," but admitted "Reese . . . should develop into a major league star with another year or two of experience." Part of the deal was that Reese would finish the 1939 season with the Louisville team.

Reese was disconsolate about the deal with the Dodgers. He would later recall that he was "crushed" by being sent to the eternally cellar-dwelling franchise, but he admitted that the sale "turned out to be the greatest break of my life."

In Brooklyn, Reese apprenticed with another player-manager who was a shortstop. But an aging Leo Durocher was both less skilled and less vain about his playing skills than Cronin, and he quickly realized that his best move as manager was to bench himself in favor of the rookie. Durocher did not retire immediately, and even played in a few games in 1945, but the arrival of Reese marked the point when Durocher stopped being an everyday player. One common story about the relationship between the two had Durocher trying to put Reese through a tough infield workout in spring training, before finally conceding himself, saying, "He'll do. I'll be the bench manager." Aside from three years of military service, Reese was a Dodger fixture for almost two decades. By ending up in Brooklyn, Reese inadvertently became part of one of the greatest stories in baseball history with his own role in the integration of the sport by Jackie Robinson. As Brooklyn's everyday shortstop in 1940, he batted .272, stole 15 bases, and played excellent defense at shortstop. One author noted that Reese "distinguished himself as a slick fielder and a first class base runner." A troubling 1941 season followed, as Reese struggled with an ankle injury and hit just .229.

Reese's 1942 season saw a return to form, as he first married his sweetheart Dorothy Walton in a double play of weddings on the same March 29th date as Pete Reiser and his girlfriend, Patricia Hurst. Reese's batting eye returned, as he hit .255 that season, and also drew 82 walks against 55 strikeouts, earning his way onto his first All-Star team.

But after that season, Reese enlisted in the US Navy, which placed his baseball career on hold for three years. Reese spent most of his time in the service in the Pacific Theater with a construction battalion. When baseball entered the picture at all, Reese had to wonder what his future with the Dodgers held, whenever the war ended. The reality was unimaginable to Reese, and it would change his life forever.

In late 1945, Reese was on a ship returning home from the service, taking the long route home from Guam. The news of Jackie Robinson signing with Montreal had somehow reached the ship, and one of the other sailors told Reese, "Hey, Pee Wee, did you hear? The Dodgers signed a nigger." Reese was playing cards with friends and, not being exceptionally interested, he continued his card game. The intrepid reporter then added, "And he plays shortstop." This brought the matter home to Reese.

A latent issue in the topic was that of players returning home after their service time. Obviously, many players left America as big-league regulars and came home in somewhat different status. But Reese was on different ground—to many observers, the only thing worse than a white veteran losing his job would be his losing it to a black man. In a split second, Reese instinctively knew how to respond.

He thought to himself, "My God, just my luck, Robinson has to play my position!" But he considered the matter, and his confidence in his own skills, and answered, "Well, if he can beat me out, more power to him." This was the code that made Reese a leader. Whatever differences might exist between himself and another man, baseball was the ultimate arbiter. He later reflected on his mentality of October 1945 by saying, "If he's man enough to take my job, I'm not gonna like it, but dammit, black or white, he deserves it."

For the time being, Robinson was taking jobs only on the Montreal Royals, and Reese had to go about the business of returning to the Dodgers. In 1946, Reese returned not only to the Dodgers but also to the National League All-Star team. He hit .285, scored 79 runs and knocked in 60, and played so well in all facets of the game that he finished sixth in the National League MVP balloting. Reese and second baseman Eddie Stanky, along with outfielder Dixie Walker, helped the Dodgers make a run for the NL pennant, which the team lost in a best-of-three playoff with the Cardinals after the regular season.

It was easy to be cavalier about Robinson when he was in Montreal, but in the spring of 1947, Reese had to come to terms with the man rather than the idea of playing beside him. It was an important spring—for Robinson, for Reese, and for the development of the Dodgers.

First, while the team was in Havana for spring training, word flowed through the grapevine that a few of the less supportive Dodgers either intended to prepare or possibly had prepared a petition to the effect that they would not play with Robinson. The existence and details of this petition are among the most controversial aspects of the integration of baseball, because admitting involvement is tantamount to placing oneself firmly on the wrong side of history. Legend has it that Dixie Walker, Bobby Bragan, and Kirby Higbe were among the players who either circulated the petition or sought support for such a cause. The trio of white, southern Dodgers approached Reese, expecting that he would join their stance.

"I'm not signing that," Reese allegedly told the group. "No way."

Humble about his motivations, Reese denied that he was making an exceptionally principled stand. "I just wanted to play baseball," he said. "I'd just come back from serving in the South Pacific . . . and I had a wife and daughter to support. I needed the money. I just wanted to get on with it."

This sort of pragmatism dovetailed neatly with the approach taken by anticipated Dodger manager Leo Durocher, who heard of the petition, convened a team meeting, and told the rabble-rousers to shove the petition up their asses. Like Reese, Durocher didn't make his stand as a matter of human rights—he made it as a matter of improving the prospects of the Dodger team for World Series bonus money. Whether this was aiming too low or not, it apparently worked.

Reese, as a proud Southerner and a veteran Dodger, found himself dealing with the situation on more than one occasion. Early in 1947, he played cards with Robinson, which drew the ire of Dixie Walker.

Soon thereafter, Walker cornered Reese and demanded, "How can you be playing cards with him?"

Reese was matter of fact. "Look, Dixie," Reese replied, "You and Stell travel with a black woman who takes care of your kids, who cooks your food, who you trust—isn't that even more than playing cards with a black?"

Walker responded, "But this is different."

Rapidly, it became apparent to Reese that it was different. Robinson wasn't merely somebody he trusted; he was a teammate in the truest sense of the world. Codes of gentility and southern manners aside, Pee Wee Reese found that he and Jackie Robinson might not have shared a skin color, but they shared an approach to baseball. Years later, Leo Durocher looked back on his years of managing against Robinson and marveled, "He doesn't just want to beat you. He wants to shove the bat right up your ass." He could have said the same of Reese, and it was that intensity that helped link Jackie and Pee Wee forever.

The sixth and final point in Branch Rickey's plan to integrate baseball was for Robinson to have the support and respect of his teammates. It seems to have been an issue on which Rickey spent an especially large amount of time, perhaps because there was little he could ultimately do to make Robinson's path any easier.

The Dodgers could be broken down into three essential groups. One was the players—mostly young, mostly from the North, who were either used to integrated life and athletic competition, or who had played with Robinson in Montreal, or later, who came up after him and thus already regarded his conquest of baseball as a fait accompli. In this group were players like pitcher Ralph Branca, who was from New York and who had lived in a thoroughly mixed-race neighborhood as a young man. Branca recalled making a point to shake Robinson's hand on his first day in the clubhouse, and he famously caught Robinson on a pop foul that left him stumbling into the Dodger dugout late in the 1947 season. Branca recalled in his autobiography, "In describing the scene, someone said that Jackie and I looked like a married couple."

Branca's original assessment of Robinson came in part based off a scouting report from outfielder and fellow Californian Duke Snider. Snider had watched Robinson play football and basketball in his college days and told Branca, "I wouldn't want to play against him. Thank God I get to play with him."

Carl Erskine, after he joined the Dodgers in 1948, was another Robinson backer. The Indiana native remembered Robinson taking time to offer him some praise after a spring training game. Erskine was from a racially integrated community, and one of his best boyhood friends was African American. Erskine later wrote, "Life was about people's souls, not their race or religion or anything else."

The second group extended in the opposite direction. There were certain players within the Dodger organization—most often those named included Dixie Walker, Bobby Bragan, and Hugh Casey—who were against the very idea of playing with Robinson. The exact identity of this core group is a matter of some dispute, as only Bragan and to a lesser extent Walker ever owned up to being on the wrong side of history. But a rough accounting would probably place a group firmly against Robinson as roughly equal to those supporting Robinson.

This left the critical third group—those who were somewhere between the polar extremes. The youngest players tended to support Robinson, and some of the veterans were the most vociferous in objecting to him. Northerners tended to support; Southerners tended to object. But the heart and soul of the team probably lay objectively with Reese—a player who was enough of a veteran to be a two-time All-Star but was barely older than Robinson, a player who was from right on the Mason-Dixon line.

As a Dodger who was neither brought up to be comfortable with an integrated team nor predisposed to rebel against such an idea, Reese's support for Robinson was a crucial pivot point in the locker room. The vast majority of Dodger players were probably watching the team leader, the player with a reputation for being an affable friend to anyone.

Perhaps the earliest point of contact between Reese and Robinson came in the multitude of card games that the Dodgers ended up playing on trains, in hotels, in clubhouses, or anywhere else. Robinson was a competitive card player, and most of his peers who were close to him remember playing cards with him. Reese was no exception. He told Jules Tygiel in an interview, "I played an awful lot of cards with him on trains."

But even the card games were slow to come early in Robinson's testing time in Brooklyn. To be sure, some of the social aspects of card playing were a simple attempt at any form of diversion in a dead period. But on another level, the card table was often the testing ground for Robinson as a man. He recalled an incident when Georgia-born relief pitcher Hugh Casey asked him during one card game, "You know what I used to do down in Georgia when I ran into bad luck? I used to go out and find me the biggest, blackest nigger woman I could find and rub her teats to change my luck."

Casey, who was infamous for his drinking problem, may have been well into his cups. Or he may have been seeing just how much Robinson could stomach. His comment met a stone silence, and Robinson swallowed his anger and simply asked another player to deal the cards. Just as Robinson's ability to tolerate hatred and ignorance on the field earned him respect, it had the same effect on his Dodger teammates, perhaps especially Reese.

One turning point that was not lost on Robinson came on June 20th. The Dodgers were scheduled to play an exhibition game against their minor-league squad from Danville, Illinois. When the team arrived around noon, Robinson and Wendell Smith decided to take advantage of a rare hole in the Dodger schedule to get in a round of golf at the local country club. Four holes into their day, Robinson and Smith caught up with the golfers ahead of them—Reese, Dodger pitcher Rex Barney, Dodger traveling secretary Harold Parrott, and *New York Times* columnist Roscoe McGowan.

It was Reese who sized up the situation and asked, "Why don't you two join us? We can make this a six-some, although that's against the rules. There aren't many people out here today and it won't make much difference." The six men played the remaining 14 holes together.

Writing about the incident in the *Pittsburgh Courier*, Smith noted that Robinson "is now definitely one of the Dodgers." He noted that Reese, Barney, and Robinson joked with each other throughout the golf game, and "without saying it to each other, they admitted that each had something in common."

What Robinson had in common with all of his teammates was his high regard for Reese. The golf club incident, thanks to Smith being part of the game, was reported. But the message that was doubtlessly carried behind clubhouse doors and hotel lobbies was that Reese was a man who didn't especially care about what the previous rules of conduct had been—like that day on the golf course, it ultimately didn't make much difference.

⌐

Reese accepted Robinson as a teammate and a friend in that initial 1947 season, but it was 1948 when the two grew into something deeper. There is a spiritual connection in a double-play combination. Consider Tinker to Evers to Chance, Franklin P. Adams's trio of Chicago Cubs who barely spoke to each other but are immortalized in baseball's literary history as forever linked by virtue of constituting a double-play tandem. In 1948, Robinson moved from first base to second, replacing Eddie Stanky, whom the Dodgers had dealt to the Boston Braves. At the same time, a young catcher named Gil Hodges was installed at first base. Hodges was the third member of the double-play triumvirate, a quiet, dependable player whose strength complemented the ferocity of Robinson and Reese in defining the Dodger core for the 1950s.

While Robinson and Reese had gotten along before, as middle infielders, they had to learn to read each other's thoughts and reactions dependably. To say that they did so would be an understatement.

Robinson played second base next to Reese from 1948 to 1952. In those five seasons, he was four times the National League's top second baseman in number of double plays turned—the other year was 1948, when he finished second.

But greater than the statistical feats of defensive certainty was the unbreakable bond that emerged between the two middle infielders. Exactly how unbreakable that bond was became the point where history and legend tend to collide.

~

There may be no single story of Jackie Robinson's career and life more famous than the day when Pee Wee Reese ambled over in response to racial taunts and jeers from a visiting crowd against Robinson and placed his arm around Robinson's shoulder during a brief chat. The only problem is that as famous as the incident is, no two accounts tell the story in quite the same way, which has led many critics of the narrative to deny that it ever happened in the first place. The web of the myth of the arm around the shoulder in many ways is more fascinating than what probably did occur.

Some stories say that the event happened in 1947, when Robinson was a rookie, probably on one of the Dodgers' very first road trips. Carl Erskine (who wasn't even there) wrote that it happened that season in a trip to Cincinnati. Ralph Branca, who was there, agreed, saying it was the first trip to Cincinnati in 1947. Rex Barney similarly placed the event on the first road trip to Cincinnati—specifically, he said that he was warming up to pitch the bottom of the first inning after Robinson had popped out to end the top of the first when the event happened. (In fact, Barney pitched the seventh and eighth innings that day, Robinson grounded out for the second out in the top of the first, and the only time Robinson hit once Barney was in the game, he singled and scored a run.) Traveling secretary Harold Parrott placed the incident on the first road trip to Philadelphia in 1947. Gene Hermanski agreed.

As demonstrated, not only when the incident occurred, but *where* it occurred, is still in doubt. Was it Cincinnati, Philadelphia, or, as Roscoe McGowen of the *New York Times* wrote, Fort Worth, Texas, in an exhibition game? And for that matter, Reese's gesture was intended to silence the opposing fans . . . or was it the opposing players? There are many, many different accounts, and they vary in many ways. In fact, the accounts vary in so many ways—and there is a complete lack of independent contemporary corroboration of the story—that many have indicated that they don't believe the incident happened at all, including author Jonathan Eig and filmmaker Ken Burns.

But the two men whose accounts haven't varied significantly are Reese's and Robinson's.

Reese was vague about any details of the incident, perhaps out of a lack of memory, and perhaps out of a feeling that it was somewhat unchivalrous to talk too much about his own role in the Robinson matter. In a 1977 interview for an AP column, he tentatively admitted, "There were times I helped him with a look or a word. I guess I stepped over and put my arm around him when things were the toughest." Hardly definitive, but then, consistent with Reese's own character.

Sportswriter Dave Kindred wrote in *The Sporting News* in 1999 that when he called Reese to ask him about the familiar Robinson stories, Reese told Kindred that he knew the stories better than Reese himself, and then interjected, "Just don't make me out to be a hero. It took no courage to do what I did. Jackie had the courage."

Only in an interview with author Jules Tygiel did Reese subtly let his own commentary surface. In the interview's opening minute, responding to Tygiel's first question about Robinson, Reese clearly says, "I was supposed to have put my arm around him—which I'm sure that I did—and I don't think I did it just to say, hey, I'm the Great White Father here or something. I may have done it with anyone."

That's as close to a tell-all account as Reese ever put forth—a six-word aside that he slips accidentally into a conversation in which he praised Robinson extensively. But if Reese was sure that he did put his arm around Robinson, that should count for something. His sympathy for Robinson was beyond dispute, and several 1947 accounts mention an incident when Robinson was being photographed during infield practice one day and Reese noticed and asked about the photographers, "Why don't they let the guy alone and let him play baseball?"

But more important than Reese's recollections, Robinson was certainly clear on the fact that Reese put his arm around him. Robinson mentioned a similar interaction in 1949, and in 1952, he told the full story of Reese's arm around his shoulder. It's the same version he told in 1955 and 1960 and 1972. The essential details are not only consistent, but they make sense outside of any need to craft some sort of narrative of friendship between him and Reese.

The incident—or more accurately, one particularly memorable instance thereof, as Robinson said that it happened more than once— occurred in 1948 in Boston, on the Dodgers' first road trip to play the Braves. Reese's actions were intended to respond to some particularly vicious heckling, not from Boston fans, but from the Braves dugout. The back story here was that Robinson's move to second base put the skids on Eddie Stanky, and resulted in his trade to these same Boston Braves. Stanky was a player who had initially experienced some reservations about playing with Robinson, had proved helpful to him later in 1947, but now was in the opposing dugout. Contemporary newspaper accounts mention some particularly vicious bench jockeying between Stanky and Leo Durocher. The apparent next step would have been heckling Reese, a Southerner, the former double-play partner of Stanky—something to the effect of how do you guys like having Robinson out there instead of Stanky, except with a host of profane nicknames likely substituted for Robinson's name. Bear in mind that Robinson had struggled through spring out of shape and was still dealing with some nagging injuries. In fact, Robinson barely played in that first game in Boston on April 26th, when he entered the game in the eighth inning for defensive purposes. But he did presumably take infield practice before the game, which is when the hateful bench jockeying prompted Reese.

In a July 1952 magazine article, Robinson told an interviewer, "Fellows like Branca . . . and Reese, who is a great fellow, have always been wonderful to me. We were in Boston in '48, and the Braves were 'giving it' to Reese for playing alongside me. Peewee [*sic*] came over from shortstop, put his arm around my shoulders, as if he had something to say. Actually, he just wanted to show where he stood. The jeers subsided."

In a 1949 column, Robinson told a similar story, although without some of the key details. Specifically, he said:

> I'll never forget the day when a few loud-mouthed guys on the other team began to take off on Pee Wee Reese.
>
> They were joshing him very viciously because he was playing on the team with me and was on the field nearby. Mind you, they were not yelling at me; I suppose they did not have the nerve to do that, but they were calling him some very vile names and every one bounced off of Pee Wee and hit me like a machine-gun bullet.
>
> Pee Wee kind of sensed the hopeless, dead feeling in me and came over and stood beside me for a while. He didn't say a word but he looked over at the chaps who were yelling at me through him and just stared. He was standing by me, I could tell you that.
>
> Slowly the jibes died down like when you kill a snake an inch at a time, and then there was nothing but quiet from them. It was wonderful the way this little guy did it. I will never forget it.

Admittedly, that description differs in no mention of the arm around the shoulder, or of Boston or exactly when it occurred, except that as Robinson told the story in August 1949, it narrows the possibilities substantially. So while Robinson was *clearly* telling the story in early 1952, he may have been telling it, with minor variations, in mid-1949.

The story pops up again by 1953, although at this point, Robinson had gotten positively sloppy on the details. Talking to Milton Gross of the *New York Times* that year, Robinson rhetorically asked, "In 1947, can

I forget what Reese did for me in Boston? The way he called time when they were on me and came over and put his arm around my shoulder?"

While this account varies from the others, it is worth noting that the only variation here is that Robinson placed the incident in 1947 instead of 1948, and that he apparently placed it during the game instead of during infield practice.

That said, he was soon back to his earlier version of events. Perhaps most intriguing, he told the story to *Look* magazine in 1955:

> Pee Wee was great to me in 1948 when Eddie Stanky went to the Boston Braves and I moved to second base. He took a lot of bitter abuse around the circuit because of it. Pee Wee comes from Louisville and the bench jockeys kept asking him how it felt to be playing beside a Negro. The first day we played in Boston that spring the Braves tried to give us a real bad time. But Pee Wee shut them up. He walked over to me and put his arm around me and talked with me in a friendly manner, smiling and laughing. There was no more trouble after that from the Braves. He did the same thing later in other parks.

All of the vital details of the story are consistent, save that Robinson did not mention that the incident apparently took place during pregame infield practice . . . although nothing he said is inconsistent with that version of events, either. But most intriguing is that tag noting that Reese "did the same thing later in other parks." Perhaps then, those who remembered the incident in Cincinnati or Philadelphia or Fort Worth weren't entirely wrong, either?

Robinson told the same basic story thereafter, although a few details were vague, and the need to contextualize the event apparently struck him as the years passed.

In 1960's *Wait Till Next Year*, Carl T. Rowan, who wrote the book with extensive interviews from Robinson, placed the incident "in Boston

. . . shortly after Jackie was shifted to second base," which would be 1948. Rowan also placed the incident during infield practice, and offered a few relatively cleaned-up samples of the jockeying from the Braves bench.

"As the calls got louder," Rowan wrote, "he strode over to Robinson and put his arm around his shoulder. They talked for a minute in buddy-buddy fashion—oddly enough, neither Robinson nor Reese remembers a single word they said—and the Braves' players fell silent."

Rowan then editorialized, using what were likely Robinson's own words, considering how closely Jackie's later accounts square with the comments. "Reese had said, simply but with force: Robinson and I are teammates, and we came here to play baseball. . . . That ended the race heckling."

In 1972's *I Never Had It Made*, Robinson repeated the story, although the details were not very extensive. He wrote, "In Boston during a period when the heckling pressure seemed unbearable, some of the Boston players began to heckle Reese. They were riding him about being a Southerner and playing ball with a black man. Pee Wee didn't answer them. Without a glance in their direction, he left his position and walked over to me. He put his hand on my shoulder and began talking to me. . . . As he stood talking to me with a friendly arm around my shoulder, he was saying loud and clear, 'Yell. Heckle. Do anything you want. We came here to play baseball.'"

Robinson's command of the details was evident in a 1971 speech he gave when *Sport* magazine honored him as its "Man of 25 Years," which was the duration of the magazine's lifespan. That night, in his acceptance speech, Robinson told the audience:

> Back in 1948 as we took our positions for infield prac-
> tice, some Boston players thought, I imagine, that Reese
> being a southerner would react to their taunts about
> playing alongside of me on the Dodgers. There wasn't
> the viciousness as compared to the taunts of Ben Chap-
> man and some of his Phillies. But it was strong enough!
> Well, Reese did react! He left his shortstop position,

came over to me, placed his hands on my shoulder and said something. I don't remember the words and I am sure he doesn't either, but his actions had great meaning. The heckling stopped. . . . Pee Wee by his gesture, simply said, yell and scream as much as you like, we are a team, we came to play ball together. Because of attitudes like that . . . we made our mark on . . . the game and the nation.

That is the case for the great Reese/Robinson incident. Of course, there are no photographs. Unfortunately, there was no contemporaneous press coverage—although the idea that scribes would not pay much heed to a random occurrence during pregame infield practice doesn't seem *that* unbelievable. Admittedly, Reese was always very vague (modest?) in his shared recollections. But Robinson's grasp of the situation is remarkably consistent. And who would remember it best? Probably not Reese, who went out of his way to say many times that he treated Robinson like a teammate, nothing more or less. Probably not a sportswriter under deadline—and many sportswriters were very selective in how Robinson's story was or was not reported. It was, after all, Robinson who felt support, whose cause was taken up by a popular, white, Kentucky-born infielder. If we can't take his word on this point, might that not say more about those researching the point than it does about Robinson himself?

Reese had long since been one of the team leaders of the Dodgers, but his acceptance of Robinson and ability to remain on working terms with all of the subgroups of players within the Dodger clubhouse cemented his status. Photos from the old Dodger clubhouse seem to be a treasure trove of Reese with his teammates, looking equally comfortable in a happy group of players with Jackie Robinson or with Dixie Walker.

Branch Rickey certainly understood Reese's leadership powers. In 1948, he presented Reese with a copy of General Eisenhower's *Crusade in Europe* "to Harold, that he may develop into a leader of men." He was apparently pleased enough with Reese that in 1949, he chose to name him as the team's captain, telling Reese, "You're not only the logical choice, you are the only possible choice; the players all respect you." The Dodgers had not had a captain during Rickey's tenure in Brooklyn, so the honor was intended to be more than ceremonial.

At this point, Reese picked up another nickname—he was Pee Wee, the Colonel, or the Captain. Robinson stated, "He took charge of us out there, in a way to help all of us. . . . When Pee Wee told us where to play or gave some of us the devil, somehow it was easy to take. He just has a way about him of saying the right thing."

Robinson was far from the only player to note Reese's excellent hand in management. Carl Erskine later recalled, "Pee Wee was like the captain of the captains. He had the respect. He had a personality, and he was an extension—always an extension of who was managing."

Sometimes, Reese's role as captain extended beyond field director and assistant to the manager. Robinson later wrote that he could not have remained in perhaps his greatest game if not for Reese. It was the final regular season game of 1951, when the Dodgers had to win to force a playoff for the NL pennant. With the game tied at 8 in the 12th inning, Robinson made a difficult diving catch of Eddie Waitkus's bases-loaded line drive to keep the season alive for Brooklyn.

Robinson recalled, "I thought I had killed myself. I jammed my elbow into my stomach when I was falling and I landed unconscious and face down in the dirt. Rachel started to cry when she saw me from the stands. She was sure I was dead."

Of course, he wasn't dead, but he had been knocked out.

"I would have quit the game if it wasn't for Pee Wee," recalled Robinson. "He talked to me and kidded me and pulled me together. Only because of him, I stayed in there."

Robinson stayed in and hit the game-winning home run in the 14th inning on what he called "my greatest day in baseball." Near the end of his Dodger career, Robinson wrote in a private letter to his wife, "The fellows are all very nice," but he admitted, "there are only a very few that

I would like to socialize with." One of the names he singled out was, of course, Reese, whom he termed "a fine team man."

⌐⌐

Getting along well with others may have been a strength of Reese, but it was an issue for Robinson, even above and beyond the initial prejudice he absorbed from teammates who didn't want to play on the same team as a black man. Ironically, some of the players whom Robinson struggled in relating to were black players who had followed his lead into professional baseball. Perhaps his greatest foil as a Brooklyn Dodger was fellow star and African American Roy Campanella.

In fact, color and excellence of play were about the only things Robinson and Campanella had in common. Campanella was born to an Italian father and an African-American mother, and he grew up in Philadelphia. While Robinson had loathed his partial season in the Negro Leagues, Campanella had quit school at 16 to join the Baltimore Elite Giants, where he played from 1937 to 1946, when he was signed as a minor leaguer by Branch Rickey.

Campanella is remembered by teammates and friends as a jovial man, one who enjoyed a joke and who was determined to appreciate the simple pleasures of life. His son, Roy Campanella II, once said of his father, "He always tried to be upbeat, and his motto in dealing with the injustices of the world was that living well was the best revenge."

Campanella's path to the big leagues was a bit easier than Robinson's. While Jackie broke in at Montreal and spent most of the season as the lone black player in his league, Campanella and Don Newcombe, then a promising 19-year-old prospect, played at Nashua, New Hampshire, and had each other for support in their pioneering experiences. Campy went to Montreal in '47, where he followed in Robinson's footsteps, as he would in '48, when he became a Dodger.

Rather than the common experiences of the two men drawing them together, they seemed to serve only to illustrate the differences between them. Journalist Sam Lacy commented, "Campanella resented

Jackie. . . . Whenever there was a group of people who came to circle around us, they always went to Jackie. They'd run past Campanella, and I think he resented it. Jackie was a symbol. . . . They went to Jackie, because he was theirs."

Historian Arnold Rampersad noted, "Campanella played one way and lived another. Dominant behind the plate, he seldom challenged white men outside this sphere, and in general deferred to Jim Crow. His easygoing manner won him friends; their white teammates respected Jack and Roy, but also loved Campanella."

Dodger traveling secretary Harold Parrott told a story that illustrated the difference between the two players. He termed it the "only time I thought Robinson was close to saying the hell with it and quitting." When the team bus stopped near a roadside restaurant in spring training of 1948, Robinson and Campanella were not welcomed into the dining facilities. Parrott had to personally carry food out to the bus. He remembered Robinson being "politely grateful—but seething at the put down." Parrott wondered, "[W]hat was the good of all the 'big experiment' when here he was, still on the outside?" He also remembered Campanella "pleading to avoid a scene" and then "laying aside his fat cigar with all the éclat of an orchestra leader putting down his baton" before he "tore into the meal." Robinson, wrote Parrott, "didn't touch a bite."

The divide between the two grew deeper after the 1949 season when Robinson led a barnstorming tour that included Campanella and many other contemporary players, including Newcombe and Cleveland's Larry Doby. Robinson received a much larger share of the profits from the tour than the others, and when they learned this, the group confronted Robinson. He didn't apologize, telling them, "I made my deal, you made your deal, and I can't be responsible." Author William Kashatus wrote, "Campanella returned home $5,000 richer but resentful of Jackie, who he felt had exploited him." He concluded, "Like all heroes, Jackie Robinson was disappointingly human."

But it was Robinson who was disappointed in the next deep fissure between the two stars. In 1954, Robinson decided that he was going to integrate the Chase Hotel in St. Louis. In his previous trips to St. Louis, he and other black teammates had stayed at the Adams Hotel, which lacked air-conditioning, among the other accoutrements that greeted the white Dodgers. Pee Wee Reese recalled Robinson getting off the train in St. Louis and telling him, "I'm going to the Chase with you." Reese recalled the other black Dodgers—Campanella, Newcombe, and Jim Gilliam—trying to talk Robinson out of that decision, but Robinson refused to budge.

Newcombe later related that he and Robinson had integrated the Chase in 1954. Campanella, though, remembered that in 1955, after Robinson had integrated the Chase, he approached Campanella, who continued to stay at the Adams. Robinson told Campy that "winning a victory over the Chase Hotel" was a significant step in that it signified the Dodgers "really becoming a team with all members . . . treated equally." Campanella rebuffed Robinson, mumbling, "I'm no crusader."

Campanella later claimed that his decision to stay at the Adams was based on the fact that even the "integrated" Chase still barred blacks from eating in the dining room, sitting in the lobby, or swimming in the pool. He remembered telling Robinson, "I've been coming to St. Louis for seven years and if they didn't want me all this time, then I don't want them now."

For a variety of reasons, Campanella was often at odds with Robinson. The relationship only thawed after Campy was paralyzed in an auto accident in January 1958. The two men grew closer with age, with Robinson asking Campanella to contribute to his 1964 book *Baseball Has Done It*, in which each man spoke frankly about his experiences with integration.

Perhaps the best story about the dueling natures of Campanella and Robinson comes from Don Newcombe. He recalled, "As much as Roy helped me, one of the reasons I was successful as I was had to be Jackie." Newcombe recalled a game in which the Dodgers led the Pirates 11-0 in the third inning. Letting up with a big lead, Newcombe quickly loaded the bases with no one out. Robinson came over and told him, "You should go to the clubhouse and take your uniform off and go home, because you don't want to pitch. You've got no business here in the big leagues, Newk. You ought to go home because here you are, fooling around." Newcombe got angry, struck out the side, and cruised to a victory. Robinson told him after the game, "I knew that you could be a better pitcher when I made you mad, and I made you mad on purpose." Remembering his combative teammate, Newcombe admitted, "Many times I wanted to take a punch at him. Shit, Jackie'd kick the shit out of me."

Newcombe continued, "Now Roy is a different type of man. If you talk about Jackie and Roy, you're mixing apples and oranges. . . . And I put Pee Wee in the same category as Roy. Soft-spoken." Biographers recalled Campanella encouraging Newcombe during difficult stretches, chattering out to him, "It's just you and me, roomie!" or "You're going to win this one." The big pitcher admitted, "I'd call Campy a stabilizer. Roy stabilized fractious attitudes on the team, especially between Jackie and me."

The variety of personalities within the Dodgers kept things interesting, but it was ultimately Reese who was the glue within the team. As the captain, he waved the other starters out onto Ebbets Field before the first pitch. As the 1940s turned into the 1950s, the mix of talented young players gave the Dodgers one of the best teams in baseball. In the 10 years that Reese and Robinson played together in Brooklyn, the Dodgers claimed six NL pennants, and in two other years, they missed them in their last game of the season.

However, the rub for Robinson, Reese, and the rest of the Dodgers was their inability to get over the hump that was the Yankee dynasty and claim a Dodger World Series title. Not for nothing was the rallying cry of the borough "Wait 'Til Next Year." The current year always seemed to come up just short, and for competitive, proud athletes like Reese and Robinson, the near-misses wear difficult to bear.

In Robinson's rookie year of 1947, the Dodgers took the Yankees to seven games before falling in the decisive game, 5-2. Robinson and

Reese were a combined 0-for-7 in that final game. In 1949, the Yankees blew past the Dodgers in five games.

The year 1952 looked as though it could be the breakthrough season in the Series. Reese batted .345, and again the Dodgers pushed the Yankees to a decisive seventh game. With the Yankees clinging to a 4-2 lead in the seventh inning and the bases loaded, Robinson had perhaps the most important at-bat of his career to date. He popped the ball up on the infield, but gusting breezes and the momentary confusion of the Yankees made the play an adventure. The tying and lead runs sprinted toward home for the Dodgers as the Yankees stood stupefied. At the very last instant, second baseman Billy Martin rushed in and snagged Robinson's pop-up ankle-high on a dead run. The Dodgers didn't threaten again, and the 4-2 score was the final.

In 1953, Robinson batted .320, but the Dodgers again dropped the Series to the Yankees in six games.

By the time the 1955 World Series came around, Jackie Robinson was not the same player he had been—and neither was Pee Wee Reese. Robinson failed to make the All-Star team for the first time since 1948, played in just 105 games, and found himself spending most of his time at third base. Reese similarly ended a streak of All-Star appearances that had stretched back to his World War II military service. He hit a respectable .282 and finished ninth in the NL MVP voting, but it was his last good year as well.

Robinson's Series was particularly unproductive, as he hit just .182, although he did electrify the crowd by stealing home in Game 1 of the Series. When the Series perhaps inevitably extended to a Game 7, Walter Alston did not put Robinson in the lineup, starting Don Hoak at third base. The Dodgers scored single runs in the fourth and sixth innings, with Reese scoring the second tally on a Gil Hodges sacrifice fly. In the bottom of the sixth, Dodger manager Walter Alston removed second baseman Don Zimmer, moved Gilliam to second base to fill his spot, and inserted Cuban outfielder Sandy Amoros into left field.

When the first two Yankee batters of the sixth reached base and lefty Yogi Berra sliced a vicious line drive that looked destined for the left field corner, it was the speedy Amoros who flagged the ball down and turned it into a double play. Amoros had the advantage of being a left-handed fielder, so Berra's drive sliced toward his glove rather than away from a right-handed player like Gilliam. Of course, there was a certain sad irony in the fact that if Robinson could not be on the field for the pivotal play, it was made by a dark-skinned player who may well not have been on the field at all if not for Robinson.

Rookie pitcher Johnny Podres held the 2-0 lead, and the final Yankee out came when Elston Howard, the first African-American Yankee, hit a grounder to Reese. Podres recalled, "When I saw the ball heading for Pee Wee, I couldn't help but thinking how ironic it was that all those years Pee Wee had been trying to beat the Yankees, and now the final out of Brooklyn's first world championship was going to Pee Wee." As he had throughout his career, Reese made the play under pressure and ended the wait for next year. The Dodgers were champions.

Reese and Robinson were together for only one more year. In 1956, Reese's average slid to .257 and he was in his last year as a starting regular. Robinson rebounded to .275 from a .256 mark the previous year, and played in 117 games, but the two friends were becoming old men. They reached one more World Series, but again lost in seven games to the Yankees, despite Jackie winning Game 6 with a walk-off hit to score Gilliam.

After the season, the Dodgers traded Robinson to the Giants for Dick Littlefield and $35,000. Robinson had already decided to retire, although he had just signed his new employment contract with Chock Full o'Nuts when he learned of the trade. Because of a deal he had made with *Look* magazine to carry the exclusive news of his retirement, Robinson sat quietly for a few weeks, even posing for some publicity shots with a Giants pennant. But he was gone.

A year later, so were the Dodgers, the team leaving Ebbets Field for Los Angeles after 1957. Reese batted .224 that year and posted an identical batting average in his final season, 1958. And slowly, Brooklyn's vaunted Boys of Summer faded away. Robinson and Reese retired, Campanella was paralyzed, Newcombe looked lost in L.A. and was promptly traded to the Reds. The younger Dodgers remained—Snider, Hodges, and a shaky young pitcher who turned out to be Sandy Koufax.

Reese spent a season as a Dodger coach but then became a broadcaster, first with CBS for six seasons and then for three more years with NBC. He broadcast games for the Cincinnati Reds for two seasons before he settled into employment with Hillerich & Bradsby, the maker of Louisville Slugger baseball bats.

Occasionally, Reese and his former teammates ran into one another, although the first of many sad occasions for meeting came when Gil Hodges, then the manager of the New York Mets, died of a sudden heart attack in April 1972. Reese and Robinson were among the many mourners at the funeral, but when Robinson was led to a seat, he was surprised to hear Pee Wee's voice. "When I said hello, he apologized," Reese remembered. His health failing rapidly, and almost completely overtaken by blindness, Robinson told him, "Pee Wee, I just can't see."

But Robinson didn't have to see, because Pee Wee saw him. Pee Wee Reese had seen the hanging tree, had witnessed the destruction that hate brings, and when he needed to see another way, Jackie Robinson saw him. That is, perhaps, what teammates do. The beauty of the team concept lies in the fact that a group of men together are something greater than they could ever be apart. A great leader is first a great visionary, because he must see not what is, but what can be.

But a more telling version of the friendship between Reese and Robinson came in their final meeting, on October 15, 1972, just nine days before Robinson died. The two old friends were in Cincinnati for the World Series. It was Robinson's final public appearance. Reese and Joe Black, another old Dodger, were talking with Robinson, who was updating them about his ill health. Robinson talked about his vision problems and then said he would need to have his leg amputated.

Black and Reese were understandably horrified. Robinson was 53 years old, and in their minds he was doubtlessly still the eternally fierce athlete. And yes, he still was.

"I'll take a while and get an artificial leg," he told the men. "And I'll learn to walk and I'll play golf, and you know what, Pee Wee? I'll still beatcha."

In 1984, Reese was elected to the Baseball Hall of Fame. The final sentence on his plaque reads, "Instrumental in easing acceptance of Jackie Robinson as baseball's first black performer."

Reese battled cancer in the late 1990s before passing away on August 14, 1999. He was survived by his wife, Dottie, of 57 years, and their two children. He is buried at Rest Haven Memorial Cemetery in Louisville, the hometown he adopted as a child. While the Meade County landmark that changed his life is nearby, most of the world has traveled many miles from that hanging tree. Pee Wee saw that path to a better way and helped a multicultural Dodger squad blaze it into reality. He was the Captain—or more accurately, he truly became the Captain after he became friends with Jackie Robinson.

Chapter Nine

DIXIE WALKER: "I FEEL LIKE I'VE LEARNED."

Fred had a dilemma, one which many fathers of teenaged girls face at some point in time. His 17-year-old daughter, Susan, had met a boy—well, not so much a boy as a man in the eyes of Fred. She had received a letter from a 22-year-old graduate student she had bumped into at the University of Notre Dame. He was northern, Irish, and Catholic. Fred—and thus his daughter also—was southern, from English ancestry, and, well, not Catholic. These matters may not seem earth-shattering today, but they were of greater significance in Alabama in 1960.

Susan wanted to go North herself, to attend college, and to at least answer the letter from that nice boy she had met at Notre Dame. Fortunately, she had an ally in her mother, Estelle, who was herself a Yankee and a Catholic, albeit one who had to marry Fred outside of her faith because he was not Catholic. Against her father's wishes, Susan did go North, attending St. Mary's of the Woods in Terre Haute, Indiana. When she got off the train from Birmingham, the graduate student, Ed, and his best friend were there to meet her. Five years later, she married Ed.

Susan and Ed have enjoyed a long and healthy marriage, with five children of their own. In time, Fred came to admit his error. "Eventually he told her that he had been wrong on both counts," recalled Ed, referring to both Susan's education and her marriage. "He didn't mind admitting he was wrong and he offered apologies."

People change. The art of changing people takes not only great lives colliding with ordinary ones, but it also takes maturity, honesty, and wisdom from the changed. Perhaps people should be more remembered for learning than for failing to have known the difficult lessons in the first place.

Fred lived 71 years and was a successful businessman and a respected community member. His life could be remembered for the number of wise decisions he made—such as marrying Estelle, who again, grew up in very different circumstances than those he knew or understood. He might be remembered for having the courage to ply his chosen vocation, despite the admonition of his own mother, "You'll never make any money. Your father never did." He could be remembered for setting up a hardware business with his brother in part to keep that same father happy, self-sufficient, and off the bottle. He could be remembered for making friends with a local Catholic priest, who agreed to a second marriage ceremony for Fred and Estelle years later, this time sanctioned by the church she knew and loved. He could be remembered for spending his time and energy helping to establish a pension plan for older baseball players, or for coaching younger players to success in the later years of his life.

He isn't. Fred "Dixie" Walker is most remembered for the decision that he himself came to call "the dumbest thing I did in all my life." Dixie Walker is the man best known for resisting Jackie Robinson's integration of the major leagues. Walker's own comments and moreover his life after 1947 attest to the fact that he did not maintain the attitudes about African Americans that he held pre-Robinson. Indeed, before the 1947 season was over, the player who had asked to be traded, who had apparently started a petition to keep Robinson off the Dodgers, was the same player who asked Branch Rickey to allow him to withdraw his trade request. Instead, a trade that probably had much more to do with aging talent than with racial equality helped cast him as an eternal scapegoat.

As an elderly man, Walker freely admitted his mistake. He spent his own years of baseball penance, the man who had decried against playing alongside of black players using his time and talent to coax the best hitting performances out of young batters, many of whom happened to be black. But the historical die had been cast. If the Robinson story is chock-full of heroes, Dixie Walker became a villain.

Frederick Ewart "Dixie" Walker was born in a log cabin in Villa Rica, Georgia, on September 24, 1910. Walker's paternal grandparents were English, and they had immigrated to the United States in 1886. A year later, their son, Ewart Gladstone Walker, who was Dixie's father, was the first of his family to be born in America. Ewart was born in Pennsylvania, but early in his childhood the family moved to Alabama in search of warmer climes and better jobs.

The Walkers were miners, and it was an escape from the coal industry that doubtlessly drove Ewart Walker to baseball. He was a big, hard-throwing, right-handed pitcher, whose sandlot acumen drew the notice of the Washington Senators. After a couple of years in the minor leagues, young Ewart, who was himself promptly nicknamed "Dixie" in celebration of his southern heritage, made the Senators roster in 1909. While the emphasis of Walker's southern-ness may seem odd, as he was born in Pennsylvania practically just off the boat from Britain, it is worth noting that he was likely the first major-league player from Alabama.

Ewart was pitching in Washington when Dixie (although no one applied this nickname to him for many years) was born at his grandparents' home in Georgia. Ewart quickly became another has-been Washington Senator, as a sore arm drove him from big-league baseball after four seasons with a 25-31 lifetime record. His brother Ernie spent three seasons with the St. Louis Browns.

Ewart soon became a minor-league coach and manager and supplemented that income by returning to the mines in the offseason. As a result, his wife, Flossie, drew a fairly narrow opinion of professional baseball. The game had taken some of the best years of Ewart's life, and sent him home as a dream-chasing miner with a penchant for the bottle.

As young Dixie grew, his mother pushed him away from baseball. He quit school early, and was quickly pursuing a life of backbreaking labor by either age 13 or age 15, depending on which accounting is correct. His daughter, Susan, noted, "My dad never really had a normal childhood. . . . Flossie used to tell him the mines would always be steady work, not like that baseball." Walker himself later recalled working in a

Birmingham steel mill, telling an interviewer, "I really believe that all that lifting work . . . strengthened my forearms for hitting a baseball."

Perhaps it was the game in his bloodlines. Perhaps it was the opportunity to escape from horrific labor. In any case, baseball soon got into Fred's heart. He played for the Tennessee Coal and Iron Company and found his own path into the game. He was at first a shortstop, a lefty at the plate and right-handed in the field. But his team added a new player, Ben Chapman, who pushed Walker into the outfield, where his baseball future lay.

Incidentally, Chapman would become a longtime friend and a future big leaguer himself. He and Walker played together for the New York Yankees, and Chapman became the manager of the Philadelphia Phillies by 1947, just in time to become even more infamous than Walker as the foremost persecutor of Jackie Robinson. But that was all some years in the future at this time.

Dixie Walker was approached by a scout of the Birmingham Barons, who asked him if he would like to try out. The scout invited Walker to a two-week tryout, but TCI wouldn't let him off work. "I decided if they wouldn't let me off, I'd get laid off," Walker later recalled. While operating a crane, he carelessly dropped a vat of hot metal. He was laid off for two weeks without pay. "The next day, I went to work out with the Barons," he recalled.

His mother was furious—some say she drew from him a pledge that if he wasn't a big leaguer in three seasons, he would give up the game. In any case, the game did not immediately cover Fred with glory. The 17-year-old played a few games in Greensboro, North Carolina, then a few in Albany, Georgia, and was sent on to Gulfport, Mississippi. He hit everywhere he played—batting .293 at Gulfport, where he spent most of the season. He had netted a $500 signing bonus and a $130 monthly salary, and still his mother warned him, "You'll never make any money."

He didn't make much quickly, as he hit .318 in Vicksburg in 1929 with just two home runs. But in 1930, at 19 years old, starting to grow into an adult physique, Dixie's hitting came on in a hurry. Splitting the season between Greenville and Jersey City, he hit .367 with 35 doubles,

19 triples, and 18 home runs. Moreover, the move to Jersey City had been engineered by the powerhouse New York Yankees, who had signed him in midseason. It was in Jersey City that an enterprising journalist, Jim Ogle, connected Fred Walker with his father Ewart, the original "Dixie" Walker, and applied the same nickname to the younger Walker. Call him whatever you would, Walker looked destined to be the next great Yankee star.

Baseball is an eternally humbling game, and even for those select few with the ability to compete at the highest level, the sport can create twists and turns that could hardly be anticipated, much less endured. Dixie Walker's odyssey with the Yankees was just such an experience. After impressing the Yankees in spring training of 1931, Walker found himself promoted to the big-league squad two weeks into the season after injuries sidelined Babe Ruth and other normal Yankee outfielders. Walker went 3 for 10, and then went back to Toledo a few weeks later.

He spent most of 1931 and 1932 simply awaiting his chance. He always hit—.305 in 1931, and .350 in 1932, with 105 RBIs earning him an All-Star spot—but at the Newark Bears' International League squad, not the Yankees' American League group.

Finally, in 1933, Walker became a regular starter for the Yankees and made much of his chances. In 98 games, he hit .274 with 15 home runs in 328 at-bats. But that was basically the extent of Walker's run as a Yankee. He injured his shoulder late in the 1933 season, crashing into a catcher at home plate and dislocating it. Given his relative inexperience, Walker tried to play through the pain. He told one interviewer years later that Yankee manager Joe McCarthy "hated to see a ball player on the rubbing table" and thus, Walker toughed out the remainder of his 1933 season.

While stardom was again forecast for him in 1934, he instead was unable to play, reinjuring his shoulder, apparently by sliding into second base in an exhibition game. His spot on the Yankees was reserved to merely pinch-hitting and pinch-running on occasion, going 2 for 17 at the plate for the entire season. The healing was slow, and Walker was so desperate that at one point, he had his tonsils removed (for the second time) in the belief that it would help his shoulder heal. Nothing really did seem to help.

In early 1935, Walker again injured his throwing shoulder and was given little chance to contribute by the Yankees. He batted 13 times for the Yankees that year, but when he was sent to Newark, he again produced, hitting .293 with 17 home runs.

In May 1936, Walker was now five years removed from his initial call-up with the Yankees. He batted a total of 388 times as a Yankee, spending most of his time either trying to nurse his eternally injured arm back to health or in Newark. A less determined man might have given up altogether. After all, the elder Dixie Walker was driven from big-league ball by a sore arm at a similar point his career.

But Walker was persistent, a quality that served him well off the field. By May 1936, he had met and even become engaged to a New York native, Estelle Shea, who was the assistant to talent scout Sonny Werblin at the Music Corporation of America talent agency, which produced *Your Hit Parade*, on which Shea often worked. Shea's vocation kept her involved in the society of the city, and her daughter noted, "She was on a first name basis with legendary performers—Harry James, George Gershwin, Ira Gershwin, Benny Goodman, Glenn Miller, and many others. She knew them, she knew their wives, she knew their families."

People who remember her and Walker indicate that the vast differences between the two somehow cemented their relationship. She was city; he was country. She was northern; he was southern. She was a Roman Catholic, and he, while more or less unaffiliated, was not Catholic. She, accustomed to the high life of the city, didn't mind to spend a dollar. He, with his mother's warnings still ringing in his ears, preferred to save. But they loved each other, and their relationship went from serious to very serious on May 1, 1936.

On that day, the Chicago White Sox claimed Walker on waivers from the Yankees. A new team, a new city, and a new start sounded appealing to Walker, but he knew who he didn't want to leave behind. The following day, he and Estelle were married by a justice of the peace, and he went with her to her office, where he told Sony Werblin that Estelle was leaving the city and her job for her new life.

Unfortunately for the Walkers, Dixie's beginning in Chicago resembled his last five years in New York. Given the opportunity to play every day, Walker was hitting .296 for the year, but after three weeks, he collided with Browns first baseman Jim Bottomley, again dislocating his shoulder and knocking him out for most of the season.

Finally, Walker got the treatment he needed—fairly revolutionary shoulder surgery from Dr. Phil Kreucher of Chicago, who basically constructed a new shoulder socket for Walker. At least one biographer compared the extent and revolutionary nature of the procedure to Tommy John ligament replacement that came about 40 years later. And after years of bouncing from injury to injury, in 1937, Dixie Walker was finally ready to play.

In his first full season, Walker played every game for Chicago, hitting .302, leading the AL with 16 triples, and knocking in 95 runs. It was the kind of season that validated Walker's patience in light of his multitude of injuries. It was the kind of season that should have made him a Chicago icon, particularly after the White Sox managed a third-place finish that season, ahead of their usual pace.

Instead, it got Walker traded to Detroit, allegedly after he declined a salary hike that was tied to the team's attendance. Instead, Walker's salary went from $6,000 with the White Sox to $10,000 with the Tigers (roughly $180,000 in current value). Walker's popularity also went from fairly high to rock bottom, due to no fault of his own, but because the trade to obtain him sent Gee Walker from Detroit to Chicago. Tiger fans disdained the loss of Gee and took it out on Dixie, booing him throughout his Tiger tenure.

For his part, Dixie hit .308 twice in Detroit—in 127 games in 1938, and then in a shorter span in 1939, due to a torn knee ligament that sidelined him for much of the season. Still taking heat from their fan base for the loss of Gee Walker, the Tigers decided after the injury to cut their losses, and so left Dixie available on the waiver wire, where he was snapped up on July 24th by the Brooklyn Dodgers.

The change in the career of Dixie Walker which followed was remarkable—in fact, it was one of the preeminent baseball stories of the early 1940s. Had Jackie Robinson integrated baseball in some other city or in some other time, the story of Dixie Walker becoming a Brooklyn icon would be his legacy. Even as it is, the halcyon days of Dixie and the Bums are worth a second look.

⌒

In 1939, Larry MacPhail had taken control of the Dodgers, and given the woebegone nature of the Brooklyn franchise, he was determined to deliver a team better known for good baseball than for hijinks and antics. At that point in time, the Dodgers' last pennant had come in 1920, and they hadn't even finished in the upper half of the National League since 1932.

MacPhail picked up young prospects like Hugh Casey, Pete Reiser, and Pee Wee Reese. He traded for Kirby Higbe, and signed Joe Medwick. And he claimed Dixie Walker from Detroit. Walker had known New York from his years with the Yankees. Or more accurately, he had known the Bronx, and the Yankees' stuffy insistence on superiority. And when he met Brooklyn, with leather-lunged Hilda Chester and the Dodger Sym-ph-ony, tiny Ebbets Field, and a tradition of aiming not so much to succeed as to at least fail colorfully, well, it was the start of something special.

Walker batted .280 over the remainder of 1939, and Brooklyn manager Leo Durocher reluctantly installed him in center field. Walker and Durocher never got along, but the relationship of convenience solidified as Walker stayed healthy and productive and helped the Dodgers to the relative highlight of a third-place finish in the NL.

In 1940, Walker became a Brooklyn star. He batted .308 with 37 doubles in 143 games, and so complete was his comeback to health and top form that he finished sixth in NL Most Valuable Player balloting. When he hit well over .400 that season in head-to-head competition against the hated Giants, the relationship between Walker and Brooklyn became almost familial. Within the next year, news stories began to surface that called Walker first "The People's Choice" and then, in an affectionate Brooklynese corruption, "The People's Cherce."

The feeling was mutual. Walker later said, "Those . . . years I spent in Brooklyn were my favorite seasons in baseball. The people just were so kind to me and I grew so close to them." Indeed, Walker put down roots in the community, buying a liquor store and using the offseason to make a few dollars speaking to small groups of his baseball experiences, often surprising them with a song in the bargain. He kept his usual residence in Birmingham and opened a hardware store there, but during the season he, Estelle, and soon their children lived in Rockville Center.

Not everyone was as enamored of the Walker/Brooklyn pairing as Dixie and his loyal fans were. Durocher, always looking to replace Walker, engineered the signing of Pirate legend Paul Waner after the 1940 season, and announced that Waner would play over Walker. Brooklyn was outraged, with a petition supporting Walker drawing 5,000 signatures.

Waner was over the hill, and eventually Walker found his way back to starting in right field, where he promptly helped lead the Dodgers to the NL pennant. Playing in 148 games, Walker batted .311 with nine home runs, 71 RBIs, and a 10th-place finish in the NL MVP voting. After a decade in the major leagues, Walker had finally experienced consecutive seasons both healthy and playing for the same team. The results were hard to argue with.

The war years only deepened Brooklyn's regard for Walker and provided him with additional chances to earn the love of his appreciative followers. While the war did tap the baseball talent pool, any medical examiner who had read the sports pages knew that Walker was an incredibly brittle person with a laundry list of serious injuries. Accordingly, it was not surprising that he was classified 4F during the war and spent the duration with the Dodgers.

Brooklyn did not win another pennant during the war, but they finished second in 1942 and third in both 1943 and 1945. While 1944 was hardly a golden season for the Dodgers, whose roster was ravaged by the military and who thus fielded half a roster of has-beens or never-would-bes, it went swimmingly for Walker. He batted .357, which won him the NL batting crown, adding 13 home runs and 91 RBIs. He finished third in the MVP voting for the seventh-place Dodgers, and was the starting right fielder for the National League in the All-Star game.

While Walker could not fight in the war, he did join a USO-run entertainment program after the 1944 season, spending much of his off-season in public service. The following year, he "slumped" to a .300 average, but he also led the National League with 124 RBIs. Walked turned 35 years old just before the end of that season and was regarded as one of the sure things on a Dodger team that was completely retooling after the war. He was a popular star athlete, a man beloved in his home city, and that city fervently hoped for more pennants, maybe even a World Series title with Walker in the middle of things.

One day in October 1945, Walker's telephone rang at his home in Birmingham. Walker had been busy, taking advantage of some downtime to paint his house. The reporter asked Walker if he was aware of the signing of Jackie Robinson. Walker admitted that he was not, but pointed out that Robinson had apparently signed with the Montreal Royals team. "As long as he isn't with the Dodgers, I'm not worried," said Walker, and presumably went back to painting his house, unaware that his life had changed forever.

In 1946, Jackie Robinson wasn't with the Dodgers, and Dixie Walker still was. Not only did the two men not play together, they would have barely seen each other in spring training. Walker continued his fine play, making the All-Star team again, batting .319 and knocking in 116 runs. He finished second to St. Louis' Stan Musial in the NL MVP voting, reversing the batting race of 1944 where he had finished first and Musial came second.

Not only in Brooklyn was Walker popular. When the Major League Baseball Players Association was established in 1946, Walker was chosen as Brooklyn's representative and also the representative for the entire National League. In the beginnings of baseball's early labor stirrings, the group set out to establish a pension plan for big-league players, which was completed the next season.

The Dodgers challenged for the NL pennant but lost to the Cardinals in a playoff after the season. Some speculation was that Robinson, who was having a fine year with Montreal, should have been called up to the Dodgers in September. Rickey apparently didn't feel that would be fair conditions to integrate baseball, and so for another season, the status quo prevailed. But things changed in a hurry in 1947.

The battling of Walker and Robinson famously began during spring training of 1947. Kirby Higbe apparently got drunk one night and confided in Dodger traveling secretary Harold Parrott that a petition either had been created or was being created with an aim toward keeping Robinson off the team. The common story had Higbe telling Parrott, "The old man [Rickey] has been fair to Ol' Hig. Ol' Hig ain't going to join any petition."

The very existence of the petition is still a matter of uncertain record. At least once, Walker denied not only his involvement in the existence of such a document, but as far as his knowledge extended, any awareness of same. On another occasion, he apparently admitted signing it. The recollections of others involved are just as tangled.

Pee Wee Reese recalled being asked by Walker, whom he acknowledged was "one of my best friends on the ballclub," if he would "sign that I wouldn't play with a black man." Reese continued, "I looked at it, and I just flatly refused. I just said, 'Hey look, man, I just got out of the service after three years. I don't care if this man is black, blue or what the hell color he is. I have to play ball.'" Reese recollected Pete Reiser being in the room and also being approached by Walker.

Reiser related that he told Walker of an experience he had in the army when he was in Richmond, Virginia. His daughter had gotten sick and so Reiser had telephoned a doctor, who told him to bring his daughter down. When he arrived, the doctor was African American. Reiser recalled, "I didn't think anything of it. What the hell was the difference?" The doctor treated the child, who got better. Reiser told the story to Walker and asked him what he would have done. Walker said he would have walked away from the black doctor. Reiser remembered, "I told him I thought he was a Goddamned fool, and then I told him what he could do with his petition."

Duke Snider remembered being approached with a petition, down to the wording of it, which according to the Duke was, "I will not participate in a game that Jackie Robinson is in the lineup." Snider related, "[N]obody signed it. Just the four guys that took the petition around, they were the only ones that signed it. They brought it to me and I said, 'What are you talking about?'" Snider had grown up watching Robinson excel in several sports, and rather than resisting, he was excited to have Robinson as a teammate.

Higbe, who was apparently responsible for leaking word of the petition to Dodger management, oddly enough recalled signing the petition. He admitted, "I felt real bad about this," and recalled discussing the matter and signing the document, reasoning curiously, "I said to myself, 'What's the difference? It ain't gonna hurt nobody.' So I signed." Higbe noted that a group of Dodgers had gone to Branch Rickey with their objections to Robinson, and that the group had originally been him, Walker, Bobby Bragan, Carl Furillo, and Pee Wee Reese, who quickly changed his mind about Robinson.

Furillo initially denied having anything to with a petition, but did admit ultimately that he had not only seen but signed such a document. Furillo related that Ed Head, Hugh Casey, and Dixie Howell were the players who had approached him with the document. "They said if I didn't sign it the niggers would have my job. I signed it," recalled Furillo.

Backup catcher Bobby Bragan, who was one of the few Dodgers who would admit that his initial inclination was against Robinson, was often cited as a signer of the petition. Bragan admitted to resisting integration and to asking Branch Rickey to trade him, but he denied any knowledge of the petition.

Truculent infielder Eddie Stanky would have been a likely candidate to join a petition. Stanky famously told Robinson during the 1947 season, "You're on this ball club and as far as I'm concerned that makes you one of 25 players on my team. But before I play with you I want you to know how I feel about it. I want you to know I don't like it. I want you to know I don't like you." Stanky is generally absolved from the petition, but author Roger Kahn does include Stanky on the list of signers.

In any case, a handful of Dodgers felt strongly enough about keeping Robinson off the team that they were willing to take some sort of definitive action. For their troubles, they were first rebuffed by Leo Durocher, and second, Branch Rickey met individually with each of the men who were holdouts.

Some remembered the meetings as individual affairs; others indicated that it was a meeting of the small group. But regardless of the details of who was or wasn't present, the message that was delivered was apparently uniform. If anybody didn't want to play with Jackie Robinson, they could be traded. Of the group, only Bobby Bragan became famous for candidly admitting that yes, he would in fact prefer to be traded. Little was said of Walker's meeting with Rickey.

Dixie himself professed to have been taken unaware by Rickey. He was gone from spring training because of an illness in his family when the Robinson storm broke. When he caught up with the team in Havana, he recalled Rickey sitting him down in the Hotel Nacional. "He really reamed me out," recalled Walker in 1981. "I was so mad at him accusing me of being a ringleader [in the move against Robinson] that a few days later, I wrote him . . . requesting to be traded."

Unlike the petition, unlike any accurate accounting of those who were opposed to Robinson, Walker's letter has survived. It is remarkable in both its brevity and its vagueness, and the facts fit both the version given by Walker and that generally accepted by others, which is that the sole impetus behind the letter was the oncoming call-up of Robinson to the Dodgers. It reads:

March 26, 1947

Dear Mr. Rickey

Recently the thought has occurred to me that a change of Ball clubs would benefit both the Brooklyn Baseball club and myself. Therefore I would like to be traded as soon as a deal can be arranged.

My association with you, the people of Brooklyn, the press and Radio has been very pleasant and one I can truthfully say I am sorry has to end. For reasons I don't care to go into I feel my decision is best for all concerned.

Very sincerely yours,
Dixie Walker

Walker would later clarify his admittedly flawed reasoning for not wanting to play with Robinson. In 1976, he supposedly told author Roger Kahn, "I organized that petition in 1947, not because I had anything against Robinson personally or against Negroes generally. I had a wholesale hardware business in Birmingham and people told me I'd lose my business if I played ball with a black man." Dixie's brother, Harry Walker, who became a successful player and manager himself, once said, "We didn't have much contact with black folks, and when Dixie said what he did it was like a man seeing a green door and not wanting to open it because you didn't know what was behind it. I think we just didn't know what it would be like when the blacks came into baseball."

When Bobby Bragan discussed his own prejudice years later, his reasoning was along the same lines as Walker's. Author Jonathan Eig wrote, "Bragan's biggest worry was how he would explain the circumstance to his friends and family back in Alabama." Bragan himself commented, "We just grew up segregated. People thought whites were supreme."

For that matter, Pee Wee Reese admitted to taking some flak from his own family and friends over his decision to play with Robinson. Reese went out of his way to expose his family to Robinson, because in time, Jackie won them over just as he had Pee Wee. But even for those inclined to see Robinson's side, getting around lifelong traditions of prejudice was a sticky matter.

While the sentiment of other players—particularly southern ones—may have aligned close to Walker's, Brooklyn fans didn't see things that way. Walker's disdain for the integration experiment was readily acknowledged. Wendell Smith, writing in the *Pittsburgh Courier*, summed up the attitude of various Dodgers in regard to Robinson and wrote of Walker, "He is against Robinson. Would rather have him elsewhere." Much the same news was carried from other sources. Suddenly, the "People's Choice" turned into the object of the people's booing, at least for a time. The Brooklyn *Daily Eagle* wrote on April 13, 1947, after an exhibition game, "The booing of Dixie Walker on the occasion of the Dodgers' first game at Ebbets Field this season was a disgraceful performance, linked as it was with the first appearance here of Jackie Robinson in action." Wendell Smith counseled patience, urging fans, "[D]on't go to Ebbets Field and boo players like Dixie Walker."

Branch Rickey was angry enough about Walker's salvo demanding to be traded that he was initially inclined to accommodate him. A memorandum survives written to Rickey from H. Roy Hamey of the Pittsburgh Pirates, reading, "Pittsburgh agrees to accept player Walker for $40,000 cash Gionfriddo and Kalin." But Rickey decided he needed more than $40,000 and a pair of reserve outfielders in exchange for Walker. Later in 1947, Rickey was close to moving Walker to Pittsburgh for $40,000 and pitcher Nick Strincevich, but around this time, outfielder Pete Reiser, as he had a bad habit of doing, nearly killed himself on an outfield wall, and Rickey again couldn't afford to part with Walker.

So for the time being, Robinson and Walker were Dodger teammates. On Opening Day, when photographers flocked to Ebbets Field and thought they might snap a photo of the two together, interim manager Clyde Sukeforth intervened. "I have tried to get you everything you need," he remembered telling the press, "but Walker is in business down South and it would not do him any good if his picture was in a news service photo." Sukeforth told this to Walker later, and recalled the latter saying, "That is exactly right. I would not object otherwise."

For his part, Robinson was fine leaving things in a deep thaw. During spring training, he admitted at one point that if the Dodgers didn't want him on the team, that he did not wish to impose. Teammates remembered him in 1947 as a rookie who tended to speak when spoken to, and not often otherwise. If many of the Dodgers were somewhat reluctant about their new teammate, they generally wouldn't remain so for very long.

Any tension within the Dodger team was quickly eclipsed by that coming from outside the team. Walker's old friend Ben Chapman is generally regarded as the most foul and virulent of the bench jockeys, based on both contemporary evidence and Robinson's later memories. Robinson said that the first game against the Phillies "brought me nearer to cracking up than I had ever been." Faced with torrential vulgarity and insults from Chapman and the Philadelphia team, he thought, "To hell with the image of the patient black freak I was supposed to create. I could throw down my bat, stride over to that Phillies dugout, grab one of those white sons of bitches and smash his teeth in with my despised black fist." But of course, Robinson realized that was exactly what Chapman and those like him wanted. He answered on the field—and his teammates began to rally to his cause.

It was Eddie Stanky, who had told Robinson that he didn't like him only weeks before, who eventually answered the barrage. "Listen, you yellow-bellied cowards," he shouted at the Phillies dugout. "Why don't you yell at somebody who can answer back?"

Some accounts have Walker approaching Chapman and telling him that he was going too far. In any case, popular indignation moved against Chapman, who found himself asking Robinson to pose for a publicity photo to help demonstrate that there were no hard feelings. The barely restrained hatred of each for the other practically leaps from the photograph—both men are handling the same bat, not even shaking hands. Walker, observing the scene, is alleged to have said, "I never thought I'd see Old Ben eat shit like that."

Chapman and Robinson would meet again. Fired as the Philadelphia manager, Chapman coached for the Reds in 1952. He made a cutting remark about Robinson to Pee Wee Reese during a spring training game that year. Robinson walked over and told him, "Look, Chapman, you son of a bitch. You got on me for two years and I couldn't say a word. Now you open your mouth to me one more time during this game, I'm gonna catch you and I'm gonna kick the shit out of you." Pee Wee Reese, who remembered the incident, stated, "Chapman did not say another word."

For all of the drama and hard feelings over the pairing of Robinson and Walker, the actual relationship between the two men, such as it was, was quiet and businesslike. In the Dodger clubhouse before an early-season game, Robinson was getting a pregame rubdown from the trainer and Walker approached Robinson with some hitting tips. Robinson recalled Walker offering tips on hitting behind runners, staying out of double plays, and shifting his feet for fly balls to the opposite field, "adding percentage points to my future batting average." Walker remembered offering Robinson "just a suggestion" and humbly noted, "I think it worked."

Many things worked, both for Robinson and for Walker, on the field. Walker related that his bat speed was declining in 1947, as he was increasingly hitting the ball to left field rather than pulling pitches. Still, he hit .306 with 94 RBIs. Robinson, of course, hit .297, stole 29 bases, and was voted Rookie of the Year. One of the first to acknowledge his role on the Dodgers was Walker. He told *The Sporting News* late in the season, "No other ballplayer on this club with the possible exception of Bruce Edwards has done more to put the Dodgers up in the race than Robinson has. He is everything Branch Rickey said he was when he came up from Montreal."

Indeed, with the Dodgers winning the pennant and Walker clearly growing more comfortable expressing support for Robinson, there was no reason that the players wouldn't continue playing together in 1948. Walker spoke to Rickey and essentially rescinded his trade request. But Walker's ultimate sin for Rickey wasn't racism as much as age. Always a proponent of trading a player a year early rather than a year late (this is the man who later tried to trade Stan Musial from the Cardinals), Rickey decided to move the 37-year-old Walker after the season, and eventually dealt him to the Pittsburgh Pirates on December 8th with pitchers Hal Gregg and Vic Lombardi in exchange for infielder Gene Mauch, pitcher Preacher Roe, and third baseman Billy Cox. In Rickey's defense, he offered Walker a job as manager of the Saint Paul squad before trading him. Walker felt he had a couple years of good baseball left and turned down the managerial job. Considering Rickey's support of Robinson, his moves to hire Bragan as a minor-league manager and to hire Walker suggests that he certainly didn't regard either man as a threat to the harmony of his integrated baseball teams.

But Walker became a Pittsburgh Pirate. He told the media, "Naturally I regret leaving Brooklyn. . . . In nine years with the Dodgers I made many close friends. I love those Brooklyn people." Obviously, Walker never said he loved Robinson. Walker would later recall him as "a very antagonistic person in many ways." He acknowledged, "Maybe he had to be to survive. . . . I don't know if I could have gone through what he did."

Time was not kind to Walker, and he subsequently had his own cross to bear. He was the man who didn't want Robinson on the Dodgers, who led the petition against him, who demanded to be traded, and ultimately was traded. And while much of that is misunderstood or overstated, it generally seems to be accurate. But of course, it wasn't the whole story. Walker may have been done with Robinson, but Robinson was not done with Walker. Or Bobby Bragan. Or Ben Chapman. Or America.

Dixie Walker's time in Pittsburgh was neither lengthy nor exceptionally memorable. Walker hit .316 for the Pirates in 1948 but was limited to 408 at-bats for a fourth-place Pittsburgh club. One highlight of his season was that on his first return visit to Ebbets Field, the Dodgers held a Dixie Walker Day and presented him with several gifts, including a new car. "Right field doesn't look right without Walker," proclaimed Judge Sam Leibowitz, in presenting the fans' tribute to Dixie. Walker knocked in two runs in an 8-4 Pirate victory.

But if Rickey's judgment that Walker's best days were past may have been a bit hasty, time caught up with Dixie all the same. In 1949, he played in only 88 games, and led the NL in pinch hits while posting a .282 overall mark in just 181 at-bats. Walker had been reluctant to return for the 1949 season and did so only when Pirates GM Fred Haney told him that after the season, he could choose among becoming manager or GM of the New Orleans minor-league squad, coaching for the Pirates, or becoming a scout. After the season, Walker asked Haney which job he could have. When Haney demurred, Walker saw the uncomfortable truth and said, "To hell with that. Just give me my pink slip and I'll go home."

Walker did not stay unemployed. Today, Walker is generally cast as a clubhouse cancer, but baseball GMs and owners often hurried to hire him. In December 1949, he was signed to manage the Atlanta Crackers of the Southern Association. In his first season, Walker led the Crackers to win their league pennant, and he led the team to a second-place finish in 1952. He became a coach with the St. Louis Cardinals in 1953, but he ended up managing their Houston minor-league affiliate. Walker went on to manage the Rochester Red Wings and the Toronto Maple Leafs, managing in the minor league for virtually the entire decade of the 1950s. Walker was 814-722 as a manager, and was successful enough that when the Dodger managerial job came open after the 1953 season, Walker's name was occasionally mentioned as the potential successor to Charlie Dressen. Certainly, this would have been interesting because it would have meant that Robinson would have been playing for Walker in Brooklyn.

Walker's path of penance would not go in that direction, as Walter Alston got the Dodger job. Instead, Walker continued to manage in the minors, but by 1959 he had grown tired of the job, and he quit Toronto a week before the end of the season. He became a scout, working under his old Dodger teammate Bobby Bragan in that capacity, and later as Bragan's hitting coach. He was out of baseball before he wrote a letter to Dodger owner Walter O'Malley late in 1968, volunteering his services. O'Malley and Alston decided to hire Walker to replace outgoing hitting coach Duke Snider as a Dodger after the 1968 season.

The year 1968 was a year of horrific turmoil in America—Martin Luther King Jr. and Robert Kennedy were felled by assassins, the Democratic National Convention broke out into riots, and Vietnam continued to cost an enormous toll both on American morale and the lives of American soldiers. But when Walker was hired by the Dodgers, it began his full-circle turn of redemption from the mistakes he had made in 1947. While 1968 was a dark year for America, it was a chance for Dixie Walker to begin making amends.

The men who had been opposed to Jackie Robinson changed their minds slowly. It wasn't as if one morning, these men woke up and realized that the southern creed and culture had betrayed their morality. It was in exposure to African Americans—starting with Robinson and continuing with a series of other baseball ambassadors—that the ignorance of bigotry melted into the intelligence of experience.

Even Ben Chapman, longtime friend of Walker and the bench-jockeying manager of the 1947 Phillies, was able to admit, "A man learns about things and mellows as he grows older. I think that maybe I've changed a bit." Chapman told the reporter, "[T]he world changes. Maybe I've changed too. Look, I'm real proud that I've raised my son different." Chapman went on to say that his son, a local football coach, coached black players. "And he gets along with them," said Chapman. "They like him. That's a nice thing, don't you think?"

Dodger resister Bobby Bragan became a major-league manager himself. The same obstinate qualities that had led him to face down Branch Rickey and tell him that no, actually, he did not intend to play with an African-American teammate had impressed Rickey. He later reflected, "He showed me a lot when he stood up for his beliefs in Panama. It made me believe in his future as a leader."

Bragan managed the Dodgers' Fort Worth affiliate in 1948, and he held the job until 1952. Rickey, who had moved on to Pittsburgh, hired Bragan to manage the Hollywood Stars, and then the Pirates themselves. Bragan was fired from Pittsburgh late in his second season, and although the Pirates won the World Series three years later, Bragan wasn't around to see it. He was back in the Dodger organization then, managing the Spokane Indians, where among his players was a young black player named Maury Wills.

Wills was not highly regarded by the Dodger brass and was perhaps more of a suspect than a prospect at this point in his career. Bragan helped change that, building up Wills's skills and confidence to the point where he could go on to become a Dodger star.

One day the two talked, and Wills asked Bragan why he hadn't wanted to play with Robinson. "I was just raised that way, Maury," Bragan confessed sadly. Wills knew a different Bobby Bragan. Author Michael Leahy wrote, "Wills would come to believe that Bragan was placed by God in Spokane to help him, and that he himself had been assigned to play in Spokane so that Bragan could teach him to switch-hit and make amends for the wrongs done to Robinson. . . . Bragan's life had taught him about the possibility for change and redemption."

"Bobby, don't worry about it," Wills said that day.

In 1959, Wills was a nobody with a manager who took him as something of a personal quest. In 1962, Wills was the National League Most Valuable Player, as well as an All-Star, a Gold Glover, and the first man in decades to steal 100 bases after he swiped 104.

Bragan wrote in Robinson's 1964 compendium on race and baseball, *Baseball Has Done It*, "My association with Maury Wills when I managed out in Spokane is one of my finest memories of this game." He continued, "I've had under my wing Roman Mejias, Roberto Clemente, Lino Dinoso . . . Henry and Tommy [Aaron] and many others. . . . All of this adds up to a tolerant attitude, a little more understanding of the situation than if we'd never left Alabama."

Of course, things changed in Alabama as well. George Wallace, the segregationist governor and sometimes presidential candidate, had pledged his eternal fidelity to the segregationist cause. Wallace was a figure well-loved by white Alabamans, and in fact, he inducted Dixie Walker into the Alabama Sports Hall of Fame in 1973. Wallace had his own slow conversion away from the segregationist cause, which he later said was well underway by the time of that induction dinner for Walker. Wallace was shot and paralyzed in 1972, and seven years later, in a speech at the Dexter Avenue Baptist Church in Montgomery, which had been bombed by bigots during his administration, he told a mostly African-American crowd, "I have learned what suffering means. . . . I know I contributed to that pain, and I can only ask your forgiveness." In another speech the same year, he admitted more directly, "I was wrong. Those days are over, and they ought to be over."

Dixie Walker's move toward equality was neither as dramatic as George Wallace's or as readily observable as Bobby Bragan's, but it was very much a real thing, and it made a tangible difference in the lives of many young African-American men. The same man who had rebelled against the idea of a black teammate spent the twilight years of his baseball career teaching the tricks of his hitting trade to ballplayers. Given the diversity that has always been a staple of the Dodger organization, Walker taught baseball to all players, white, black, Latino, and mixes between. It wasn't headline-grabbing work, but Walker invested himself in it, and he changed young lives.

Dodger center fielder Willie Davis was one quick study of Walker's methods. Davis had never hit .300 in a season in his first eight years, and he promptly did so in his first three years of working with Walker. He admitted at the time, "If I'd been swinging in past years the way I'm doing this spring, why I really believe I could be making $150,000 a year instead of $50,000 a year. You know all Dixie Walker has been doing is saying, 'Line drives. I want to see nothing but line drives.' And when I stop swinging from my heels it comes easy. I can do it." Davis's strikeout totals decreased, his batting average increased, and after the 1972 season, he signed for a $100,000 salary the following year.

Another Dodger who benefited from Walker's help was Jimmy Wynn. Wynn had struggled to get along with his manager in Houston, who was Dixie's brother, Harry. Dixie did his best to smooth over that issue, and then helped Wynn raise his batting average by 51 points and knock in 108 runs in his first year as a Dodger. "Our relationship has been beautiful," Walker told the media.

Dixie stepped down as the Dodgers' full-time hitting coach after the 1974 season, but he still worked as a minor-league instructor and would sometimes moonlight with the big-league club. In 1976, Walker worked throughout the spring with Dodger acquisition Dusty Baker. Walker was effusive in his praise of Baker, noting that the young outfielder had approached him on his first day at the team's Vero Beach training camp. "I find him a player who's determined to reach his potential," said Walker. Indeed, Baker became a two-time All-Star as a Dodger. He also became a manager, winning 1,863 games in that capacity, which currently ranks him 15th in the history of major-league baseball.

While Walker didn't make any sort of grand pronouncement about his views on race, he was honest when questioned about it. In spring training of 1972, he told columnist Ira Berkow, "My attitude has changed over the years. I feel like I've learned. You associate with Negro players, as a manager and a coach, day in and day out, and you get to know them like you do white players." Of course, the topic brought about a discussion of that first black player who Walker got to know, and he admitted, "I've grown and Jackie knows it."

When Robinson died later that year, Walker said, "I'm as sad as I possibly could be about his death. . . . At that time [1947] I was resentful of Jackie, and I make no bones about it. But he and I were shaking hands at the end."

In a 1981 interview, Walker observed, "[Robinson] had the instinct to always do the right thing on the field. He was a stem-winder of a ballplayer. But you know we never hit it off well. Over the years, though, Robinson and I would meet at Old-Timer's Day games and we sat and chatted some." Walker had recently seen a television program that had discussed various African-American civil rights pioneers, and he was surprised that Robinson was never even mentioned in the program.

"It surprised me," he said. "I mean, how soon people can forget."

⌒

Dixie Walker retired from baseball after 1976, and he returned home to Birmingham, where he died on May 17, 1982, of colon cancer. His widow, Estelle, survived him by 20 years, and he was also survived by three of his children. He was, unfortunately, also survived by the stigma of being the great villain of the Robinson story, the all-but-white-hooded outfielder who couldn't stand his black teammate.

If it is surprising how quickly some people do forget the monumental contributions of Jackie Robinson (1980s MLB star Vince Coleman feigned ignorance of who Robinson was less than a full generation after his death), it is perhaps somewhat surprising that people also forget the world that existed before Jackie Robinson changed it. Dixie Walker, Bobby Bragan, Ben Chapman, and George Wallace were all products of a different time and culture.

There were some men who played with or against Jackie Robinson who were wise enough, compassionate enough, or just plain lucky enough to give the man the benefit of a doubt. Pee Wee Reese is chief among those players, but there were others who became longtime friends and true teammates of Jackie Robinson. There were others who failed to avail themselves of that same opportunity, and by their own testimony and evidence, most of them spent the rest of their lives kicking themselves for their mistake.

George Wallace was fortunate enough to experience a public forgiveness from many of the people he wronged. When he said that he was wrong to stand in schoolhouse doors and pledge to keep out black students, many Alabamans chose to forgive him and honor his courage in changing the path of his life.

Bobby Bragan managed Maury Wills and Hank Aaron. Dixie Walker coached Willie Davis and Dusty Baker. Even Ben Chapman's son coached young African Americans with what had to be appreciably more restraint and fairness than his father had used as a manager.

Dixie Walker was a remarkable player, a man who built an excellent career out of perseverance and love of the game of baseball. He was a dedicated manager and coach, and helped establish the early pension plan that planted the seeds that grew into baseball's current economic boom. He is remembered for one tragic mistake. He repudiated the mistake, and he lived out his baseball career by the code that Jackie Robinson built—treating players equally regardless of color, and coaching based on work ethic and ability, not on complexion.

It is not for us to forgive Dixie Walker. It is not for us to remove his terrible mistake from history. But it is for us to see it not as the final word on his life, on baseball, or on history. Jackie Robinson won him over. It is the Dixie Walkers of Robinson's story, the men who had to wrestle profoundly with their own heritage and learned behaviors, who are the final proof of the story's success. The story of Dixie Walker and Jackie Robinson would have been a tragedy had it ended where it started. It didn't. Walker and Robinson both had a role in the changes that followed, and that is where they will forever be linked.

It is for us to allow people to change, even to encourage them to change. Jackie Robinson brought about a cultural revolution that started with one man, and he affected everyone differently, but none more than those who tried to resist him. He was too right to be resisted, and the proof is in the changes that he made just by being himself. The final chapter in the life of Dixie Walker, and of most of those like him, is one of redemption. Our mistakes are not irrevocable, and right can still win if we are malleable enough to let it. Change comes hard for some, but it still comes, and 100 years after his birth and 46 years after his death, that is the ultimate legacy that Jackie Robinson leaves.

ACKNOWLEDGMENTS

If you have ever watched a sporting event and wondered why an athlete struggles to string together coherent thoughts seconds after ending a significant competition, well, the same thing happens to authors. Next time, I'm going to write this before the book and not after, but until then, my apologies in advance to those I omit in the fatigue of the moment.

As always, my family has been kind, helpful, and unselfish in their time and love. I feel sorry for people who don't have a spouse as wonderful as my wife, Julie, but that basically means I feel sorry for everyone. She is a fine team woman, among many other things. Much love to our children, Natalie and Ryan. I hope that baseball continues to reward you as much as it has rewarded me, and that you each follow your own paths with the courage and boldness of Jackie Robinson. Love to Mom and Teresa for their constant love and support and to Dad for those Friday mornings in the car with Red Barber and Bob Edwards. Thanks also to the Costellows for including me in their family in a million ways, all of which are appreciated.

Thanks to my friends at Cole, Loney & Cox for supporting my other career and for being friends. Not unlike the old Brooklyn Dodgers, it takes all kinds to make a team, and on our good days, I'd like to think we could win a pennant or two.

Thanks to all of the writers who have handled these topics previously. Arnold Rampersad and Lee Lowenfish contributed what I would consider definitive biographies of Robinson and Rickey, and they each made my life easier accordingly. Red Barber was a great writer as well as a great broadcaster, and this book wouldn't exist without him or Doris Kearns Goodwin, whose books surpass even their high reputations. John Paul Hill is a kind and helpful author, despite being a fellow Western Kentucky University alum.

Thanks to my editor, Rick Rinehart, and production editor Meredith Dias, copy editor Desiree Reid, layout artist Joanna Beyer, and proofreader Susan Barnett. A big "thank you" also to Ryan Schroer, who helped me dodge a couple of big errors in the manuscript.

The ideas make no difference without all of the people who make them more readable, more accessible, and more enjoyable, and they all do it well.

Thanks to the Baseball Hall of Fame, particularly Matt Rothenberg, Cassidy Lent, and John Horne, who always go above and beyond.

Last but far from least, thanks to my readers everywhere. I hope you've enjoyed this, and I hope we can do this again soon.

—Joe Cox
September 2018

NOTES

CHAPTER ONE: "YOU KNOW DOGGONE WELL YOU'VE GOT A GIRL."

2. Biographical information of Rachel Isum and her family drawn from multiple sources, including Rampersad, 75–77.

2. "seemed to favor me": Ibid., 76.

2. "I got fifty cents": Ibid., 77.

2. "I don't know where": *McCall's Magazine*, June 1951.

2. "pretend[ing] I was a needy student": Ibid.

2. "those good people": Ibid.

2. "Right now it certainly": Ibid.

3. Rachel's academic record per Rampersad, 76, 78.

3–4. Jackie Robinson's family background from multiple sources, including Rampersad, 10–17.

4. Incident of Robinson, taunting girl, and rock fight from multiple sources, including Jackie Robinson (*I Never*), 5–6, and Rowan, 24.

4. Incident of local police and aquifer: Rowan, 31.

4–5. Mack Robinson biographical information and jacket story: Rampersad, 31.

5. Significance of Downs: Jackie Robinson (*I Never*), 7–8, and Rachel Robinson, 18.

5–6. Robinson's early athletic excellence is per multiple sources, including Rampersad, 27, 37, and Robinson (*I Never*), 9.

6. Junior college athletic feats from multiple sources, including Rampersad, 42, 54.

6. Robinson's police scuffle is per Mann (*The Jackie Robinson Story*), 44.

7. Robinson working as a janitor: Rampersad, 72.

7. Robinson's discomfort with women and wariness of white women: Rowan, 58–60.

7. Rachel's initial impressions of Jackie: Jackie Robinson (*I Never*), 11.

7. "handsome, proud, and serious": Rachel Robinson, 22.

7. "we both were shy": Ibid.

8. Rachel's dislike of Jackie's white shirts: Rampersad, 78.

8. "I thought to myself": Ibid.

8. "He wore his color": Ibid.

8. "fun but never completely comfortable": Ibid.

9. "I could see no future": Jackie Robinson (*I Never*), 12.

9. "In this time of sorrow": Ibid., 11.

9. "My father's death": Rampersad, 88.

9. "There are few people": Jackie Robinson (*I Never*), 11.

9. Robinson's NYA job and Rachel's keepsake: Rampersad, 84, 89.

9. "I was thrilled": Ibid., 89.

10. Football time in Hawaii: Ibid., 86–87.

10. Rachel's work and busy schedule: Rachel Robinson, 27–28.

10. Robinson's OCS block and incident with Major Hafner: Rowan, 70, 73.

10. "How would you like": Ibid., 73.

10–11. Football racism and departure: Ibid., 74–75.

11. "If you ever": Jackie Robinson, unpublished manuscript for *My Greatest Day*, 13, located in Jackie Robinson Papers, National Baseball Hall of Fame.

11. Robinson's engagement: Rampersad, 94, places it in 1943. Rachel Robinson, on the other hand, said in an interview with Carl Rowan, circa 1958, within the Jackie Robinson Papers, National Baseball Hall of Fame, that "We were engaged about 5 years before we were married."

11. Zellee Isum's support: Rampersad, 79, 94.

11. "Tell her to either": Ibid., 95.

11. Robinson's military information: Jackie Robinson Papers, National Baseball Hall of Fame.

11–12. Rachel's plans and Jackie's reaction per Rachel Robinson, Rowan, 86–88.

12. Rachel's actual motivations: Rampersad, 98.

12. Rachel's return of Jackie's ring: Ibid., 99.

12. Robinson's military information: Jackie Robinson Papers, National Baseball Hall of Fame.

12. Account of reunion with Rachel: Unpublished *My Greatest Day* manuscript, Jackie Robinson Papers, National Baseball Hall of Fame.

12. "I set some sort": Ibid.

12. Rachel's travel plans: Rampersad, 124–25.

13. "never again to allow": Unpublished *My Greatest Day* manuscript, Jackie Robinson Papers, National Baseball Hall of Fame.

13. Robinson's encounter with Alexander and employment: Jackie Robinson (*I Never*), 24–25.

13. Working with Downs at Samuel Huston: Rampersad, 113–14.

13–14. Robinson's issues with the Negro Leagues are per multiple sources, including Jackie Robinson (*I Never*), 24–25.

13. "I began to wonder": Ibid., 25.

14. "Jack no doubt seemed priggish": Rampersad, 118. Story with Sammie Haynes is from Ibid.

14. Rachel's activities: Ibid., 124.

14–15. Rickey's opening question and much of the ensuing dialogue from many sources, including Jackie Robinson (*I Never*), 30. The exact exchange cited here is from Rowan, 113–14.

15. "We were engaged": Rachel Robinson, unpublished interview with Carl Rowan, circa 1958, Jackie Robinson Papers, National Baseball Hall of Fame.

15. Rickey's instructions and "[H]e would only tell me": Rampersad, 128.

16. "Rachel began to think": Ibid., 132.

16. Wedding information from Rachel Robinson, 41, 43. Jackie forgetting to book a room is per Rowan, 127.
16. "finally clos[ing] the door": Rachel Robinson, 43.
16. Spring training travel issues from multiple sources, including Ibid., at 46, 48.
16. "we had the survivor's": Ibid., at 48.
16. "I could have lost my temper": Unpublished *My Greatest Day* manuscript, Jackie Robinson Papers, National Baseball Hall of Fame.
17. "We found that our marriage": Rachel Robinson, unpublished interview with Carl Rowan, circa 1958, Jackie Robinson Papers, National Baseball Hall of Fame.
17. "[M]y role had begun to unfold": Rachel Robinson, 52.
17. "With this closeness": Rampersad, 144.
17–18. "had hoped for a year": Ibid.
18. "We can't miss": Ibid.
18. "In Montreal, Jack would leave": Rachel Robinson, unpublished interview with Carl Rowan, circa 1958, Jackie Robinson Papers, National Baseball Hall of Fame.
18. "I never told Jack about": Rampersad, 155.
18. "[Y]ou try to be sensitive": Rachel Robinson, unpublished interview with Carl Rowan, circa 1958, Jackie Robinson Papers, National Baseball Hall of Fame.
19. Jackie's nervous issues documented variously, including Jackie Robinson (*Jackie Robinson*), 105.
19. "I managed to get in": Rachel Robinson, 57.
19. Maltin's famous line was actually "the large group of Louisville fans . . . couldn't fail to tell others down South of the 'riots,' the chasing of a Negro—not because of hate but because of love." *Pittsburgh Courier*, October 12, 1946.
20. Account of the return and Rachel's pep talk: Jackie Robinson (*Jackie Robinson*), 114–15.
20. Rachel's recollection of the living situation and Jackie Jr.'s health problems: Rowan, 190.
20. "utter nightmare": Ibid.
20. Ibid., at 191.
21. "Gradually I began to learn": *McCall's Magazine*, June 1951.
21. Rachel's Opening Day experience: Rachel Robinson, 62.
21. "She spent most of her days": Tygiel, 201.
21. "As we traveled back": Rachel Robinson, 72.
21. "[S]he tried hard to make": Rampersad, 180.
22. Threatening letters and Cincinnati is per FBI file, Jackie Robinson Papers, National Baseball Hall of Fame.
22. "[I]t wasn't in a period of kidnappings": Tygiel, 201.
22. Jackie Robinson Day accounts: Rampersad, 185.
23. "Though we shared a few": Rachel Robinson, 90.
23. "Jack and I really don't need": *McCall's Magazine*, June 1951.
23. Robinsons' friendships: Rachel Robinson, 89–90.
23. "It was nothing to her": Rampersad, 196.

23. "She was a very demanding": Ibid.

23–24. Christmas tree story and "In California, we knew": Ibid., at 197.

24. "The children liked it": Ibid.

24. Housing discrimination: Rachel Robinson, 129–31.

24. "Sometimes it was hard to tell": Jackie Robinson (*I Never*), 105.

24. "The friendship Andrea and I shared": Rachel Robinson, 132.

25–27. Conversation with O'Malley and the two Robinsons: Rowan, 256–58.

25. The 1952 date is based on minor injuries Robinson suffered in spring training. Robinson is called the best attendance draw in baseball in the *Cincinnati Enquirer*, March 21, 1952.

26. "She had never become involved": Jackie Robinson (*I Never*), 99.

27. Robinson's hiring and the details thereof: Falkner, 249–50.

27. "Jack experienced my move": Rachel Robinson, 147.

28. "We had created": Ibid., at 148.

28. "I needed greater freedom": Ibid., at 147.

28. Rachel dropping her books and "reducing myself to the stature": Ibid., at 161.

28. Jackie waiting for Rachel and "I felt we were close": Ibid.

28. Rachel's employment information is per Ibid., at 172, 176.

29. Afternoon of Jazz: Ibid. at 182, 184–85.

29. "To be very honest": Jackie Robinson (*I Never*), 159.

29. "Rachel realized": Ibid., 160.

29. "I am proud that my wife": Ibid., 159.

29. "Rachel has told me": Ibid., 161.

30. Jackie's political difficulties per many sources, including Falkner, 288–93, 307–10.

30. "I've had more effect": Rampersad, 423.

30. Jackie's medical issues per multiple sources, including Falkner, 340–42.

30. Sharon's story and "First Mr. Rickey": Rampersad, 449.

31. Death of Jackie: Rachel Robinson, 216.

31. Jackie Robinson Foundation statistics are per "The Jackie Robinson Foundation," www.jackierobinson.org.

31. "I don't know if I'll be there": MLB.com, "Robinson Accepts O'Neil Award." Embedded at www .mlb.com/news/rachel-robinson-gets-hofs-buck-oneil-award/c-245206626 (7/29/17).

31. "I am one of the fortunate ones": Rachel Robinson, 223.

31. "Jack and I had modest plans": *McCall's Magazine*, June 1951.

32. "I feel that the legacy": Rachel Robinson, 226.

CHAPTER TWO: ATTENDANCE, JESUS, AND AMERICA: THE MOTIVATIONS OF BRANCH RICKEY

33. "I felt like": Polner, 22.

33. Orla teaching Branch baseball: Ibid.

33. Meeting and Rickey's scribbling of "Attendance," "Jesus," and "America": Ibid., 137.

34. The controversy over Rickey's birthplace is documented in his player file at the National Baseball Hall of Fame. His family information is per multiple sources, including Polner, 17.

34. Influence of Rickey's parents and "I felt as though": Ibid., 18–19.

35. Wesley influence and "Give all you can": Ibid., at 21. Same information with slightly different wording on the quote from Lowenfish, 17.

35. Fight with student is indicated in Lowenfish, 13, and Polner, 25. Meanwhile, Rickey's own version was less dramatic and is given in Mann (*Branch Rickey*), 17–18.

35. Petition to keep Rickey and "those Xs of poor people": Lowenfish, 15.

35. Rickey falling in love: Ibid., 17.

35. Rickey's father disapproving of college: Polner, 28.

35–36. Rickey's college career and loss of amateur status: Lowenfish, 20–22.

36. Charles Thomas story is recounted from many sources, including Lowenfish, 23–24, and Polner, 37–38, and Mann (*Branch Rickey*), 215–16.

36. "I never felt so helpless": Lowenfish, 23.

37. Rickey and the Reds's disagreement on Sundays from multiple sources, including Lowenfish, 26–28.

37. Rickey's sorrow at the idea that his mother kept him from playing documented at Lowenfish, 27, and Mann (*Branch Rickey*), 36.

37–38. Rickey's future plans: Lowenfish, 35.

38. Rickey's inability to throw: Ibid., 39–40.

38. Tuberculosis scare and recovery: Ibid., 43–48.

38. Struggling law practice and baseball future: Ibid., 54, 59.

39. "tremendous sense of intellectual challenge": Ibid., 59.

39. Cardinal farm system ideology per various sources, including Polner, 83, and Lowenfish, 122.

39. "Pack up and come home": Lowenfish, 122.

39. "buy raw talent": Ibid.

39–40. "In time . . . you will see": Ibid., 150.

40. Cardinal tryout camps: Ibid., 156.

40–41. Clashing of Landis and Rickey per multiple sources, including Polner, 110–11.

41. "You are both guilty": Ibid., 103.

41. Discussion between Rickey and Landis: Lowenfish, 281.

41–42. "The farm system is not": Mann (*Branch Rickey*), 166.

42. Loss of player value is per Lowenfish, 283, and Rickey's contract bonus is detailed in various sources including Polner, 103, and Mann (*Branch Rickey*), 172–73, which clarifies that Rickey's 10 percent bonus extended only so far as the team declared a net profit for the business year.

42. Rickey's move and new contract: Lowenfish, 318.

42–43. The Powers/Rickey feud and the statistics included: Mann (*Branch Rickey*), 238–39.

43. Rickey's 37-page reply: Polner, 128–29.

43. Erskine's story of two bonuses and Dizzy Dean: Vincent, 112–14.

44. "we got at the table": Falkner, 105.

44. Segregation of Sportsman's Park and visit from Thomas: Lowenfish, 24.

45. "I don't mean to be a crusader": Falkner, 114.

45. "When I hired Jackie Robinson": *Civilization*, September/October 1995, 57.

45. "trouble ahead" and "That's the way it is": Lowenfish, 376.

45–46. The six-part plan is detailed from multiple sources, including Mann (Branch Rickey), 214–15.

46. Meeting with McLaughlin and "We are hoping": Polner, 133–34.

46. "If you're doing this": Ibid., 134.

46–47. Latin-American scouting: Lowenfish, 350.

46. O'Malley's alleged attempts to sign Garcia: Kreuz, 46–47.

47. Rickey first asking Robinson about having a girl is confirmed in multiple sources, including Mann (*Branch Rickey*), 220, Jackie Robinson (*I Never*), 30–31, and Lowenfish, 373–74.

48. Rickey asking Robinson about his religion is not as well documented, but it was apparently not uncommon practice and is corroborated at Lowenfish, 374, and Long and Lamb, 2. Obviously, the later tone of discussion also reflects this as probable.

48. Rickey asking Robinson about his contract is per Mann (*Branch Rickey*), 220–21, Jackie Robinson (*I Never*), Rowan, 114. Considering that Rickey had Robinson sign a statement indemnifying him and the Dodgers, it was doubtless verified by Rickey.

48. "In ten minutes": *Reader's Digest*, October 1961, 98.

48. Rickey's investigation with Smith and "I didn't want to tell": Long and Lamb, 48.

48. "understood that what might": Lowenfish, 369.

49. "I know you're a good ballplayer": Lowenfish, 375, and Jackie Robinson (*I Never*), 31. While others render the line slightly differently, it was a key point of the conversation.

49. Rickey's theatrics are widely reported, including Mann (*Branch Rickey*), 222–23, and Rowan, 116–18.

49. The use of Papini's book and the specific lines are from multiple sources, including Rowan, 118–19, which says he handed the book to Robinson, and Mann (*Branch Rickey*), 221, which says Rickey read it aloud.

49. "I have two cheeks": Many sources, including Mann (*Branch Rickey*), 223. Rowan, 118, renders the quote slightly different, but to the same import.

49. "I'm looking for a ballplayer": Jackie Robinson (*I Never*), 33.

49. "No army, no owners": Ibid., 32.

50. "pointed out that an incident": Sukeforth/Rickey memorandum, from Arthur Mann Papers, National Baseball Hall of Fame.

50. "I had to do it": Jackie Robinson (*I Never*), 34.

50. "If you want to take this gamble": Sukeforth/Rickey memorandum from Arthur Mann Papers, National Baseball Hall of Fame.

50. "I thought the old man": Honig, 191.

50. "Why a good respectable": *Pittsburgh Courier*, November 3, 1945 (from a column summarizing reactions to Robinson signing).

50. "Those who were good enough": Ibid.

50. "we don't believe Jackie Robinson": *New York Daily News*, March 12, 1946.

51. Rickey's bombshell and "the biggest threat": various sources, including Mann (*Branch Rickey*), 254–55, and Lowenfish, 417, although the exact text differs slightly in places on the second source.

51. "If any individual": Ibid.

52. "You can't afford to miss": Jackie Robinson (*Jackie Robinson*), 76–77.

52. Rickey's encouragements: Jackie Robinson (*I Never*), 44, 56.

52. Robinson's incident with Stanky: Polner, 163.

52. Rickey's choice of Hopper and his instructions: Red Barber (*Rhubarb*), 274.

53. Rickey's reliance on *Essay on Man*: Lowenfish, 429, and Polner, 177.

53. Clay Hopper's conversion: Jackie Robinson (*I Never*), 52.

53. Hopper desiring to having Robinson back in 1947: Polner, 164.

53. Rickey's resistance to the petition: Mann (*Branch Rickey*), 256–57, and Lowenfish, 418–19.

53. "a few idiots": Reed, 32, although he argues that the story is probably apocryphal. Furillo's change of heart was not.

53–54. Walker and Bragan not concurring: Eig, 44–45.

54. Pennock conversation: Lowenfish, 430–31. Rowan, 183, repeats the story but says it was Phillies president Bob Carpenter.

54. "When he poured out": Rowan, 183–84.

54. *The Sporting News'* award and "The sociological experiment": *The Sporting News*, September 17, 1947.

55. "You will have to promise": Polner, 153.

55. "I've heard Rickey say": Red Barber (*When All Hell*), 61.

55. Sukeforth/Rickey memorandum from Arthur Mann Papers, National Baseball Hall of Fame.

56. "All along I had known": Rowan, 199.

56. "Jackie, you're on your own now": Jackie Robinson (*I Never*), 77.

56. "The idea that Branch Rickey": Rampersad, 207.

56. "Some have made it seem": Rachel Robinson, 88.

56. Van Cuyk incident: Rampersad, 206.

56. "better be rough on me" and context of controversy: Rowan, 236–37.

57–58. Rickey's sale of interest in Dodgers well documented, including Mann (*Branch Rickey*), 282–85, and Lowenfish, 487–92.

58. "It is certainly tough": Jackie Robinson Papers, National Baseball Hall of Fame.

58. "Sometimes my family believed": Rampersad, 231.

59. Robinson's defense against "El Cheapo" in many sources, including *Our Sports*, July 1953, 34, et seq.

59. Rickey's approval of Clemente: Lowenfish, 528–29.

60. Necciai information: O'Toole, 75.

60. Continental League information: Lowenfish, 539–48.

60. Continental League as key to expansion: Ibid., 574–75.

61. Rickey's clashes with Cardinals and desire to rid the team of Musial: Ibid., 585–89.
61. "a man who has been": Lowenfish, 580.
61. Rickey's hospital visit to Robinson: Rampersad, 370.
61. Rickey's repeated health problems: Polner, 163, 230.
61. "That's not important": Ibid., 252.
61–62. Rickey's last speech and death: Lowenfish, 1–5.
62. "As I mourned for him": Jackie Robinson (*I Never*), 260.

CHAPTER THREE: TRICKY NAVIGATION: HAPPY CHANDLER, JIM CROW, AND JACKIE ROBINSON

64–65. Chandler's early biography: Holtzman, 46–47.
64. "just a wide place in the road": Chandler, 8.
64. "the foremost and most satisfying": Ibid., 10.
65. "Every day we filled": Ibid., 12.
65. Death of Chandler's brother: Ibid., 15.
65. Chandler's encounter that led to his education: Ibid., 19.
65. Chandler's arrival at college: Ibid., 21, and Holtzman, 46.
65. "Thank God he didn't": Ibid., 22.
65. Baseball in college and with Lexington Rios: Holtzman, 47.
65. Chandler's departure from Harvard and return to Kentucky: Chandler, 46.
66. Chandler's meeting with and falling in love with Mildred Watkins: Ibid., 52–54.
66. Chandler's split with Lafoon: Ibid., 101–2.
66. Maneuver to establish primary elections: Ibid., 102.
66. Chandler's disdain for Roosevelt and Truman: Ibid., 151–52, 164–65.
66. Chandler's praise for Nixon: Ibid., 148.
66–67. Roosevelt campaigning for Barkley and Chandler losing Senate race: Ibid., 134–41, and Roland, 146.
67. NAACP disfavor of Chandler: Hill, 33.
67. Chandler's vice-presidential aspirations: Pearce, 46.
67. Owners' meeting and MacPhail's support: Holtzman, 44-45.
68. "Chandler's biggest problem": *New York Mirror*, April 25, 1945.
68–69. Overview of Jim Crow documented by many historical sources, including Zinn, 194–205.
69. "We consider the underlying": *Plessy v. Ferguson*, 163 U.S. 537, 551 (1896).
70. Berea college case: *Berea College v. Kentucky*, 211 U.S. 45 (1908).
70. Previous Kentucky statutes on a list obtained from a now-defunct website, which was located at www.jimcrowhistory.org. This list, which was four pages long and included not only the list of the statutes in question but also dates, was an excellent resource that will hopefully be restored. In the meanwhile, it can (at least momentarily) be viewed at http://sourcesfinding.com/sitebuildercontent/sitebuilderfiles/jimcrow-lawskentucky.pdf.
70. "The general trend": *Pittsburgh Courier*, May 5, 1945.

70. "I doubt if Chandler": *The* (Baltimore) *Evening Sun*, April 25, 1945.
70. "I'm for the Four Freedoms": Polner, 174.
70. "Once I tell you something": Tygiel, 43.
71. Baseball's history of segregation is well documented, including Tygiel, 10–29, which is perhaps the best treatment of same.
71. "He was the best catcher": Ibid., 15.
71–72. The inefficiency of the baseball's old power structure is per Holtzman, 22–23.
72. The installation of Landis: Holtzman, 24–28.
73. Landis/Durocher incident: Tygiel, 31, but further documented in column below.
73. "Landis Steps to Bat": Unidentified column within integration file at National Baseball Hall of Fame and Museum, dated July 17, 1942, in pencil, likely from *Brooklyn PM*.
73. Bill Veeck's story is documented (and questioned) in many sources, including Tygiel, 40–41, and Eig, 181–82.
74. "[I]t's nice to know": Hill, 36.
74. Rickey's discussion of the clandestine meeting in his Wilberforce speech: Lowenfish, 449–50.
75. Reactions from Carpenter and Griffith: Ibid., 451.
75. Lack of official comment: *Dayton Daily News*, February 21, 1948.
75. "for the purpose of letting": Chandler, 226.
75. Robinson not on meeting agenda: Falkner, 147.
75. No minutes taken at meeting: Chandler, 226.
75. Chandler's account of meeting: Ibid., 226–27, and *Sports Heritage*, May–June 1987, 21–25.
75. "flat out said if we let": Tygiel, 81.
75. The report was located within the A. B. "Happy" Chandler Papers, University of Kentucky. This author viewed a copy of same at the National Baseball Hall of Fame, in its Integration file, and all quotes are from the document itself.
76–77. Bavasi's recollection and quotes from same: Holtzman, 71.
77. Rickey's Ménière's disease: Lowenfish, 385–87. This was the issue that had him in poor health at the time of the public announcement of Robinson's signing.
77–78. Chandler's account of the private meeting with Rickey in Versailles and all quotes therein: Chandler, 227–29.
78. First reference to same: *The Sporting News*, February 6, 1965.
78. "would not have fit Rickey's behavior pattern": Hill, 38.
78. Hill also takes exception with the details on approval of Robinson's contract: Ibid., 39.
79. "Dad would say to someone": Falkner, 151.
79. "uncanny ability to make people": Ibid.
79. McLaughlin and Barber's indication of initial confidences are well documented. As for King, that is per Falkner, 151.
79. Rickey's YMCA meeting is equally well documented, including Lowenfish, 417.
79. Chandler acting toward the Louisville Colonels: Hill, 39.

79–80. Contact between Chandler and Herb Pennock regarding bench jockeying: Ibid., 40.

80. Chandler's retention of John DeMoisey to protect Robinson: Chandler, 230.

80. The Cardinals strike account: *New York Tribune*, May 9, 1947.

80. The bounce back with Frick and Shotton: *Philadelphia Inquirer*, May 9, 1947.

80. "Baseball is an American game": Unsourced newspaper column, "Breadon Denies Frick Story Cards Planned Strike over Robinson," National Baseball Hall of Fame Integration File.

81. Letter from Posey: National Baseball Hall of Fame Chandler Correspondence File.

81. Return letter to Effa Manley and letter requesting reserve lists: Ibid.

81. "At best, one can describe": Tygiel, 82.

81. "Chandler is political minded": Ibid.

82. Mexican League issues: Holtzman, 48–52.

82–83. Durocher controversy: Ibid., 53–66.

83. Chandler's issues with Saigh: Ibid., 80.

83. Chandler's investigation of Del Webb: Ibid.

83. Dick Wakefield ruling and "out to get my job": Hill, 45.

83. Danny Lynch and Jack Lohrke deals: Holtzman, 82.

83. Chandler credited his work on integration for costing him the job frequently, such as *Cleveland Plain-Dealer*, March 22, 1982 ("The decision that hurt 'Happy' Chandler").

84. Chandler's work on television rights and player pensions: Holtzman, 78–79.

84. "If Jesus Christ": Chandler, 238.

85. Chandler's account of Sturgis incident: Ibid., 257.

85. "The tank had to sit in Clay": Ibid.

85. "I will never forget your part": *Sports Heritage*, May–June 1987, 25, which includes a photo of the letter.

85. "I had everybody in high places": *The Sporting News*, May 22, 1965.

85. Robinson's employment with Black and his rise within the NAACP from many sources, including Rampersad, 301–7.

86. Robinson's acknowledged support of Nixon discussed: Jackie Robinson (*I Never*), 135–40.

86. Robinson loses newspaper column over Nixon endorsement: Falkner, 281.

86. Robinson's attachment to Rockefeller: Jackie Robinson (*I Never*), 162–75.

86. Conflict with Malcolm X and quotes: Ibid., 176–82.

86. Conflict with Dr. King: Rampersad, 416–17.

87. Chandler's conflict with Wallace: Chandler, 270.

87. Chandler's friendship with Rupp: Ibid., 122–23.

87. Kuhn's support of Chandler: Ibid., 280.

87. Wilkinson and voting on UK Board of Trustees: Ibid., 292.

87–88. Chandler controversy and "You know, Zimbabwe": *Albany Times-Union*, April 7, 1988.

87–88. Chandler's further remarks regarding the offensive slur and potential boycott: Ibid., and *Albany Times-Union*, April 8, 1988.

88. "slap more backs": *Louisville Courier-Journal*, June 16, 1991.

CHAPTER FOUR: WENDELL SMITH AND THE POWER OF THE PRESS

89. American Legion game and "I wish I could sign you": *Chicago Tribune*, July 28, 1994.

89. Wish Egan's scouting background: *Baseball Digest*, July 1951.

90. "That broke me up": Lamb (*Blackout*), 17.

90. Smith's links with Ford: *Chicago Tribune*, July 28, 1994.

90. Smith's background and high school experience: Lamb (*Conspiracy*), 83.

90–91. West Virginia State's background: Haught, 101–7.

91. Academic tradition of State is per West Virginia State University, "Our History Runs Deep": www.wvstateu.edu/About/History-and-Traditions.aspx (8/31/18).

91. Smith's athletic background (including credit for jump shot innovation): *Detroit Free Press*, November 27, 1972.

91–93. History of African-American journalism from multiple sources, including Simmons, 9–51.

93. The role of the Communist press: Tygiel, 36–37, and Falkner, 95–101.

94. Smith writing in favor of integration: *Pittsburgh Courier*, May 14, 1938.

94. Smith's poll on integration: Falkner, 96, and Rampersad, 121.

94. "upheld baseball's unwritten ban": *Smithsonian*, October 2000, 120–32.

95. "Negroes are not barred": *St. Louis Star and Times*, July 17, 1942.

95. "Col. Larry MacPhail" and "few and far between": *The Sporting News*, November 1, 1945.

96. 1943 owners' meeting and ire of Lacy: Lamb (*Blackout*), 97.

96. Lewis's speech and Murphy's plan: Lamb (*Conspiracy*), 236.

96. Lack of reaction and "I guess that's all": Ibid.

96. "Don't interrupt Robeson": Ibid.

96–97. Muchnick and his pressure on the Boston teams: Tygiel, 43–44.

97. Pirates's failed tryout: Ibid., 40.

97. McDuffie and Thomas tryout: Ibid., 45–46.

97. Postponing of tryouts and Egan's reaction: Ibid., 44.

97. Workout, "You boys look" and "Get those . . . ": Ibid.

97. "We'll hear from the Red Sox": National Baseball Hall of Fame, "Wendell Smith and the Boston Red Sox," https://baseballhall.org/discover-more/stories/wendell-smith/355 (8/31/18).

98. Collins's letter to Smith: Wendell Smith Papers, National Baseball Hall of Fame.

98. Cronin's memories: Tygiel, 44–45.

99. Excellence of other Negro League prospects from many sources, including Tygiel, 58, and Rampersad, 122.

100–101. Conversation between Rickey and Smith and comments: *Chicago Tribune*, March 31, 1997.

100–101. Follow-up phone conversation between Rickey and Smith: Ibid.

101. Rickey signs Smith as a scout: Ibid.

101. Smith's letter to Rickey and Rickey's reply: Wendell Smith Papers, National Baseball Hall of Fame.

101. The Robinsons' hellish trip documented from several sources, including Jackie Robinson (*I Never*), 39–41, and Rachel Robinson, 46, 48.

101. "Well, I finally made it": Long and Lamb, 72.

102. Robinson's desire to quit and his further arrangements: Ibid.

102. Robinson and traveling party fleeing town: Lamb (*Blackout*), 88–89.

102. New housing arrangements: Ibid., 90–91.

102–3. Cancellation in Jacksonville and game in DeLand moved: Ibid., 136–40.

103. Robinson pulled off the field in Sanford: Ibid., 154–55.

103. "vicious old man": Rampersad, 148.

103. "I wanted to produce so much": Lamb (*Blackout*), 164.

103. Wright as superior prospect: Ibid., 115.

103. "If he was white": Tygiel, 117.

103–4. Robinsons' appreciation of Montreal: Jackie Robinson (*I Never*), 47, and Rachel Robinson, 54, 57.

104. Robinson's first game: Lamb (*Blackout*), 171–72.

104. Smith's dual roles: National Baseball Hall of Fame, "Wendell Smith and Jackie Robinson," https://baseballhall org/discover-more/stories/wendell-smith/447 (8/31/18).

104. Incident in Baltimore: Long and Lamb, 80.

104. Incident in Syracuse: Jackie Robinson (*I Never*), 49.

104. Smith writing about the nervous condition: Long and Lamb, 80.

105. "You're a great ballplayer": Jackie Robinson (*I Never*), 52.

105. Hopper's spring training comment: Lowenfish, 392.

105. "Wendell would always say": *Los Angeles Times*, April 14, 2013.

105. "Jackie needed somebody": Ibid.

105–6. Smith not being welcome and "They wouldn't even let him": Ibid.

106–7. Transition to Cuba and Smith's unfamiliarity with same: Wendell Smith Papers, National Baseball Hall of Fame.

106. Correspondence regarding possibility of Robinson call-up: Ibid.

106. Dodger housing arrangements: Tygiel, 165.

107. Harold Parrott's involvement in lodging: Ibid., 185.

108. "The things the Phillies shouted": *Pittsburgh Courier*, May 3, 1947.

108. "[T]he column was really designed": Burroughs, "That Time Jackie Robinson Was a Columnist for the Pittsburgh Courier" www.theroot.com/that-time-jackie-robinson-was-a-columnist-for-the-pitts-1790854857 (4/4/16).

109. "[N]ot only is [Robinson]": *Pittsburgh Courier*, April 19, 1947.

109. Extent of commentary provided Ibid., and numerous other examples in the *Courier, Chicago Defender*, and other papers.

110. Decline of Negro Leagues: Tygiel, 299–302.

110. Yankee Stadium attendance: Eig, 192.

110. "considerable apprehension": *Pittsburgh Courier*, August 9, 1947.

110. Letters with Rickey: Wendell Smith Papers, National Baseball Hall of Fame.

111. "The Negro Leagues were": *New York Times*, May 12, 2003.

111. Admission of Smith: Wendell Smith Papers, National Baseball Hall of Fame.

111. Decline of Courier circulation: Taylor, "The History of the New Pittsburgh Courier," https://newpittsburghcourieronline.com/the-history-of-the-new-pittsburgh-courier (2/2/18).

111–12. Errors in *The Jackie Robinson Story*: Rampersad, 207.

112. "This, it seems": *Pittsburgh Courier*, March 14, 1949.

112. Dick Young story and "When I talk to Campy": Tygiel, 327.

113. Smith's crusade against segregation in spring training: Lamb (*Blackout*), 179.

113. Smith helping to elect Negro League players into Hall of Fame: National Baseball Hall of Fame, "Wendell Smith and the Hall of Fame," https://baseballhall.org/discover-more/stories/wendell-smith/452 (8/31/18).

113. Robinson acknowledges debt to Smith: Jackie Robinson (*I Never*), 29.

113–14. Smith's illness and "He never backed down": *Los Angeles Times*, April 14, 2013.

CHAPTER FIVE: CLYDE SUKEFORTH AND THE RESIDUE OF DESIGN

115. Scouting information: Scouting file, National Baseball Hall of Fame.

116. Sukeforth's childhood and comments on same: Clyde Sukeforth (Maine Memory Network), www.mainememory.net/artifact/8617 (1998).

116–17. Sukeforth's education: Ibid., and Ray, 69–70.

117. Sukeforth's early career: Ray, 70.

117. "[W]hen I'd get to hit": *Sports Collectors Digest*, February 18, 1994.

117–18. Injury to Sukeforth: Ray, 70.

118. Reference to Sukeforth as "one of the best catchers": *The Sporting News*, November 26, 1931.

118. Postinjury playing: Ray, 70.

118. Marriage: Ibid., 71.

118. Sukeforth's early managing: Ray, 70.

118. Sukeforth's run-in with the Bi-State League president: *The Sporting News*, August 6, 1936.

119. Becoming a coach and "wasn't my ambition": *Sports Collectors Digest*, February 18, 1994.

119. Sukeforth "too good a fellow": *The Sporting News*, November 26, 1942.

119. Scouts who followed Robinson: Lowenfish, 368.

119. Greenwade's erroneous credit and seeing Robinson 20 times: Kreuz, 47–48.

119. Rickey's use of USL as a smokescreen: Lowenfish, 367–68.

119–120. Assessment of Robinson: Tygiel, 59, and Kreuz, 48.

120. Sukeforth's recollection of beginning to follow Robinson and seeing other players: Sukeforth/Rickey memorandum from Arthur Mann Papers, National Baseball Hall of Fame.

120. Sukeforth's attempts to find Robinson: Ibid.

121. Sukeforth tipping elevator operator: Honig, 186.

121. Sukeforth asking Robinson about army discharge and Robinson talking about ankle injury: Sukeforth/Rickey memorandum from Arthur Mann Papers, National Baseball Hall of Fame.

121. Robinson's curiosity about Rickey's motives and dialogue regarding same: Honig, 186, 188.

121. "The more we talked": Ibid. at 188.

121. Sukeforth's memorandum: Arthur Mann Papers, National Baseball Hall of Fame.

122. Train journey and trip time line: Lowenfish, 372–73.

122. Sukeforth's memories of Rickey/Robinson meeting and quotes from same: Sukeforth/Rickey memorandum from Arthur Mann Papers, National Baseball Hall of Fame.

124. Sukeforth instructions not to overdo throws and Robinson ignoring same: Lamb (*Blackout*), 94.

124. "Clyde showed his support": Jackie Robinson (*I Never*), 45.

124. Rickey coaching Robinson and "He is apt": Rampersad, 145.

124. "had the greatest aptitude" and "in one half hour": Ibid.

124. Rochelli and Breard being helpful: Ibid., 145–46.

124. Sisler coaching Robinson and "[H]e played that first base": *Sports Collectors Digest*, February 18, 1994.

124–25. "the old-time baseball men": Rampersad, 117.

125. Gene Benson and his advice to Robinson: Falkner, 120–21.

125. "kept encouraging him": Rowan, 180.

125. Sukeforth's letter to Rachel Robinson: Jackie Robinson Papers, National Baseball Hall of Fame.

125. Sukeforth as source of information on petition: Kahn, 118.

126. Argument that the suspension of Durocher jeopardized Robinson's progress: Falkner, 157, and Red Barber (*1947*), 115–16.

126. Sukeforth tabbed as interim manager: Lowenfish, 426.

126. "I knew that he was": Jackie Robinson (*Jackie Robinson*), 125.

126. "I didn't tell Jack anything": Ray, 71.

127. "The guys on the team": *Pittsburgh Courier*, May 24, 1947.

127. Sukeforth's role in Magerkurth's bench clearing: *The Sporting News*, May 21, 1947.

127. Sukeforth restrains Robinson: Tygiel, 204.

127. Shotton's offense of Robinson and Sukeforth's role in clearing it: Jackie Robinson Papers, National Baseball Hall of Fame.

128. Questionnaire from Robinson: Jackie Robinson Papers, National Baseball Hall of Fame.

129. "They're both OK": Erskine, 41.

129. Sukeforth's account: Clyde Sukeforth (Maine Memory Network), www.maine-memory.net/artifact/8617 (1998).

129. Robinson watches Thompson touch the bases: Rampersad, 240.

129. Sukeforth's second marriage: Ray, 71.

129. Sukeforth's support of Clemente: *Sports Collectors Digest*, February 18, 1994.

130. "[T]here's a question": Clyde Sukeforth (Maine Memory Network), www.maine-memory.net/artifact/8617 (1998).

130. Sukeforth turning down Pirates job: *The Sporting News*, August 14, 1957.

130. "I knew Jack wasn't feeling well": *New York Times*, March 30, 1997.

131. "I didn't expect to have": Ibid.

131. Letter from Robinson included in Jackie Robinson Papers, National Baseball Hall of Fame.

131. "That was kind of him": *New York Times*, March 30, 1997.

132–33. Proliferation of mental skills coaches: *USA Today*, April 3, 2018.

CHAPTER SIX: KINDLY OLD BURT SHOTTON: "I CANNOT POSSIBLY HURT YOU."

134. "We'll get you": McCarver, 17.

134. "I am falling out a window": Polner, 131.

134–35. Consideration of managerial search: Various sources, including Mann (*Branch Rickey*), 260, and *Saturday Evening Post*, August 20, 1949.

136. McGraw as father of modern baseball managers: James, 34–37.

136. "did more to establish": Ibid., 54.

136. McGraw and Mack as establishing baseball orthodoxy: Ibid., 55.

136–37. "He'd fine players": Ibid., 48.

137. "Mack's philosophy": Ibid., 65.

137. "McGraw's approach": Ibid.

137. "If Durocher spoke a sentence": Eig, 39.

137. "While Durocher thrived": Ibid.

138. "I don't care": Tygiel, 170.

138. "I don't agree": Golenbock, 93.

138–39. Shotton's early years: Gough, 14.

139. Shotton's nickname and early baseball career: Ibid., 15.

139. Shotton's marriage: Ibid., 19.

140. "Rickey was the first manager": *Saturday Evening Post*, August 20, 1949.

140. "I tell you": *Baseball Magazine*, February 1917.

140. All-Star selection: *Saturday Evening Post*, August 20, 1949.

141. "The younger players responded": Gough, 35.

141. "If I had a father": *Saturday Evening Post*, August 20, 1949.

141–42. hidden ball trick and catching foul ball: Unsourced article, Dated October 16, 1945, Burt Shotton file, National Baseball Hall of Fame.

142. Telegram and Mary's admonition: Gough, 5.

142. Shotton's supposition about the reason for meeting: *The Sporting News*, August 11, 1962.

142. Shotton's lack of a contract: Edelman, 75–76.

142. Shotton lost getting to ballpark: Lowenfish, 428.

142. Shotton not dressing in uniform: Edelman, 76.

142. Shotton's apparel: *Saturday Evening Post*, August 20, 1949.

143. "You fellas can win": Golenbock, 169.

143. "Every day, when Burt": Eig, 84.

143. "As a manager": Gough, 83.

143. "Shotton knew in short order": Red Barber (1947), 191.

143. "Unlike other managers": Gough, 58.

144. "Jackie's admirers": *Saturday Evening Post*, August 20, 1949.

144. "a perfect gentleman": Ibid.

144. Shotton's comment about dealing Robinson for two pitchers: Burt Shotton File, National Baseball Hall of Fame.

144. "one of the happiest moments": Gough, 87.

144. Shotton's next job: Edelman, 77.

145. Durocher's reaction to Robinson: Lowenfish, 448.

145. "Robinson will shag flies": Ibid.

145. "[I]f you had a winning team": Jackie Robinson Papers, National Baseball Hall of Fame.

146. Shuffle of managers between Dodgers and Giants per multiple sources, including Lowenfish, 460.

146. Perfume flap: Rampersad, 236.

146. Laraine Day insulting Robinson in regard to the All-Star game: *New York Daily News*, June 19, 1950.

147. Newcombe's encounter with Shotton: Golenbock, 238–39.

149. Shotton's departure from Dodgers: Gough, 118–19.

149. Robinson's appreciation of playing for Dressen per multiple sources, including unpublished interview with Carl Rowan, Jackie Robinson Papers, National Baseball Hall of Fame.

149. "Alston has known": Same interview with Rowan, Jackie Robinson Papers, National Baseball Hall of Fame.

149. "Out there alone": *Look Magazine*, January 24, 1955.

149–50. Reese as player-manager: Edelman ("Pee Wee Reese"), 193.

150. "Shotton was a good sound": Jackie Robinson Papers, National Baseball Hall of Fame.

150. Further thoughts on Shotton per Ibid.

150. "I love to play": *Saturday Evening Post*, August 20, 1949.

150. "I think Shotton has a great way": Edelman ("Burt Shotton"), 79.

150–51. Other players' thoughts on Shotton: Ibid.

151. "My managers know": Unidentified magazine article, Jackie Robinson Papers, National Baseball Hall of Fame.

151. "I am extremely proud": Transcript of Robinson's comments, Jackie Robinson Papers, National Baseball Hall of Fame.

152. Shotton's death and Fraley's obituary: discussed in Edelman ("Burt Shotton"), 78–79, and Gough, 129.

152. "His managerial theory": Gough, 128.

152. "Wisdom in handling men": Ibid.

153. Alvin Dark incident: *New York Daily News*, November 14, 2014.

153. "You know, for a colored player": Bouton, 308.

153. "I knew we had nine Pirates": *Baseball Digest*, September 1995.

154. Lasorda's Spanish and behavior per viewing of the 1981 World Series official video.

154. "The only thing": *Saturday Evening Post*, August 20, 1949.

154. "Joe's done a good job": *Chicago Daily Herald*, October 7, 2016.

154. "He very rarely tries": Ibid.

CHAPTER SEVEN: MEN AND BROTHERS: RED BARBER AND JACKIE ROBINSON

156–57. Barber's meeting with Rickey: Red Barber (*Rhubarb*), 266–70.

156. Barber's plans to teach: Ibid., 141.

158–59. Barber's early life: Ibid., 181–83.

158. Barber's love of sports and show business: Ibid., 106–10.

159. Barber's decision to attend college: Ibid., 110–11.

159. Barber's end of football and finding odds jobs; Ibid., 118–22.

159–60. Barber's radio debut and conversation with Major Powell: Ibid., 142–45.

160. Progression of broadcasting and decision to leave school for work: Ibid., 155–60.

160. "The day I got out": Ibid., 138.

161. Beginning of radio broadcasting: Walker, 21–25, which indicates that Rice did not broadcast the World Series games.

161. McNamee's rise and "McNamee described": Bryson, 147.

162. New York City broadcasting ban: Golenbock, 185.

162. Lack of coverage of Vander Meer: Red Barber (*Rhubarb*), 218–19.

162. "The Nation's Station" and broadcasts reaching to Europe or South America: *Cincinnati Enquirer*, December 10, 2013.

162. WFBE and Harry Hartman information: Shea, 97.

163. Barber's path to Cincinnati: Red Barber (*Rhubarb*), 182–87.

163. Barber hired by WLW: Ibid., 190.

163. "It was a new world": Ibid., 193.

163. Opening game and "the most joyous day": Ibid., 200, 203–5.

163. Broadcasts being "quite casual" and no money changing hands: Ibid., 199.

164. Barber working the World Series: Ibid., 221–24.

164. Barber broadcasting and being watched by McNamee: Ibid., 224–26.

164–65. MacPhail and Brannick argument: Golenbock, 185.

165. Dodgers covering all games (road games being re-creations until 1948): Shea, 137, 143.

165. "the most influential sportscaster": Ibid., 137.

165. "was by far the most detail-oriented": Ibid., 138.

165. Barber's 14 pieces of advice: *The Sporting News*, December 14, 1939.

165–66. "When I took the job": Red Barber (*Rhubarb*), 40.

166. "Red Barber was an indelible": Golenbock, 187.

166. "In our household": Oliphant, 82.

167. "scrupulous grammar": *New York Times*, October 23, 1992.

167. "In time, despite my southern accent": Red Barber (*Rhubarb*), 41.

167. Barber's memories of blood drive: Ibid., 78–80.

167. "When we arrived": Lylah Barber, 97–98.

167. "I was raised": Red Barber (*Rhubarb*), 269.

168. Barber's recollection of his mother's death and "My anger grew": Red Barber (*Show Me*), 42–46.

168. Barber family tragedies and Red's decision to go to church: Ibid., 47–54.

168. "I was an instant convert": Ibid., 55.

168. Red is confirmed as an Episcopalian: Ibid., 55–56.

169. "I knew Red": Lylah Barber, 160.

169. Barber's memories of his father's advice: Red Barber (*Rhubarb*), 270–71.

169. "I had been carefully taught": Ibid., 271.

169. "How much control": Ibid.

169. "Men and Brothers" and Barber's understanding: Ibid., 272.

170. Barber's memories of Landis directing him to report: Red Barber (*1947*), 64–65.

170. Barber's memories of Bill Klem umpiring the ball: Red Barber (*Rhubarb*), 273.

171. "Barber was another important": Edwards, 93.

171. "Robinson on base": Red Barber (*1947*), 191.

171. "Barber and Allen": *The Sporting News*, October 8, 1947.

171. "It was more than that": Edwards, 94.

171–72. The Barbers and their old friends from Gainesville: Lylah Barber, 160.

172. Barber working in television: Shea, 143.

172–73. Beginning of Barber's friction with O'Malley: Red Barber (*Rhubarb*), 282.

173. "I was a close friend": Ibid.

173. O'Malley asking Barber about a manager: Ibid., 282–84.

173. "was just a combination": Ibid., 285.

173. Barber turning down the World Series: Ibid., 285–89.

173. Barber's relationship with Allen: Ibid., 300–1.

173. Barber's duties with Yankees: Shea, 186.

174. "On TV it's the director's show": Red Barber (*Rhubarb*), 304.

174. Barber's disapproval of Garagiola: Ibid., 313–14.

174. Barber is let go by the Yankees: Ibid., 328.

175. Ketzel Levine and Barber: Edwards, 18–19.

175. Barber's spots on NPR: Edwards, 20–21.

175. "[F]or many listeners": Ibid., 172.

176. "Barber's decline and death": Corbett, 292–93.

176. "Rickey and Jackie Robinson": Red Barber (*Walk*), 199.

176. "a converted white man": Ibid., 202.

177. "[I]f there is any thanks": Red Barber (*Rhubarb*), 276.

CHAPTER EIGHT: PEE WEE REESE: "STANDING BY ME."

178. The lynching of Ernest Dewley is per *The Nashville American*, May 1, 1902. No one names Dewley as the man who died on the lynching tree, but his lynching is by far the most well documented that occurred in the area, and its timing would allow Carl Reese to remember it.

178. "When a n----r": Kahn (*Into My Own*), 93.

178. "there was definitely an emotion": *New York Times*, March 31, 1997.

179. Reese's childhood: Edelman ("Pee Wee Reese"), 189.

179. "The part [of town]": Unpublished interview with Jules Tygiel, circa 1980, Jules Tygiel Papers, National Baseball Hall of Fame.

179. Reese's memory of himself and his brother running away: *New York Times*, March 31, 1997.

180. Reese's marble tournament fame: *Louisville Courier-Journal*, May 21, 1933.

180. Reese's small size and odd jobs: Edelman ("Pee Wee Reese"), 190.

180. "Climbing up and down": Ibid.

180. Reese ending up with Dodgers despite "working agreement" of Louisville and Boston: *The Sporting News*, July 27, 1939.

181. "crushed" and "turned out to be": Edelman ("Pee Wee Reese"), 191.

181. Durocher takes himself out and "He'll do": Ibid.

181. "distinguished himself as a slick": Ibid.

181. Reese's injury and marriage: Ibid.

181–82. Reese enlists in the navy and out of baseball for three years: Ibid.

182. Reese told of Robinson and reflects on that news: *New York Times*, March 31, 1997.

182. "If he's man enough": Edelman ("Pee Wee Reese"), 192.

183. Reese approached with the petition and his response: *New York Times*, March 31, 1997.

183–84. Incident with Walker: Ibid.

184. "He doesn't just want to beat you": Lowenfish, 448.

185. "In describing the scene": Branca, 82.

185. Snider and his feelings: Ibid., 69.

185. Erskine and his feelings: Erskine, 6.

185. Players who were opposed to Robinson from various sources including Rampersad, 164.

186. "I played an awful lot": Unpublished interview with Jules Tygiel, circa 1980, Jules Tygiel Papers, National Baseball Hall of Fame.

186. Hugh Casey incident: Jackie Robinson (*I Never*), 65.

186–87. The golfing incident with Reese and Robinson: *Pittsburgh Courier*, June 28, 1947.

188. Erskine places event in Cincinnati: Erskine, 62.

188. Branca also places event in Cincinnati: Branca, 75.

188. Barney's erroneous details: Golenbock, 161.

189. Roscoe McGowan places event in Texas: *The Sporting News*, December 19, 1956.

189. "There were times": *Des Moines Tribune*, July 19, 1977.

189. Conversation with Dave Kindred and "Just don't make me out": *The Sporting News*, August 30, 1999.

189. "I was supposed": Unpublished interview with Jules Tygiel, circa 1980, Jules Tygiel Papers, National Baseball Hall of Fame.

190. "Why don't they let the guy alone": *Look Magazine*, January 6, 1948.

190. Newspapers mentioning bench jockeying between Stanky and Dodgers: *Boston Globe*, April 28 and April 30, 1948.

190–91. "Fellows like Branca" and Robinson's first full account of the event: *Focus Magazine*, July 1952.

191. "I'll never forget the day" and 1949 account of event: *Washington Post*, August 28, 1949.

191–92. "In 1947, can I forget" and 1953 account: *Pittsburgh Post-Gazette*, November 10, 1953.

192. "Pee Wee was great" and 1955 account: *Look Magazine*, February 8, 1955.

192–93. "in Boston" and supporting details: Rowan, 227–28.

193. "Reese had said": Ibid., 228.

193. "In Boston during a period": Jackie Robinson (I Never), 64.

193. "Back in 1948": Jackie Robinson Papers, National Baseball Hall of Fame.

194–95. Rickey's gift to Reese: Polner, 124.

195. "You're not only the logical choice": Edelman ("Pee Wee Reese," 193).

195. "He took charge of us out there": Ibid.

195. "Pee Wee was like the captain of the captains": Vincent, 138.

195. "I thought I had killed myself": Working draft of *Wait 'Till Next Year*, Jackie Robinson Papers, National Baseball Hall of Fame.

195–96. "The fellows are all very nice": Rampersad, 290.

196. Campanella's background: Kashatus, 64–80.

196. "He always tried to be upbeat": Rampersad, 292.

196–97. "Campanella resented Jackie": Ibid., 291.

197. "Campanella played one way": Ibid., 228.

197. Parrott's story of the "only time I thought Robinson": Golenbock, 196–97.

197. Barnstorming tour and hard feelings: Kashatus, 132–33.

198. "I'm going to the Chase": Ibid., 157.
198. Newcombe's version: Ibid.
198. Campanella's version of the dispute: Ibid.
198–99. "As much as Roy helped me": Golenbock, 239.
199. "Now Roy is a different type": Ibid.
199. "I'd call Campy": Kashatus, 131.
201. "When I saw the ball": Golenbock, 404.
201. Robinson staying quiet after trade, going to Chock Full o'Nuts: Rampersad, 305–6.
202. "When I said hello": Falkner, 341.
203. "I'll take a while and get": Ibid., 342.

CHAPTER NINE: DIXIE WALKER: "I FEEL LIKE I'VE LEARNED."

204. The romance of Susan Walker and her future husband: Allen, 38–39.
204. Walker changing his mind about his son-in-law: Ibid., 93.
205. "You'll never make any money": Ibid., 57.
205. "the dumbest thing": Kahn (*The Era*), 35.
206–7. Walker's youth and background: Allen, 46–50.
206. Ewart Walker's sore arm and postbaseball days: Ibid., 50.
206. Walker either quit school at 13 (Allen, 50) or 15 (Spatz [*Dixie*], 11).
206. "My dad never really": Allen, 50.
207. "I really believe all that lifting": Spatz (*Dixie*), 11.
207. Chapman joins Walker's team: Allen, 53.
207. Walker gets laid off to make his tryout: Ibid., 54–55.
207. Walker's baseball money and his mother's reaction: Ibid., 55–57.
208. Jim Ogle calls him Dixie: Ibid., 60.
208. Walker's injuries and "hated to see": Ibid., 67.
209. tonsils removed: Ibid., 68.
209. "She was on a first name": Ibid., 89.
210. Estelle departs with Dixie for Chicago; Ibid., 90–91.
210. Walker's radical shoulder surgery: Ibid., 71–72.
210. Walker traded because of contract issue: Ibid., 72.
210. Detroit fans booing Walker: Spatz ("Dixie Walker"), 38.
211. MacPhail turns around the Dodgers: Golenbock, 33.
212. The People's Choice: Spatz ("Dixie Walker"), 39.
212. "Those . . . years I spent": Allen, 111.
212. Liquor store and frequent public speaking: Ibid.
212. Petition in support of Walker: Ibid., 116.
213. Walker's reaction to Robinson and "As long as he isn't": Ibid., 138.
214. Walker as Brooklyn representative and NL representative, working on pension: Ibid., 134–35.
214. Higbe talking to Parrott: Tygiel, 168.

214. Walker appears to deny the petition in *New York Times*, December 10, 1981. Five years earlier, he apparently acknowledged his role in the petition per Kahn (*The Era*), 35.
214. Reese's memories of petition: Golenbock, 148.
214–15. Reiser's memories of the petition: Ibid.
215. Duke Snider's memories of the petition: Vincent, 58–59.
215. Kirby Higbe's admission of signing: Golenbock, 149.
215. Furillo's comments on petition: Allen, 178.
215–16. Bragan's memories of petition: *Ithaca Journal*, April 5, 1997.
216. "You're on this ball club": Barber (1947), 115.
216. Stanky noted to have signed petition: Kahn (*The Era*), 34.
216. Individual meetings with Rickey: Lowenfish, 419.
216. Walker on his meeting: *New York Times*, December 10, 1981.
217. Walker's letter to Rickey: text in *New York Times*, December 10, 1981. Copy of letter within Branch Rickey Papers, National Baseball Hall of Fame.
217. "I organized that petition": Kahn (*The Era*), 35.
217. "We didn't have much contact": Allen, 172.
217. "Bragan's biggest worry": Eig, 42.
217. "We just grew up": Ibid., 43.
217–18. Reese's thinking on Robinson: Rowan, 229.
218. "He is against Robinson": Spatz (*Dixie*), 171.
218. Booing is per *Brooklyn Daily Eagle*, April 13, 1947.
218. "[D]on't go to Ebbets Field": *Pittsburgh Courier*, April 26, 1947.
218. Trade memorandum within Branch Rickey Papers, National Baseball Hall of Fame.
218. Second trade canceled because of Reiser: Spatz (*Dixie*), 168.
218–19. "I have tried to get you everything you need": Sukeforth/Rickey memorandum from Arthur Mann Papers, National Baseball Hall of Fame.
219. "That is exactly right": Ibid.
219. Robinson not wanting to be an unwanted teammate: Eig, 38.
219. Ben Chapman and Robinson's near breakdown: Jackie Robinson (*I Never*), 58–59.
219. Stanky's retort: Ibid., 60.
219. Walker telling Chapman he was going too far: Lamb (*Conspiracy*), 322.
220. "I never thought I'd see": Golenbock, 163.
220. "Look, Chapman, you son": Kahn (*Boys of Summer*), 325.
220. "adding percentage points": Jackie Robinson (*Baseball Has Done It*), 57.
220. "just a suggestion": *New York Times*, December 10, 1981.
220. "No other ballplayer": *The Sporting News*, September 17, 1947.
221. Rickey's trade of Walker discussed: *Southern Cultures*, Summer 2002.
221. "Naturally, I regret leaving": Allen, 188.
221. "a very antagonistic": *New York Times*, December 10, 1981.
222. Dixie Walker Day and "Right field doesn't look right": *Brooklyn Daily Eagle*, May 22, 1948.

222. Managing promise and "To Hell with that": Allen, 201–2.

223. Walker's letter to O'Malley: Ibid., 213.

223. Chapman account: *New York Times*, May 19, 2013.

224. "He showed me a lot": Lowenfish, 420.

271–272. Bragan's conversation with Maury Wills: Leahy, 18–19.

224. "My association with Maury": Jackie Robinson (*Baseball Has Done It*), 59.

225. Wallace inducting Walker into Alabama Sports Hall of Fame: Allen, 237.

225. "I have learned what suffering means": *The Montgomery Advertiser*, September 15, 1998.

225. "I was wrong": *The Tallahassee Democrat*, August 4, 1979.

225. "If I'd been swinging": Spatz (*Dixie*), 222.

226. "Our relationship has been": Ibid., 223.

226. "I find him a player": Ibid., 224.

226. "My attitude has changed": Ibid.

226. "I'm as sad": Ibid.

226–27. "[Robinson] had the instinct": *New York Times*, November 10, 1981.

227. Coleman's ignorance: *The Tallahassee Democrat*, April 15, 1987.

BIBLIOGRAPHY

NEWSPAPERS AND MAGAZINES

Albany Times-Union
Baseball Digest
Baseball Magazine
Boston Globe
Brooklyn Daily Eagle
Chicago Daily Herald
Chicago Defender
Chicago Tribune
Cincinnati Enquirer
Civilization
Cleveland Plain-Dealer
Dayton Daily News
Des Moines Tribune
Detroit Free Press
The (Baltimore) *Evening Sun*
Focus Magazine
Ithaca Journal
Look Magazine
Los Angeles Times
Louisville Courier-Journal
McCall's Magazine
The Montgomery Advertiser
New York Daily News
New York Mirror
New York Times
New York Tribune
Our Sports
Philadelphia Inquirer
Pittsburgh Courier
Pittsburgh Post-Gazette
Reader's Digest
Saturday Evening Post
Smithsonian
Southern Cultures
The Sporting News

Sports Collectors Digest
Sports Heritage
St. Louis Star and Times
The Tallahassee Democrat
USA Today
Washington Post

BOOKS AND ARTICLES

Allen, Maury, with Susan Walker. *Dixie Walker of the Dodgers: The People's Choice.* Tuscaloosa, AL: University of Alabama Press, 2010.

Barber, Lylah. *Lylah: A Memoir.* Chapel Hill, NC: Algonquin Books, 1985.

Barber, Red. *1947: When All Hell Broke Loose in Baseball.* New York: Da Capo Press, 1984.

Barber, Red, and Robert Creamer. *Rhubarb in the Catbird Seat.* Lincoln: University of Nebraska Press, 1997.

Barber, Red. *Show Me the Way to Go Home.* Philadelphia: Westminster Press, 1971.

Barber, Red. *Walk in the Spirit.* New York: The Dial Press, Inc., 1969.

Bouton, Jim. *Ball Four: Twentieth Anniversary Edition.* New York: Macmillan, 1990.

Branca, Ralph, with David Ritz. *A Moment in Time: An American Story of Baseball, Heartbreak, and Grace.* New York: Scribner, 2011.

Bryson, Bill. *One Summer: America, 1927.* New York: Doubleday, 2013.

Carroll, Brian. *When to Stop Cheering: The Black Press, The Black Community, and the Integration of Professional Baseball.* New York: Routledge, 2007.

Chandler, Happy, with Vance H. Trimble. *Heroes, Plain Folks, and Skunks: The Life and Times of Happy Chandler.* Chicago: Bonus Books, 1989.

Corbett, Warren. "Red Barber." *The Team That Forever Changed Baseball and America: The 1947 Brooklyn Dodgers.* Lincoln: University of Nebraska Press and SABR, 2012.

Edelman, Rob. "Burt Shotton." *The Team That Forever Changed Baseball and America: The 1947 Brooklyn Dodgers.* Lincoln: University of Nebraska Press and SABR, 2012.

Edelman, Rob. "Pee Wee Reese." *The Team That Forever Changed Baseball and America: The 1947 Brooklyn Dodgers.* Lincoln: University of Nebraska Press and SABR, 2012.

Edwards, Bob. *Fridays with Red: A Radio Friendship.* New York: Pocket Books, 1995.

Eig, Jonathan. *Opening Day: The Story of Jackie Robinson's First Season.* New York: Simon & Schuster, 2007.

Erskine, Carl, with Burton Rocks. *What I Learned from Jackie Robinson: A Teammate's Reflections on and Off the Field.* New York: McGraw-Hill, 2005.

Falkner, David. *Great Time Coming: The Life of Jackie Robinson from Baseball to Birmingham.* New York: Simon & Schuster, 1995.

Golenbock, Peter. *Bums: An Oral History of the Brooklyn Dodgers.* New York: G. P. Putnam's Sons, 1984.

Gough, David. *Burt Shotton, Dodgers Manager: A Baseball Biography.* Jefferson, NC: McFarland, 1994.

Haught, Jamie A. "Institute: It Springs from an Epic Love Story." *West Virginia History Journal* 32.2 (January 1971), 101–7.

Hill, John Paul. "Commissioner A. B. 'Happy' Chandler and the Integration of Major League Baseball: A Reassessment." *NINE: A Journal of Baseball History and Culture* 19.1 (Fall 2010), 28–51.

Holtzman, Jerome. *The Commissioners: Baseball's Midlife Crisis.* New York: Total Sports, 1998.

Honig, Donald. *Baseball When the Grass Was Real: Baseball from the Twenties to the Forties Told by the Men Who Played It.* Lincoln: University of Nebraska Press, 1993.

James, Bill. *The Bill James Guide to Baseball Managers: From 1870 to Today.* New York: Scribner, 1997.

Kahn, Roger. *Into My Own: The Remarkable People and Events That Shaped a Life.* New York: Thomas Dunne Books, 2006.

Kahn, Roger. *Rickey & Robinson: The True, Untold Story of the Integration of Baseball.* New York: Rodale, 2014.

Kahn, Roger. *The Boys of Summer.* New York: Harper & Row, 1987.

Kahn, Roger. *The Era 1947–1957: When the Yankees, the Giants, and the Dodgers Ruled the World.* Lincoln, NE: Bison Books, 2002.

Kashatus, William C. *Jackie & Campy: The Untold Story of Their Rocky Relationship and the Breaking of Baseball's Color Line.* Lincoln: University of Nebraska Press, 2014.

Kreuz, Jim. "Tom Greenwade: Destined for the Hall of Fame." *Can He Play? A Look at Baseball Scouts and Their Profession.* Phoenix, AZ: SABR, 2011.

Lamb, Chris. *Blackout: The Untold Story of Jackie Robinson's First Spring Training.* Lincoln: University of Nebraska Press, 2004.

Lamb, Chris. *Conspiracy of Silence: Sportswriters and the Long Campaign to Desegregate Baseball.* Lincoln: University of Nebraska Press, 2012.

Leahy, Michael. *The Last Innocents: The Collision of the Turbulent Sixties and the Los Angeles Dodgers.* New York: Harper, 2016.

Long, Michael G. and Chris Lamb. *Jackie Robinson: A Spiritual Biography.* Louisville, KY: Westminster John Knox Press, 2017.

Lowenfish, Lee. *Branch Rickey: Baseball's Ferocious Gentleman.* Lincoln: University of Nebraska Press, 2009.

Mann, Arthur. *Branch Rickey: American in Action.* Cambridge, MA: The Riverside Press, 1957.

Mann, Arthur. *The Jackie Robinson Story.* New York: Grosset & Dunlap, 1963.

McCarver, Tim, with Ray Robinson. *Oh, Baby, I Love It!* New York: Villard Books, 1987.

Oliphant, Thomas. *Praying for Gil Hodges: A Memoir of the 1955 World Series and One Family's Love of the Brooklyn Dodgers.* New York: Thomas Dunne Books, 2005.

O'Toole, Andrew. *Branch Rickey in Pittsburgh: Baseball's Trailblazing General Manager for the Pirates, 1950–1955.* Jefferson, NC: McFarland & Company, Inc., 2000.

Pearce, John Ed. *Divide and Dissent: Kentucky Politics, 1930–1963.* Lexington: University Press of Kentucky, 2006.

Polner, Murray. *Branch Rickey: A Biography*. Jefferson, NC: McFarland & Company, Inc., 2007.

Rampersad, Arnold. *Jackie Robinson: A Biography*. New York: Alfred A. Knopf, 1997.

Ray, James L. "Clyde Sukeforth." *The Team That Forever Changed Baseball and America: The 1947 Brooklyn Dodgers*. Lincoln: University of Nebraska Press and SABR, 2012.

Reed, Ted. *Carl Furillo, Brooklyn Dodgers All-Star*. Jefferson, NC: McFarland & Company, Inc., 2011.

Robinson, Jackie. *Baseball Has Done It*. Brooklyn, NY: Ig Publishing, 2005.

Robinson, Jackie. *I Never Had It Made: An Autobiography*. New York: Harper Collins, 1995.

Robinson, Jackie, as told to Wendell Smith. *Jackie Robinson: My Own Story*. New York: Greenberg, 1948.

Robinson, Rachel, with Lee Daniels. *Jackie Robinson: An Intimate Portrait*. New York: Harry N. Abrams, Inc., 1996.

Roland, Charles P. "Albert Benjamin Chandler." *Kentucky's Governors, 1792–1985*. Lexington: University Press of Kentucky, 1985.

Rowan, Carl, with Jackie Robinson. *Wait Till Next Year: The Story of Jackie Robinson*. New York: Random House, 1960.

Shea, Stuart. *Calling the Game: Baseball Broadcasting from 1920 to the Present*. Phoenix, AZ: SABR (e-version), 2015.

Simmons, Charles A. *The African American Press: A History of News Coverage during National Crises, with Special Reference to Four Black Newspapers, 1827–1965*. Jefferson, NC: McFarland & Company, Inc., 2006.

Spatz, Lyle. *Dixie Walker: A Life in Baseball*. Jefferson, NC: McFarland, 2011.

Spatz, Lyle. "Dixie Walker." *The Team That Forever Changed Baseball and America: The 1947 Brooklyn Dodgers*. Lincoln: University of Nebraska Press and SABR, 2012.

Tygiel, Jules. *Baseball's Great Experiment: Jackie Robinson and His Legacy*. New York: Oxford University Press, 1997.

Vincent, Fay. *We Would Have Played for Nothing: Baseball Stars of the 1950s and 1960s Talk about the Game They Loved*. New York: Simon & Schuster, 2008.

Walker, James R. *Crack of the Bat: A History of Baseball on the Radio*. Lincoln: University of Nebraska Press, 2015.

Zinn, Howard. *A People's History of the United States*. New York: Harper Perennial, 1990.

INTERNET

Burroughs, Todd Steven. "That Time Jackie Robinson Was a Columnist for the Pittsburgh Courier." www.theroot.com/that-time-jackie-robinson-was-a -columnist-for-the-pitts-1790854857 (4/4/16).

Clyde Sukeforth (Maine Memory Network). www.mainememory.net/artifact/8617 (1998).

"The Jackie Robinson Foundation." www.jackierobinson.org (8/31/18).

MLB.com. "Robinson Accepts O'Neil Award." Video embedded at www.mlb.com/news/rachel-robinson-gets-hofs-buck-oneil-award/c-245206626 (7/29/2017).

National Baseball Hall of Fame. "Wendell Smith and Jackie Robinson." https://baseballhall.org/discover-more/stories/wendell-smith/447 (8/31/18).

National Baseball Hall of Fame. "Wendell Smith and the Boston Red Sox." https://baseballhall.org/discover-more/stories/wendell-smith/355 (8/31/18).

National Baseball Hall of Fame. "Wendell Smith and the Hall of Fame." https://baseballhall.org/discover-more/stories/wendell-smith/452 (8/31/18).

Taylor, Rob Jr. "The History of the New Pittsburgh *Courier*." https://newpittsburghcourieronline.com/the-history-of-the-new-pittsburgh-courier (2/2/18).

West Virginia State University. "Our History Runs Deep." www.wvstateu.edu/About/History-and-Traditions.aspx (8/31/18).

INDEX

ABOUT THE AUTHOR

Joe Cox is a member of the Society for American Baseball Research (SABR) and is the author of *Almost Perfect: The Heartbreaking Pursuit of Pitching's Holy Grail* and *The Immaculate Inning: Unassisted Triple Plays, 40/40 Seasons, and the Stories behind Baseball's Rarest Feats*. He has also coauthored or contributed to another five sports books. He lives with his wife and children near Bowling Green, Kentucky.